THREE WORLDS

Biography

THOMAS LOVE PEACOCK

JAMES BRANCH CABELL

SWIFT

SINCLAIR LEWIS

Fiction

OTHER PROVINCES

THE NINTH WAVE

Literary History and Criticism

THE AMERICAN NOVEL

CONTEMPORARY AMERICAN NOVELISTS

THE ROVING CRITIC

MANY MINDS

AMERICAN AND BRITISH LITERATURE SINCE 1890
(with Mark Van Doren)

WHAT IS AMERICAN LITERATURE?

Edited

THE CAMBRIDGE HISTORY OF AMERICAN LITERATURE

MODERN AMERICAN PROSE

AN ANTHOLOGY OF WORLD PROSE

THREE WORLDS

BY

CARL VAN DOREN

NEW YORK AND LONDON

HARPER *&* BROTHERS PUBLISHERS
MCMXXXVI

CONTENTS

I FIRST WORLD: PRE-WAR
    Village   1
    Town   58
    University   75
II SECOND WORLD: POST-WAR
    War   113
    Journalism   128
    Literature   186
III THIRD WORLD: NEW WORLD?
    Boom   245
    Depression   260
    Resolution   282

I FIRST WORLD: PRE-WAR

Village
Town
University

Village

I was born in a village then called Hope, in Illinois, and I lived there or on a farm a mile away till I was fifteen, as happy as an animal. After we had decided to leave the village for a town, I was suddenly restless. Through four or five dragging months I blamed the farm and the village, though they were the same as they had been. I resented country manners, country clothes, country grammar. Ambition in me first took the form of snobbishness. I believe this is more general than many people will confess.

My brothers were too young to have clear opinions on the change, and my father and mother had simple motives. Living in town would be easier than in the country, and there would be better schools for the boys. But all of us, whether aware of it or not, were in the drift of an impulse which in 1900 was common in Illinois and throughout the Middle West. Farming had become old-fashioned. The successful farmers were retiring, as they called it, to the towns, leaving their farms to be rented by the less successful or to be run by hired labor. The value of land, at least the price, had risen so fast in a generation that the owners had turned from working farmers into landlords. Few of them looked farther than to the county seat, or even to the nearest railroad station, but they did look and they did move from the land. It was a powerful instinctive migration which was to transform a large part of America.

When I call Hope a village I use a word for it which nobody there ever used. Hope was a church, a school, a blacksmith shop, one store at first and two after a while, and ten houses, in which, in fifteen years, not more than fifty persons lived. It lay at a cross-roads on the long slope of a terminal moraine in the middle of a prairie. The horizon was a circle on the plain, and the sky bent down and met it in a level line. The sun came up out of Indiana as if it were the ocean. The sunsets were sky-high and horizon-wide and rainbow-colored. The soil underfoot was as black as the nights, springing up annually into lavish corn and oats and hay, and some wheat, and along the roads and hedges into a tumult of weeds. In the hot summers they said you could hear the corn grow.

Corn pressed in on Hope like a tame jungle. The site of the village had been cut out of two farms which surrounded it. Behind them were others which belonged hardly less to the village than the houses in it. Most of the men saw each other almost every day at the store or the blacksmith shop. The children went five days of the week during nine months of the year to school. And everybody met everybody else at church on Sunday. Although the village was a bare cross-roads in a cornfield, it was also the heart of a community, with the bones, flesh, blood, and nerves of any community. Any community is a world.

2

Hope had theology and religion. The church belonged to one of the small sects which are the fringes of Protestantism. I never heard the name of it till I was grown. The preacher did not live at Hope but came Saturday, preached morning and evening on Sunday, and left on Monday, the guest in turn of various households of the congregation. It cannot have been easy for him to satisfy his audiences. There were still in Hope a few hardshell and hellfire pioneers who wanted sterner doctrine than they got from the sermons. There was a family of unbelievers, a man and his sons, who came occasionally to church and were believed to be listening with secret sneers. There was a family of Quakers. There were unregenerate sinners, husbands of pious wives, who behaved well enough in church but who had never joined it. And on Sunday there was always half a churchful of sleepy children who wished they could go outdoors and play.

The church at Hope was a sober club for the encouragement of good behavior. While a few members were devout or dogmatic, most of them were easy-going in whatever faith they had. The motto painted in bold letters on the wall behind the pulpit, "Christian Character the Test of Fellowship," made up the whole creed. To be honest and decent in daily affairs was all that was required of any member, and that was required rather by the community than by the church alone. At the annual revivals new members joined the church, most of them children who had come to adolescence the past year. But I never saw anything like a religious orgy at Hope. Such uproar went with camp-meetings in backward villages. Nor did the support of the church put burdens on the congregation, which paid what it chose to afford. The people of Hope were not like the Catholic Germans to the west, who, Hope believed, would let the priest get them into the church, lock the door, and tell them how much money they must raise before they could go about their usual business.

And yet the church meant more to Hope than any club. It had a kind of music that wound itself into the memory. Not the wheezing cottage organ. Not the dry hymns. Not the drone of the preacher. But the music of rich, proud words from the Bible falling upon ears that had heard them again and again and now heard them chime with old recollections. The silence during prayer. The hush at communion. All sorts of thoughts and feelings, of course, ran through the passive minds of the worshippers: vows, fears, loves, hates, lusts, resentments, repentances, forecasts, griefs, triumphs. But they had in common one strain of piety, a sense of reverence toward a ceremonial which had become a part of them, reaching back to their childhood, and bringing them at each repetition the accumulated experience of solemn hours. This piety was Hope's religion.

Sunday school was livelier. Every Sunday there was a passage of Scripture to be studied, with such comments as the teachers knew how to make, and a Golden Text to be memorized. After an opening hymn and a prayer, the classes scattered to various parts of the church's one room, the most envied class to the gallery. Nobody took much interest in the day's lesson, except to see what picture would be on the card which every child was given to help him remember the passage he was supposed to have read. When the school had reassembled it was exciting to watch one of the teachers write on a blackboard the numbers of those present in the classes and of the pennies they had contributed.

What we learned out of the Old and New Testaments stayed in us by the most unconscious assimilation. Yet I cannot now read any part of the Bible without remembering as much as reading. My memory runs just ahead of my eyes, and I catch up with it like a man visiting the house where he lived as a child.

It may be because I was so young that my mind seldom went beyond Hope in thinking about church and Sunday school, but I doubt that in this I was different from my elders. For these modes of worship had not been imposed by any alien sovereign hierarchy to which the congregation was subject. Hope had itself imported them to meet its own needs.

About the time of the Civil War, when the township had been settled only a few years, my Grandfather Butz came home one evening to find his wife gone from the house. A little later she returned, on horseback. A tall girl, already gaunt from hard work and prairie weather, she got down from her horse and faced her husband with flushed cheeks but determined eyes.

"Where in the nation have you been?" My grandfather was a Whig and a conservative.

My grandmother was a Republican and a radical. "I have been around to the neighbors to ask them to come to Sunday school next Sunday."

"What Sunday school?" Hope had then no church and nothing but a temporary schoolhouse a muddy mile away from the cross-roads.

"We're going to organize a Sunday school. I'm tired of having the men waste all their Sundays on horse races. It's a bad example for the children. Next Sunday everybody has promised to meet at the schoolhouse."

This was a long speech from my grandmother, and it was probably all she said while my grandfather objected and debated, and finally agreed and admired. On Sunday they drove, in a farm wagon for want of any other vehicle, to what was to be Sunday school.

The schoolhouse sat naked on the prairie. The first man who came tied his team to the hitching-post in front. The next one tied his to the rear wheels of the first wagon. And so on in a straggling, stamping line. The women and children went inside as soon as they arrived. The men stood outside, talking about everything but what had brought them there. Time passed with nothing done because nobody knew what to do.

My grandfather was not a patient man. "Men," he said, "we came here to organize a Sunday school. Suppose we go in and get it started." They filed in and sat down on the hard benches.

Another silence. More impatience from my grandfather, who had a tongue. He rose and called the meeting to order.

"Ladies and gentlemen, we have met to organize a Sunday school. I don't know much about Sunday schools, but I think the first thing is to elect a superintendent. Do I hear any nominations?"

There was a buzzing on the benches. Some one nominated my grandmother. There were no other nominations. My grandmother was elected. She was too shy to stand up and say a word that day. Some one thought they should have an assistant superintendent. My grandfather was nominated and elected.

With that the meeting halted. They all felt there should be some kind of prayer, but there was not a "praying man" in the house. They gave that up. Two or three of those present remembered a Sunday school hymn they had heard. They taught the others. The opening verse ran:

"The Sunday school, that blessed place!
Oh I had rather stay
Within its walls, a child of grace,
Than spend my hours at play."

They sang the verse several times, and perhaps other verses. It was the only hymn, and the only music, they had for weeks to follow.

The next Sunday Uncle Tom Snyder, a praying man and an ordained occasional preacher, came and helped them through the service. My grandmother took her horse again and rode among the neighbors till she collected seven dollars to send to Cincinnati for printed weekly lessons. After that the Sunday school was never interrupted. Hope's form of spiritual life had been set up.

A better schoolhouse was built on an acre of ground which my grandfather gave out of his farm at the cross-roads. Taxes paid for it. Voluntary pockets built a church. Though there was talk of uniting with the Methodists, the congregation chose the New Lights instead. Possibly they thought the Methodist doctrine and discipline too strict or too explicit. More likely their choice was on the whole an accident. In any case, Hope in its own way made up its own mind. It had taken its first step when it undertook to civilize its Sundays, much as it might have undertaken to improve its bridges. Church and preachers came as a natural next step. The order of worship might be imported, but the motive to import one had been native, and native motives established and continued it.

The earliest preachers, two or three of whom survived to years which I can remember, were bearded, ignorant, honest men who farmed during the week and on Sunday preached loud sermons against the grosser faults of the community. Such preachers satisfied their generation. The sons and daughters of that generation looked upon them as relics of the pioneer time, which was so recent but seemed so remote. The later preachers shaved their faces and were softer, like the new generation. The church kept pace with its world. In 1860 Hope was open prairie. In 1885, when I was born, the community was as settled in its virtues and vices as if it had been there a thousand years.

3

THESE years saw a change in the school at Hope. The earliest memory of which I can fix the date takes me back to a September day when I stood at the fence of our house in the village and watched the children playing in the schoolyard next door. I was four that day, and I boasted of it to some of them who spoke to me as they ran by. But what I remember best is seeing the teacher limp across the yard from his house just behind it. I was afraid of him, a sour, savage man who, I now know, had taught there so long that he was tolerated but had come to be disapproved. He died soon after. I have no other memories of him and no knowledge but what I gathered from the legend which outlasted him.

On the day of his marriage, one of my great-aunts told me, he left the wedding party to sit behind the stove and study an arithmetic book. My father told me the teacher had formerly believed that Chinese eyes do not move in their sockets—he had read that the Chinese have "oblique-set" eyes! My mother told me that when she was five or six the teacher had terrified her by making her sit, as punishment for some little failure, on the floor and put her finger through a knot-hole, telling her that if she were not a better girl a dreadful beast might bite her finger off. Against his cruelty, my grandmother told me, there had been a rebellion in the school itself. Once, when he had said that the next day he was going to whip some of the big girls, my mother now among them, the bigger boys, including my uncles, met after school and swore they would not permit it. They were going to bring a rope to school and, if he tried to carry out his threat, tie him up and beat him. An older man overheard, told one or two others, and warned the teacher. Knowing him and the boys, they were afraid that in the fight which was sure to take place some one might be hurt or even killed. This was mutiny, as surely as if the school had been a ship. Whatever fury the teacher may have felt, the big girls were not punished, and the affair was dropped without a word. The community knew how to look out for itself better than how to talk about it.

The good things said of the tyrant were that he kept order among the rowdiest boys who came to school only in the winter, that he drilled the elements of learning unforgettably into his pupils, and that he grounded them once for all in the distinction between right and wrong. But he passed with the old days and the old need for his kind, if there ever had been such a need. My first teacher, shortly after his death, was a young girl, and no child thought of disobeying her. The pioneer school survived only in the pioneer teacher. When he was gone, it was gone.

I did not start to school till my brother Guy, two years younger, was old enough to go with me. By that time we had moved from the village to a farm, and for the next six years we walked a mile back and forth on every school day from the first of September to the first of June. There were days enough when we had to stagger through snowdrifts or to pick our way among puddles of black mud, but I remember best the mornings in late April or early May when we were allowed to begin going barefoot. As our father was the doctor, our appearance without shoes was a prescription to the other children. Many shoes and stockings came off on those mornings, and many feet, blanched and softened since October, ran wild in a happy, wincing freedom.

All the school days of the six years seem now to have been alike. From nine to twelve, with fifteen minutes' recess, we sat at hard double desks and benches without moving or speaking except when we went forward to recite. The children who lived in the village had to go home to dinner. The rest of us raced for our dinner-pails, waiting on shelves at the back of the room, and, again in our seats, raced to see who could first be done with his hearty sandwiches, hard-boiled eggs, pie or cake, and possibly milk carried in the hollow lid of the dinner pail. Nobody went hungry and nobody was hurt by eating too fast. There was some trading in food, but most of us ate what we brought. At least once every day some boy cracked an egg shell on another boy's head. But the real business of the noon hour was not eating. In fifteen minutes we were playing rounders, or handy-over, or dare base, or I spy. In winter we built snow forts and defended and assaulted them, or went skating on the brook— called the branch—which ran just east of the village. Once when we were skating we did not hear the bell, or by a sly conspiracy refused to hear it, and had to stay in after school for three days to make up the time lost. On every other day for six years the bell at one o'clock brought us in to another three hours divided and spent like the three hours in the forenoon.

Our schooling was plain fare. Outside of a little singing and drawing and book-keeping, we gave our whole time to reading, grammar, writing, spelling, arithmetic, geography, physiology, and American history. So far as we were ever taught, the human race had had a past in only two parts of the world: in Judea, which we learned about on Sundays, and in America, during the week. The human body in our physiology had no means of reproducing itself and no impulse to do it. We did not mind. We had watched the animals and discussed our elders. Geography was maps and boundaries, capitals and principal products. When later I first saw mountains I was surprised that they were not tidy cones, as in the pictures I had seen in school.

Arithmetic came nearer home. We learned how to measure land in square rods and acres and square miles: always square measures for square land, such as we knew. Forty acres were an exact square a quarter of a mile each way, and a day's work with a cultivator in a corn-field, ten acres or a hundred rows, was a walk of twenty-five miles. We learned how many pounds make a bushel of corn in the ear, of shelled corn, oats, wheat, rye, potatoes, and how many bushels would fill how big a crib or bin. We learned how to estimate the number of shingles it would take to cover a roof, laid so many inches to the weather, or of the strips of weatherboarding for the side of a house. All the boys were interested, and most of the girls. The girls were more interested in calculations for laying carpet or putting on wallpaper. School furnished us a science for what we helped to do at home in practice. For what we might have to do when we were grown, we studied interest and promissory notes and checks and the simplest book-keeping. As a kind of adventure in arithmetic, we once organized a joint stock company and dealt in imaginary shares. Prices fluctuated by fiat of the teacher, who each day posted them on the blackboard. Guy and I bought right and left and got control. Then, again by fiat, the factory burned down, the stocks became worthless, and the undertaking ended.

I have often heard it said that in the old days people spelled more correctly than now. If this is true, it is true of older days than mine at Hope. Then, although we had a spelling match the last half-hour of many Fridays, we made the mistakes which must always be made by all but experts in the difficult English language. One winter a neighboring school held a series of public spelling bees in the evening. We thought of this as a conscious revival of a former custom. Guy and I, then perhaps eleven and thirteen, drove our bay Indian pony Dick in his red and black cart to see what the first of them would be like.

It seemed strange to be in a schoolroom at night, dark outside, dusky inside with kerosene lamps, and stranger to see men and women sitting at desks built for boys and girls. The teacher of that school took charge. About half of those who had come sat as audience. The other half chose sides and stood in lines along two walls. The teacher gave out words from a familiar spelling book, first to one side, then to the other. Each person who misspelled a word went back to his seat. When nobody was left on one side, the other was the winner. Then came the match for individuals, all in one long row. First the teacher gave us easy words. The line grew confident, and the audience restless. He turned farther toward the back of the book. Hard words thinned us out. Hard words, however, were not enough. There were wary spellers in the line. Finally he came to tricky words. The line shortened to three, a man, a woman, and a boy. He gave me the word indelible and I spelled it. Four or five turns later, he gave me deleble. I had never seen the word, spelled it by analogy with indelible, and went down. I do not remember whether the man or the woman left was the victor.

But I remember what happened on the way home. Guy and I got away with the pony ahead of most of the others. He was trotting at his usual jog along the narrow dirt road when we heard sharp hoofs behind us. By the faint moon we could see that it was our own teacher and another man, driving the showy sorrels Dexter and Rarus to an open buggy. They swung to the left and started to pass. Dick was eighteen and lazy and fat, but he loved a race better than food or drink. Guy and I were still hot with competition. The pony broke into a run and we gave him his head. Dexter and Rarus fell back for a moment. I suspect the men were astonished, and not too sure it would be safe to race with boys so young. Then the team drew closer to us. We hogged the road without a scruple, yelled at Dick, and lashed him with the ends of the reins. He ran like a dog, head down, nose out, his belly close to the ground, his unshod feet making almost no sound. For a quarter of a mile Dexter and Rarus could not pass him, and when at last they did, they had to plunge by with two wheels dangerously in the ditch at the side of the road. Dick accepted what he could not help and, blowing noisily, lagged the rest of the way home. Guy and I were wild with a triumph we would never have felt if one of us had stood up last in the spelling match. Dick had kept ahead of Dexter and Rarus for a quarter of a mile, which was his distance. We were not so wild as to tell our parents, who would have known that racing horses

in harness in the dark along a rough narrow road is one
of the best ways to break a neck. And our triumph was absolute when the next day at school our teacher praised the
pony.

Writing in school meant practice in penmanship and the
study of the forms of correspondence. The days of copper-
plate hand-writing had gone, and our grandfathers complained. In our decade we went through the general change
from a slanting to a vertical hand and came out of it writing shapelessly. Grammar was formal, parsing words and
analyzing sentences. Most of the children parsed and an-
alyzed yet spoke as ungrammatically as ever, their speech
rising no higher than its source at home.

As to reading, we did little in school besides the graded
selections in successive readers. We read them aloud in class.
We looked up the pronunciation and meaning of the hard
words. The unabridged dictionary on its metal stand had
definitions not only of hard but also of bad words. We
hunted for all we knew, and stared at them shameless in
print. What the selections we read might be about, as wholes,
we hardly noticed. I remember only two. One was a passage
from the Tempest which gave Guy what was long his favorite
term of abuse: "Ape with forehead villainous low." Through
him it entered the private vocabulary which we used only
when together or, later, with our younger brothers. The
second passage was from Ivanhoe, the account of the archery
contest at the tournament. This was my peak of romance.
I still flush with the glow of that old excitement, I still smell
the book in which I read, I still see Robin Hood and his
rivals exactly as I saw them then. No other narrative sentence
has ever seemed to me so shining and satisfying as that final
one: "His arrow split the willow rod against which it was

aimed." But when I set up a peeled willow and shot at it, my arrow realistically missed.

School was less local than church. Every year there were central examinations for all the districts of the township, and final examinations for the winners from several townships. We were not required to take them, but to pass was creditable and to be first was as honorable, if not as profitable, as if Hope had been in China. I took my central examination in the ordinary routine, and was surprised when I learned I had the highest marks. The final examination became important.

It was held at Collison, which was the nearest railroad station and seven miles away. One other boy from Hope went too. That morning I got up before daylight, saddled the pony, and rode past Roy's house, where he joined me. A belated snow had fallen all night, and was still falling, so sticky that we must have looked like snow-boys on snow-horses. It balled up on our horses' feet, which we had frequently to scrape out to keep them from slipping. Roy was loosemouthed, bragging all the way about how easily he would pass. I was nervous about myself and disgusted with him. We rode past the oak shadows of Pilot Grove and its big, quiet house. A swinging lantern moved about near the barn. I remember nothing more of the next six miles, but it was daylight when we reached Collison and stabled our horses.

Collison had a brick schoolhouse of several rooms. The contestants shuffled about the corridors until a bell called us to the day's work. Most of our teachers were there, advising and encouraging us. They got us settled at our desks, with printed questions and paper to write on. I dived into the examination and thought of nothing else for three hours.

At noon we were given an hour off and dinner, for twenty-five cents apiece, served by the ladies of the Methodist church. I liked the scalloped oysters best. We ate like school children, and went back to the examination.

During the second three hours I must have got tired, though I felt it only as impatience. A good many children had turned in their papers and left the room, to skylark in the corridors. I envied them. And I wanted, before I set out for home, to talk to Amy, a girl I liked. Though she was taking the examination, she was no scholar and had been among the first to find she had written all she knew. Seeing her at the door, teasing me, I hurried through my answers to the questions in American history, and joined her.

The teachers had read the papers as they came in, and in half an hour the marks were ready. We crowded in from the corridors. My own teacher looked sternly at me. "Don't you know what the Missouri Compromise was?" he asked. My spirit slumped. I did know but I had overlooked the question in my hurry. A girl from another township had been more conscientious, and I came out second to her. The worst thing about it was the disappointment of my father and mother that night when I rode up in the dark and had to tell them. I did not tell them about Amy.

My family were not ready to move to town as soon as I was ready to go to high school, so that my last year at Hope would have been wasted if the new teacher had not taught me algebra and ancient history in a special class which it must have been inconvenient for him to crowd into his days. I had little sense of marking time. School was the only life I knew outside of the farm, and studies were only a part of what we did there. This was a community of children, imitating the larger community in preparation for living in it. I found it pleasant, as one of the oldest boys, to have a hand in the government, and felt authority all the more because my brothers Frank and Mark, seven and five, were among the governed. Like the other older boys, too, I discovered girls. From being nuisances they had become amusements and mysteries. We talked about them a great deal, speculating. One of the girls in the neighborhood that spring climbed out a window at night and eloped with the hired man. Her father went after her and brought her back. The children hardly mentioned it to their parents, but the scandal cannot have hummed more busily anywhere than it did at school.

The boys and girls who had done the work of the eight grades were ready for whatever the community demanded, except experience. Most of the girls married early. The ambitious boys went further with their schooling, prepared to go as far as they chose. Of the five sons of a family in the next district and the five in my family, nine went to college, two became college professors, two agricultural experts, two writers, one an architect, one a broker, one a merchant, and one a salesman. Of the rest, the majority became farmers. I have never heard that any one of them all ever complained that his first school had done less for him than it should.

4

Hope was so self-contained, and I was so young when we lived there, that I observed almost nothing of its relations to the county and the state. My father was a member of the school board, but this to me meant only that we got free passes, once to a demonstration of the incredible phonograph which some traveling entertainer gave in the schoolhouse, and once to a medicine show which pitched its tent on the school grounds for a week. A great-uncle of mine, a township supervisor, had something to do with the county poor. I remember when I first learned the meaning of the word pauper, and wondered if I would ever see such a person. I used to hear some comment now and then on the political ring which administered the county at Danville. When our teacher left Hope to become county superintendent of schools, we admired him. The state was too large to interest me more than vaguely, though I went with my father and mother and Guy to the World's Fair in Chicago, to be worn out with dazzling wonders, and though I listened to violent abuse of Governor Altgeld when he pardoned the Chicago anarchists.

Our community was almost entirely Republican. Its political hero was Speaker Cannon of the House of Representatives. Vermilion County called him Uncle Joe, and when he came, as he often did, to speak at Potomac, twelve miles away, he was very friendly with my grandfather, whom Potomac called Uncle Jerry. They had known each other from boyhood in the pioneer time. They even looked alike, as I used to think so many men of their generation did, although the Speaker was a politician, and my grandfather fastidious and fanatical.

During the Presidential campaign of 1892 some of the boys wore stiff, ugly caps which had "Cleveland" or "Harrison" printed across the front, and little Republicans taunted little Democrats in doggerel:

" 'How big is Grover Cleveland, Pa, that people call him great?
Is he as big as Uncle Ben, the favorite candidate?'
'Oh no, my son, he weighs a ton, but mostly gall and fat.
He wears a number nineteen collar and a little Tom Thumb hat.' "

After Cleveland was elected the Republicans in Hope prophesied the worst, and they blamed him for all that happened in 1893.

I was not affected. I ate, dressed, slept, played, and read exactly as I would have done if there had been no crisis. That winter, or the next, we once or twice burned corn in the Round Oak stove and talked about the hot, oily fire it made. A new standing joke appeared in the community. Some man, it was said, had sent a carload of sheep to Chicago. The commission agent reported that the amount received for them would not pay the railroad charges, and asked for money to make up the loss. The man replied: "Have no money, but am sending more sheep." No matter how often we heard this, we laughed. The general distress pinched our community but did not overwhelm it. What was going on in industrial cities, we did not guess. The horror that came nearest to us was in Kansas, which grew to a legend.

Although I have since then often been in Kansas, I can never lose my childish picture of it as a treeless plain, bare from drouth, swept with hot winds, eaten up by chinch bugs. Bleeding Kansas. Starving Kansas. Burning Kansas. Several families had gone from Hope to that cheaper land, and letters as well as newspapers told us about it. Now and then movers, as we called them, in covered wagons, went miserably past our house. I remember a wagon which had, daubed on the canvas, the defeated but rebellious words:

> "I'm tired of Kansas and starvation.
> I'm going back to my wife's relations.
> Damn Cleveland's administration."

Many of the movers stopped to beg, clumsily, for food and fodder. We always gave it to them, and heard their stories. One pitiful woman, the first dirty woman Guy and I had ever seen, whined when my mother asked her if she could use a side of salt pork and a sack of corn meal: "I'd be glad to get anything." Her answer must have struck Guy, for that night at supper, when asked what he would have, he said the same words in nearly the same tone. "I'd be glad to get anything," whined, became a household sentence. We were not a heartless family, but we had had no experience of want to the point of actual hunger, and the sight of it could not sadden us long.

The Spanish-American war was an explosion and a blaze on the horizon. Nobody that I knew went from Hope to be a soldier, and nobody argued intelligently about the war's origin or purpose. It came to us as simple melodrama in the newspapers. In the lovely island of Cuba, which many of us for the first time learned was in the West Indies and belonged to Spain, an innocent people were brutally oppressed by tyrants from the Old Country—our common name for Europe. How vile these tyrants were had not been realized until they blew up the Maine. Now that the truth was known, our duty to free the Cubans from their yoke was as strong as the need to punish them for their murderous treachery to us. This was like the Revolution, which had freed the American colonists from Great Britain. This was like the Civil War, which had freed the slaves. The pulse of altruism throbbed in our veins. Once more the righteous had taken arms against the wicked. Not for years afterwards did I, or I suppose any other native of the village, regard the war with critical eyes. We believed what the newspapers told us to believe, and read nothing between their uninformed, or interested, or sinister lines. A selfish war was supported by a generous people.

In that feverish spring the past rose to a fresh life among us. Only the old remembered war. For the young, war existed in books. When it appeared in newspapers it seemed to bring something of the past with it. War was history. This was war. Therefore, this was history. The instinctive syllogism had a magic influence. It enlarged the conflict into something heroic. I did not see a single uniform or flag or rifle in Hope, but when I read the papers I was looking, I dimly felt, at history as a reality. My world, becoming wider, became deeper, touched with a large illusion. The scuffles in Cuba, the crashing assault on Manila, the breathless voyage of the Oregon around the Cape, the massacre of the Spanish fleet: these gave us epic days. Nor was this at all peculiar to me or the children of my age. The run of historical fiction which followed took countless American readers back over the whole American past. Almost as if the shabby war wished to hide its dubious face, it threw out bright, soft, sweet clouds of romance.

The facts of the war interested us, not the debates of the treaty and the peace. Those who opposed expansion into the West Indies and the Philippines were held to be a pedantic, if not an unpatriotic, crew absurdly bent on turning the clock of time back. The United States had already expanded. It was too late to wrangle. The nation's destiny was manifest, white man's burden and all. Democracy had triumphed in America for a century, and now had triumphed over a European foe. The future was immense and secure.

5

In 1933 I motored through Hope on a broad, swift highway running straight north to Chicago. My brother Paul, born at Hope, but only a year old when we moved away, drove so fast that we were upon the village before I expected to be and beyond it before I could take in more than flickering images of the church and the house where I was born. As we rushed on under the maples my grandfather had set out on both sides of the road along his farm, I looked back half-bewildered. Most of the houses were gone. Not a soul that I had known still lived there. The very name of the village had been lost since the post office was given up. Hope is a gray monument. A stranger might go by without ever suspecting that it was once the centre of life for its own society. Yet there a microcosm formed and dissolved, and there the essential story of an older America was compressed into three generations.

Two of my great-grandfathers had come to Pilot township before the Civil War. The Butzes were of Pennsylvania German stock from another Hope, in New Jersey, where my grandfather was born. While he was still a child, his father read a book about the west that stirred him, and he fell in with the movement that shifted a whole people during the Jacksonian days. The family went first to Ohio, near Sandusky, and then on to Illinois, near Decatur. From there, for some reason, my Great-grandfather Butz turned back to Vermilion County, to settle at Hope. My grandfather, driving a yoke of oxen to a wagon loaded with farm tools, almost lost them crossing an unbridged stream at the spot where Urbana later built the high school in which I, still later, peacefully studied. A boy shouting at his oxen mired down in the ford. A boy reading about the wars in Gaul. The same place, and only fifty years between.

Pilot township already had a few inhabitants who seem to have been lost in the prairie sloughs. They had not, like some of their friends, settled in the timber along the Middle Fork, holding that only land which would grow trees would grow crops. But, settled around Hope, they had found that the soil, however fertile, needed to be drained if they were not to live half the year in mud. When my great-grandfather came, they lived in mud, desolately. The first thing they asked of him was that he should make forceps and pull their teeth, which had had to ache till they stopped aching or fell out. He was a blacksmith, not a dentist, but he made the forceps and pulled the teeth.

With drainage, the prairie people soon left the timber people behind. To live down in the timber in my day was to be thought wild and backward. They used to tell the story of a man who had lived there, long before, and who never came out except on election day. Then, year after year, he would emerge, coonskin on his head, rifle across his shoulder, and make his way to the polls. Coming up to the judges of the election he invariably said:

"I cast one vote for Andy Jackson."

"But Andy Jackson," he would be told, "is not a candidate."

"Makes no difference. I cast one vote for Andy Jackson."

After Jackson's death the man from the timber would not change his vote.

"I cast one vote for Andy Jackson."

"Andy Jackson is dead. You can't vote for him."

"It's a damned Whig lie. Andy Jackson will live forever. I cast one vote for Andy Jackson."

The Tillotsons were prairie people. In the seventeenth century a Tillotson had been Archbishop of Canterbury and had written, John Dryden thought, the first modern English prose. Another Tillotson preferred Massachusetts to England. From New England certain Tillotsons spilled over into New York, where one of them married a woman, my great-great-grandmother, who brought into the family some of the blood of one of the Five Tribes. My Great-grandfather Tillotson looked almost as much Indian as Puritan, austere and proud. My grandmother, born in Indiana, had from this Red strain her high cheek-bones and perhaps her stoic silence. The Tillotsons, who settled north of Hope, became the largest and the most permanent clan in the township. The country between Hope and Armstrong swarmed with my great-aunts and great-uncles and their many children, and the annual reunion of the Tillotsons and their kin to this day brings scores and even hundreds together, few of whom come from more than fifty miles away.

When Jeremiah Butz went to the father of Rebecca Tillotson to ask for her in marriage, he found the older man chopping wood. The young man was timid, not only because he was at a natural disadvantage, but also because he could not help knowing that the substantial Tillotsons might well consider the Butzes a restless lot. He had to force himself to say what he had come for.

"Mr. Tillotson, we—that is, Becky and I—we—we think it may be foolish, but we think—we think we would like to get married."

The old gentleman went on with his ax, as if waiting

for more. My grandfather was too much frightened to speak. Finally, between strokes, the father said:

"If you think it is foolish, why do you want to do it?" And he said nothing else.

There seemed to the lovers nothing to do but run away. They drove to Danville, to a fair, got their license, happened to see a justice of the peace they knew, asked him to marry them, and, sitting in a buggy, were married by the justice, standing beside it. My grandfather, having persuaded my grandmother this far, coaxed her into what followed. They hurried home before the others, and when the substantial Tillotsons came in, wondering about Rebecca, they found her already in bed with a man who they did not yet know was her husband.

My grandfather's brothers were restless enough. Two of them moved on to Kansas, then to Idaho, and one of them to British Columbia. When he was an old man he wrote a letter in which he said he had gone as far as he could on the American continent, and had decided he would go no farther west till he went to heaven. But my grandfather was more stable, and he was married to a Tillotson. He lived for almost forty years on one farm, retired to Potomac, and lived for over thirty years more in the same house. His four sons, three of whom looked like Tillotsons, as soon as they were men all made for the Indian Territory, where the two younger married women who were both part Cherokee.

My grandfather and grandmother established themselves on the farm that lay nearest to Hope on the north and east. From him I picked up all I know about the life of his generation.

He broke the prairie sod, driving five yoke of straining oxen, stopping every hour or so to hammer the iron ploughshare to a sharper edge. Some of the grass roots, immemorial, were as thick as his arm. He said it was like ploughing through a heavy woven door-mat. He dug hundreds of rods of drainage ditch, making the tile himself. He fenced part of his land with rails brought from the timber. It was a day's work to go, split the rails for a rod of fence, and bring them back. He was one of the first to realize that the thorny osage orange would make good hedges, and to begin setting out the plants and waiting for them to grow. Remembering New Jersey, he collected and hoarded stone for years, until he had enough to lay a foundation for his barn. In those old times, he said, the deer were so plentiful that a man could stand on rising ground and at a distance see droves of them. One day in winter, when the prairie was covered with a sheet of ice, two or three men went out with a hayrack on a sled and brought back a load of deer which they had killed without firing a shot. The dogs chased them, the deer slipped and fell on the ice, and the men cut their throats.

My grandfather lived with his growing family for some years in a prairie cabin which, after he built a permanent house, was given over to the chickens. He used to tease me by saying that my mother, his third child, had been born in a hen-coop. The work he and my grandmother did must have been terrific, and harder on her than on him. She bore the children and took the burden of his impetuous hospitality. Once, when he brought a raft of visitors home for dinner, unexpected, she had nothing to give them but green corn, of which she and the girls cooked enough to fill a wash tub. But he did not spare himself. Besides all the work he had to do, he invented other work. There was the long avenue of maples he set out. It was his boast that after he was twenty-one he never let a year go by without planting trees.

And he was, as the county history called him, the elegant man of Pilot township, forever busy with improving his farm and trying to improve the community. In his later years he made his house and grounds in Potomac a gardener's paradise. He argued for hard roads, for an electric railway. He wasted money boring for oil. The older he grew the bolder he was. When he was a young man he would have knocked down anybody who had called him an Abolitionist. When he was an old man, he was a Prohibitionist. Thousands of times he declared he would never cast his vote for any party that would license an evil for revenue. When he ran for Coroner on the county ticket, he announced that if elected he would bury Republicans and Democrats with equal pleasure.

He was like most men of his generation in that older America. He looked upon the future as a perpetual adventure and never doubted that it was an endless source of benefits to come. Men had only to work and wait for them. He had seen the wild prairie blossom under his hands. Other men could do and see as much if they chose. His contemporaries at Hope, though no one of them was quite so given up to the future as my grandfather, held his general opinions. They were solid, civil squires who had prospered, whose land by 1890 was worth forty times what it had been when they had claimed it from the Government, and who had never heard of any law of diminishing returns. At the same time, they doubted that the generation of their sons, who were to inherit these farms already ploughed and drained and hedged, could ever match the fathers. The old men had a kind of patriarchal status. Every year at the Old Settlers' Day celebration they listened with pride to stories of times past, much as more ancient patriarchs must have listened to stories of the conquest of Canaan.

My father, who belonged to the generation of the sons, was in a sense as much a pioneer as any of the fathers. He was not a native of Hope, but settled there, as the one physician for miles around, after the community had been formed. He came from Kankakee County, where his father was both preacher and farmer. My Great-grandfather Van Doren had been the first of his Dutch line to leave New Jersey, first for New York State, where my grandfather was born, and then for Illinois. My father, while like all the Van Dorens before him he felt he must own land, like most of them also studied a profession, to earn more money to buy land. At the medical school in Chicago he might have been a Scottish student in Edinburgh, not only supported by the farm at home but actually fed in part on food sent from it. He began the practice of medicine as assistant to his elder brother Silas at Penfield, a dozen miles away from Hope, and came there on the urging of various men, including my Grandfather Butz, who felt that Hope ought to have a doctor of its own. My father's fortune was then his clothes, his medicine kit, and a black saddle-horse.

When, that winter, the community Christmas tree was being set up in the church and hung with presents, he dropped in with those he was to give, and slyly tucked in somewhere a silk handkerchief for himself. Hardly more than a boy, he could not bear to seem neglected when the presents were given out, and so to be marked as an outsider. He made his way to a place in the life of Hope which only a country doctor could have had. If there were doubts of him because he was young, they soon passed. One of his earliest patients was my Uncle Mark, a giant at seventeen, who had an attack of spinal meningitis in the night and was found in convulsions in a bed he had broken to pieces. When he got well the credit went to my father. Two years after he came to Hope he was married to my mother.

She was as ambitious as he. At ten she had ridden back and forth across the prairie with the mail-bags for the village, when my grandfather was postmaster. At fifteen she had begun to teach school. Though she had had only one year at a normal college, she was at twenty the best educated girl in Hope, as my father was the best educated man. But they were both too much at home there to think for years of leaving. They built a house in the village, where two sons were born. My father's growing practice and my mother's growing household were not enough. They bought a farm west of Hope and moved to it. For ten years, during which three more sons were born, they matched the pioneers for labor.

They lived in a comfortable house instead of a shack. They drove a carriage instead of a wagon. They had, from my father's practice, an income outside of the farm. It took them only that ten years, as against my grandfather's and grandmother's forty, to find themselves able to retire. Yet what they did was terrific too. Indoors my mother never had more than one servant—hired girl—if she had one, and outdoors my father had to run the farm in the intervals of a practice which never allowed him an hour in which he might not be called away. The scale of his farming was larger than Hope had been used to, the pace faster. He put in as many tile as the farm's former owner. He did more to better the fertility of the soil. He built more barns and sheds. He raised more livestock. He paid more attention to markets and Government reports, of which there were now more to pay attention to. In the end, his ambition outran my mother's, or at least became different. She valued his profession most, and wanted him to advance in it. He was absorbed in the land and believed in its future with a stubborn optimism.

But times were changing and my brothers and I were growing old enough for other schools. The boys of the neighborhood, as much used to horses as to their own legs, rushed about on bicycles, hating the hedges and the thorns which punctured tires. Two of the young women had even been seen in bloomers. An automobile—still called a horseless carriage—had driven up to ask help from the blacksmith. The telephone was coming to Hope. At our house, at least, there was an obscure sense that an age had ended. My great-grandfather had been a pioneer, my grandfather a squire. My father was ready to be a landlord and a capitalist. Rising prices and machinery had freed us to take our place with other such freedmen in the towns.

On a day in August 1900 we were startled by a long line of carriages and buggies coming toward the farm from the village. It was a surprise party, Hope's farewell to my mother and father. Almost everybody we knew piled out, and teams were hitched to the fence the whole length of the lane. Before we quite knew what had happened, the men had set up trestles and a long table on the lawn, and the women had unpacked baskets of such food as belonged to Fourth of July celebrations and Old Settlers' Day: roast chicken, fried chicken, boiled chicken with dumplings, pressed chicken in jelly, young turkey, guinea hen (red meat was for cold seasons): smearcase, hardboiled eggs, deviled eggs, pickled eggs; potato salad, bowls of lettuce with cream and vinegar dressing, pickled beets, pickled onions, green peppers stuffed with piccalilli, sour cucumbers, sweet cucumbers, mixed pickles; light bread, light biscuits, soda biscuits, salt rising bread, corn bread, raisin bread, nut bread; sun-preserved cherries, preserved strawberries and raspberries and blackberries and plums, pickled peaches, apple sauce, apple butter, peach butter, grape butter, stewed pears, apple jelly, currant jelly, apple and currant jelly, grape jelly, watermelon preserves, tomato preserves; layer cakes with white or caramel or chocolate icing, cakes with chopped walnuts or hickory nuts or butternuts in the layers or between them, marble cakes, cakes with lemon icing or red sugar on top, fruit cakes rich with citron, angel food, devil's food, cup cakes, doughnuts, crullers, cookies; fresh apple pie, dried apple pie, cherry pie, blackberry pie, gooseberry pie, gooseberry and currant pie, raisin pie, lemon pie, rhubarb pie. One man brought a wagon-load of watermelons. And, since these were modern times and Hope now had an ice-house, there were freezers of ice cream and gallons of lemonade.

We ate. Then speeches, laughter, tears, and endless talking all over the house and grounds until the guests had to go home. It was long before I realized what the occasion must have meant to my family and the community. At the time, my flushed pride was mixed with disgust for the tears. Seeing that my father and mother were moved, I told myself they were old—he was forty-three, she thirty-seven—and soft. Our ten years on the farm, I thought, were something to be left behind with the farm, decisively.

6

WHEN we moved from the village to the farm I was five, and I remember sitting on top of a load of furniture and poking at the clock so that it struck all the way there. At the next step of my memory we seem to have been as thoroughly rooted in the farm as its trees.

Between the white house and the road there was a kind of park, surrounded by a high paneled fence and planted with hard and soft maples, elms, and cedars. Among them were mulberry, pear, and plum trees, and a thicket of wild plums, and along one side, just outside the fence, a row of cherry trees from which we used to scare robins and blue jays when the fruit was ripe. The house stood in a smaller yard with a picket fence which protected its lilacs, mock oranges, peonies, asparagus, and beds of flowers from the sheep which were now and then turned into the park to keep the grass down. To the left of the house, as you faced it from the road, lay first the vegetable garden and then the orchard, and behind the house the truck garden. Beyond the orchard and the truck garden, to the west and north of the house, which fronted south to the road but had its chief entrance on the east, were artificial groves of willow, ash, and walnut, with long rows of osage orange which had been allowed to grow for fence posts. The former owner had turned a part of the prairie into a wood. My brothers and I spent almost as many hours of our summer days in the trees as under them. I still remember the shock I felt when my father allowed one of the cedars to be cut down for the church's Christmas tree.

We seldom used the driveway through the park, preferring the farm lane which, with no gate to open at the road, led past the house to the stables at the rear. To the right of the lane was the little pasture, for the pony and the horses my father used to ride or drive to see his patients, and behind that the big pasture, for the cows, the work horses and mules, and whatever other stock might need it. All the rest of the farm was field or meadow, every square rod cultivated except the small plot where the foreman lived. He was not quite a foreman, but a married man hired by the year to carry out my father's orders with the help of the unmarried men who came and went in varying numbers with the seasons.

For the whole decade of the nineties we lived there almost as independent of the world at large as if this had been still the eighteenth century. The general store in the village had staple groceries and sometimes oranges, lemons, and bananas. From the nearest butchers, miles away, my father, if he had been to Ogden, Fithian, Collison, Potomac, or Armstrong on business, might bring home fresh meat as a summer luxury. But whatever else we ate came from the farm.

We had beef when the winter cold would keep a slaughtered steer till we, and probably some other family who shared the cost, could eat the whole of it. Mutton, on our farm, was more common. When I was fourteen I could kill, skin, clean, and hang a wether in thirty minutes. Pork and chicken we had oftenest of all. No day of the year ever stirred my brothers and me more than the day we butchered. The men built a fire under a cauldron standing on iron legs in the barnyard, and set up a wooden platform beside it. The hogs, dragged from the pen, squealed wildly while they were stuck and bled. Bloody hands plunged the fat dead bodies in the boiling water, lifted them on the platform, and scraped the bristles off with the edge of a corn-knife. Butcher knives, sharpened while the water boiled, cut up the carcasses. Part of the meat was saved to be eaten fresh or ground up into sausage. Hams went to the smoke house, sides to casks of brine, bellies and the waste to kettles to be rendered into lard or boiled down to soap fat. It took the whole household days to dispose of what the men got ready for us in half a day. Killing chickens was a lighter matter. A stealthy visit to the roost at night or a short chase by day, squawks, an expert wringing of a neck, a headless flopping on the ground, hot water and wet feathers, a knife to open the bird and find the joints: a few minutes were enough, and few days went by without such minutes. When we said "squeal like a stuck hog" or "run around like a chicken with its head off" we were taking our similes from life.

Bakers were as far away as butchers. Our own oven furnished all our bread, which we liked best to eat when it was so hot that butter would melt into it as into a sponge. So with all the kinds of biscuit and corn bread. The oven was never idle. Cakes and pies poured out of it. The pantry—always called the buttery—had a special box for cakes, a rack for pies, and a stone jar for cookies. My brothers and I were not supposed to cut a cake or pie without permission, but we had the run of the cookie jar.

So long as we lived at Hope I never even heard of buying vegetables or salad at a market. Our green season began with the first rhubarb, of which we knew that name although we usually called it pie plant. After a winter diet, rhubarb was such a delight it seemed a tonic. Then, in turn, radishes, lettuce, young onions, peas, string beans, wax beans, tomatoes, celery, parsnips, cabbage, turnips, from the vegetable garden, and from the truck garden strawberries, raspberries, blackberries, new potatoes, and roasting ears. From the earliest cherries to the latest winter apples some fruit or other was always ripe. And at the end of the season there were pumpkins between the corn rows.

"We eat what we can, and what we can't eat we can," said a country jingle. Knowing we could buy nothing fresh out of season, we had to save for winter what the summer had left behind. In the fall we ploughed up bushels of potatoes and picked barrels of apples for the cellar, where kegs of sauerkraut stood beside casks of salt pork. Other apples were buried in beds of straw in pits dug in the vegetable garden. We put up few vegetables but hundreds of glass jars of fruit and preserves, which filled shelf after shelf on the cellar wall. We dried apples and the cooked meat of pumpkins. Then we settled to our winter fare: meat and potatoes, bread and gravy, canned corn and canned tomatoes, pickles and preserves, pies and cakes. We were always greedy for anything made from corn grown and ground on the farm: mush and milk, fried mush, corn bread, corn meal cakes, and lye hominy. Our hominy, in ten-gallon jars, was left in the summer kitchen to freeze and thaw till it was tender. Weeks of this winter fare, and then rhubarb again. If the food was monotonous, we did not know it.

With some help from visiting dress-makers my mother made most of her own clothes and clothes for the boys when they were babies. When we were older, some of our shirts were made at home, and sometimes our heavy woolen stockings. From the village store we got rough straw hats for summer, fleece-lined caps and mittens for winter, rubber boots for spring and fall, and overalls for every day. The rest of our clothing came from Danville or—ordered by mail— from Chicago. We even had smart tweed suits from the Lilliputian Bazaar in New York. I admired them, but was embarrassed when the other boys thought they were stuck-up. We suffered now and then from my mother's taste. She would not let us wear high boots with brass-bound toes, nor felt boots with rubber overshoes, nor exposed suspenders. She made us put on overcoats on days when we felt it would be manlier to do without. Once she insisted that I go to school in a new pair of buttoned shoes which I was sure looked like a girl's. I sat at my desk all through the noon hour, refusing to join the other children in the playground for fear they might ridicule my shoes. But I seldom thought more about my clothing than if I had been a colt. Like a colt, I was uncomfortable, at least in warm weather, when I was forced to wear shoes. Everything else I took for granted, outgrew it, and passed it on to my younger brothers.

We were a masculine household, and I do not remember a single dress my mother wore while we lived at Hope, though I do remember words I heard her and her friends use: basque, bodice, sacque, front breadth, panel, hemstitch, featherstitch, basting, pleat, gore, ruching, tuck, bombazine, calico, gingham, silk, satin, tulle, voile, cambric, challis, ribbon, lace, fast color, leg-of-mutton sleeve, sash, shawl, corset, V-front, crochet, applique, Mother Hubbard (of which my mother disapproved), shirt waist, insertion, bustle, petticoat, chemise, drawers, mitts, broadcloth. The tumbled words are clearer in my memory than the things they stood for. The one garment of my mother's which I remember is a long gray shawl she wore one day when she drove Guy and me to my grandfather's in Potomac. It was a cool day, and the bronchos, Dandy and Nelly, were skittish. Arrived at the hitch-rack in front of the house, my mother got out and went to tie the off horse first. Dandy was wild, and the wind blew her shawl in his eyes. He wheeled, taking the gentler Nelly with him, and ran off down the road, with the two little boys screaming in the seat. The horses turned in at the barn, and one of the men caught them. I can still see the shawl whip upward in the wind. After that my mother was never quite so bold a horsewoman as she had been all her life.

The fashions in women's clothing must have changed, but I did not notice that, any more than I noticed that the fashions in boys' clothing changed hardly at all, except as boys grew older and, at about twelve, rose from knee breeches to long trousers. My father, less concerned than any of us about his clothes, seems to me now to have changed most during our ten years on the farm. His high hat gave way to a derby and then to a Fedora; his Prince Albert coat to a cutaway and then to a sack; his stiff-bosomed shirts to soft shirts, though with stiff cuffs and collars. He always wore a doctor's clothes, not a farmer's, and when he took a hand on the farm, he did it in old clothes. Work clothes in Hope were likely to be old clothes. A man might scatter manure in a frock-coat, green with age, which had once been black and his Sunday best.

Indoors, my father had an office in the lower floor of one wing of the house, cut off from the rest by a hall and stairway. There he saw his patients, and there, behind a partition in one corner, he put up their medicines. He pulled aching teeth, set dislocated joints, bound fractured bones in primitive splints. Sometimes he had an assistant, always a young doctor just out of medical school who had not yet found a practice of his own. Sometimes I was my father's assistant, whittling splints out of smooth pine or holding bandages. Once, when he removed dangerous tonsils from a boy of about my age, I dropped the chloroform on the mask which my father held, and later pinned the boy's hands down during the operation. In an emergency, my father might be called on for anything. He was Hope's only specialist, as well as its only practitioner. He was also its only veterinary, though most of the farmers knew how to treat their own sick animals. Guy, resentful because my father was away so much of the time seeing sick people, once wished he were a cow doctor.

A French observer of life in the United States declares that he found in the families of country doctors the sole American instance of something like an hereditary profession, almost an hereditary rank. While two of my father's brothers were country doctors and one had been at a medical school when he died, and another was a pharmacist, none of my brothers studied medicine. But our whole family had, I think, an obscure sense of being set a little apart by the profession. I felt half-guilty when I decided I did not want to be a doctor. The same thing happened to another boy, also the son of a country doctor, at about the same time in Minnesota. I think it is fair to guess that behind the passion which drove Martin Arrowsmith in his career lay a dim sense of guilt in Sinclair Lewis. Because he was not a doctor himself, he had to imagine his doctor-hero to the uttermost, as a kind of apology and tribute to the profession he felt he had deserted.

My father must have been at home a good deal, but I remember him as forever going and coming, particularly going out in black nights which, when I was small, frightened me. Now and then, when he was treating some infectious disease, he would not let us come near him, but as a rule we swarmed around and over him like puppies, for he was amiable, gay, and patient. He seemed never to be tired. After being away all night, he would drop down on a couch, even with the boys playing in the room on a rainy day, sleep for a quarter of an hour, and wake up a new man. He seldom forgot to bring us candy from the village. When we were expecting him, we used to wait at the mouth of the lane, our eyes on the point of the road from which he could first see us. If he had forgotten, he would, however wearily, turn his powerful, hard-gaited gray horse—Prince or Billy—around and gallop back to the store. Then we would run shouting to meet him.

The formal parlor had the marble-topped center-table that most parlors had, a cottage organ, and bookshelves covering half of one wall. Guy and I took our music lessons there, resisting music, which we thought girlish, until my mother gave up hope in us. We often read in the parlor, sprawled on the ingrain carpet which was comfortably padded underneath with a layer of straw. Heated by an open fireplace, where a fire was rarely built, the parlor was likely to be cold except in summer. It was a ceremonial room. But I there came as close to violent death as I ever came. When I was still small enough to wear a pinafore, I tried to reach something from the mantel, set fire to my clothing, and ran in flames and terror to my mother, who threw me down and rolled me in a rug.

My father's office had a small stove and the kitchen of course a cookstove. The rest of the house depended on the sitting-room, with its omnivorous Round Oak which overheated that room and had something to spare, through open doors, for the parlor and dining-room, and, through iron registers in the ceiling, for the bedrooms upstairs. We went upstairs only to sleep. In cold weather, my brothers and I undressed beside the stove, and then ran up the shivering stairway to our icy beds, which in the coldest weather had had the chill taken off by hot bricks wrapped in rags. Our baths we took in a washtub in the warm kitchen after supper.

Of the house's dozen rooms, we chiefly lived in three, and the three were really one, for the dining-room was hardly more than a broad passage between the sitting-room and the kitchen. I remember the kitchen best of all, with its smell of food, and the cheerful simmering of the kettle. Our kitchen was unlike anybody else's, for the windmill stood so close to the kitchen wall that we could open a casement window to get a fresh drink from the hogshead into which the mill pumped cool hard water. From the hogshead the waste water overflowed through a pipe to the milk-trough in the buttery, with its crocks of milk and cream, and murmured out through the drain. I know now that the mill ran only when there was wind and we needed water, but I seem, remembering, to hear always the creak and hum of the wheel and the clank of the shaft—though I remember, too, the still days when we had to disconnect the windmill and pump water by hand, not only for the house but also for the horse-tank in the barnyard.

From the small brick-paved court behind the kitchen Guy and I used to climb the windmill ladder, crawl around the frame to the kitchen roof, and scramble up the shingles to our bedroom window. Nothing about the house is so vivid to me, after these years, as that little court, where on summer evenings we sat on the edge of the porch and washed our feet in a tin basin, slopping the water carelessly on the worn red bricks. To this day, when I have to determine the points of the compass anywhere, I imagine myself back on the porch, always sitting with bare feet, looking up the long moraine toward what is for me the eternal North, with the village of Hope on my right, toward the eternal East.

7

TEN years, remembered, pour over me like a tide. Separate then, they have been mixed by time into one general memory.

My life on the farm seems to be not so much an experience
ten years long as a spacious moment in which everything
happened at once. I can remember when Frank and Mark
and Paul were born, but I find it hard to remember when
they had not yet been. Unless I force my reason to correct my
sight, I see us as always seven. My father and mother, called
Papa and Mamma. Guy and I, called the big boys. Frank and
Mark, the little boys. Paul, the baby. We lived together in
a busy tumult, in a close-knit affection which the later scat-
tering of the family has never weakened.

When I tell most of my friends that I had a happy childhood, I perceive that many of them are envious, more of
them skeptical. It has become as common to abuse families
as it used to be to exalt and sentimentalize them. An unhappy childhood is rated as an asset, like a lost love: something to be hugged. Without saying how he suffered as a
child, who can hint how sensitive he is? Who can prove he is
original now without recalling that he was rebellious then?
On that lewd scapegoat, the family, its members heap their
sins. I know there are unhappy families, tyrannical fathers,
nagging mothers, quarrelsome brothers and sisters. There
were unhappy families at Hope, cats and dogs, bears and
monkeys. But I no more believe that families in general are
as unhappy as most of my friends make out than I believe
that families in general are as happy as Dickens and Thackeray insisted. In any case, I am not generalizing. I had a
happy childhood in a happy family. My father was no tyrant.
My mother, while sharp and quick in punishment, did not
nag. And though my brothers and I often fought together,
we fought, not sulked, and never carried a grudge over to
the next fight. If I had to go today to a lone island with one
companion, there is no living man I should prefer to any of

my four brothers—though I should not know how to choose which one of them.

The years at Hope, remembered more intently, seem less like a single tide than like a slow, steady wheel, turning through the seasons.

I remember early days in June. Along with the whole family, I got up at dawn. My father, if he had not been away all night, as he often was, rode over the farm or made plans with the men. My mother set about breakfast. The little boys rushed out of the house to play. Guy did various chores, and I went to drive up the cows, my special chore. In those fresh dawns nothing was pleasanter than to find a cow still lying down and, after I had roused her, to step from the cold grass into the warm spot where she had lain. I followed the cows at their sluggish, wandering gait to the cowshed, where they went to their own stanchions and waited ruminantly for me to milk them.

To have to milk two or three cows morning and evening is to be a slave to them, I know, but I felt my slavery less than my pride in being the eldest brother and bearing this responsibility. And I enjoyed milking, even the cantankerous, tough-uddered old Shorthorn and the Jersey that kicked like a horse. Milking would give me, I had been told, a strong grip. Milking was a good time for oratory. Squatting on a three-legged stool, my head pressed against the cow's flank but my eyes alert for her lashing tail, I made up patriotic speeches, orotund and magniloquent. "By the might of his own intellect," one sentence began with a rising inflection, "and by the power of his own will," it went on with a dying fall, "Abraham Lincoln rose to the highest level in the land," with a ringing statement. I remember no more of it.

Meanwhile the men were feeding, currying, and harnessing

the work horses in the barn. I could hear the horses biting at their ears of corn and stamping at the flies, the men pounding their curry combs and loudly ordering the horses to stand over.

With full pails, I went in to breakfast, after washing my hands in a basin outside the kitchen door. Breakfast was much the same as any other meal, except that it included no dessert. We ate less for refreshment after sleep than for strength for the day ahead. I hurried to the barn, led out my team, snapped their reins together, and drove them to the cornfield where I had left my plough standing the night before.

It was now six o'clock. For five hours I steered the plough back and forth along the rows, turning the grass and weeds up to the deadly sun, and leaving a wake of warm, mellow loam for my bare feet. From eleven to one I stopped work for food and a longer rest than most farmers took. Then back to the field till six again. The first hours of the afternoon were the most trying of the day, the horses lagging under the relentless sky, waves of heat rising visibly from the ground. I went again and again to the jug of water left in the shade of the hedge. Later, when the sun began to turn red, a breeze stirred the still air. Horses and boy got a kind of second wind, ploughed their final rows at a quicker pace, and came back to supper at a trot.

After I had unharnessed and fed my team, milked the cows which the little boys had brought in from the pasture, eaten my supper, turned out the cows and horses, I must have been tired as I sprawled on the grass under a tree beside the house, but I remember only a gorged, happy languor in which my mood expanded with the shadows. Not even the close, hot nights of Illinois kept me from sleep when I went to bed at eight.

On the Fourth of July we got up as early as on a work-day and drove in the carriage to Potomac for the celebration. Most people went directly to the picnic grounds, in a grove just west of town. We went first to my grandfather's, left the team in his stable, out of reach of firecrackers, and walked the rest of the way. The official part of the celebration was always the same. On a raised platform, draped with bunting and a flag, the same kind of orator made the same kind of speech. On hard plank benches the same audience listened with the same nods of agreement. The same band played badly the same anthem which the same patriots sang worse. The place of the ceremony was a sober oasis in a desert of hilarious noise: the crack and rattle of small crackers, the roar of giant crackers, the bang of torpedoes, the whine of balloon whistles, the call of hawkers and barkers at the stands, the stamping and whinnying of horses tied at the racks, babies crying, boys shouting. The smells of the day were as insistent as its sounds: bruised grass and broken weeds underfoot, popcorn and peanuts, acrid dust, horse-dung, and patriotic gunpowder everywhere.

After the speaking, the plank benches were shoved to-gether to make tables, stuffed baskets came from the carriages, and enormous meals appeared. Families ate in clans, we with the multitudinous Tillotsons. Later came a baseball game, some sly courting, much talking, and at last the tired hour, hated by boys and girls, at which the annual ecstasy started to break up. Most of the country people went home for milking. We stayed at my grandfather's house for supper, watched the fireworks, and drove back to Hope under the stars which we seldom saw in summer. I remember the night when I kept awake the whole trip and discovered that Potomac's moon was Hope's moon too.

By the Fourth the corn was generally laid by, and we turned to hay-making. I drove the rake which piled the swaths of timothy or clover in windrows and then, strad-dling the windrows, into rough cocks for the forks of the men who pitched and loaded them on hayracks. At the barn, I led the single horse which with a rope and pulleys could lift a quarter of a load at a time, draw it to the ridgepole, carry it spinning along the track, and, when the fork was tripped, drop the hay into the mow. Rain, of course, was always the hay-maker's risk and enemy, but in fine weather hay-making was the cleanest, sweetest work of the year.

After hay-making, threshing. No farm at Hope was large enough to need a threshing outfit of its own. A dozen or so farmers would organize a ring, hire a thresher, and arrange among themselves how many men and teams each farmer was to furnish and in what order they were to take their turns.

Our turn came. Chugging and coughing, a steam engine brought the high, huge red threshing-machine along the road, made a wide turn at the lane gate, manœuvered its slow way to the place where the year's strawstack was to stand. There the engineer and his firemen pegged the thresher and the engine as far apart as the wide leather belt would reach. Men with teams and hayracks rattled to the field where the oats had already been cut and bound and set in shocks to dry. The first two hayracks loaded drew up alongside the thresher, another team backed a wagonbed under the spout out of which the threshed oats would pour, the feeder settled himself at the mouth of the machine with his cutters. With a hoot of the whistle the engine let loose its power till the thresher hummed. The men on the hay-racks pitched sheaves upon the sloping tables on each side of the feeder, his helpers with quick knives cut the bands, and he with expert motions, now right hand now left, swept the sheaves headfirst into the humming throat, which growled as its iron teeth caught them. Then began a rhythmic thunder which stopped only at noon and night. A steady stream went as sheaves into the mouth, was broken up in those roaring bowels, and came out either as oats by the spout or as straw through the blower, which swung back and forth in an arc like the new moon.

This process was Hope's chief experience of what it means when machinery calls the dance and sets the pace. While the thresher ran no man could step aside, and all men must work together. The loaded hayracks came, the unloaded hayracks went, without any interval. The knives of the cutters never rested and had always to be careful of the feeder's hands, which never rested except when one feeder spelled another. The stackers, working in the chaff with handkerchiefs around their necks and sometimes over their mouths, wallowed back and forth under the blower. The men or boys who waited at the spout kept shoveling the oats forward in their wagonbeds. Loaded, they started off for Fithian, eight miles away, urged their horses up the incline to the elevator, and saw their oats dumped into a bin which might be emptied that very day into a box-car going to Chicago. Then where? There was no philosopher in Hope to brood over the process, no poet to celebrate it, but it stirred us all by the loud noise and ruthless purpose which dominated us in our brief turn at tending the long line which at harvest reached from how many fields to how many mills, from seed in the ground to the nourished flesh of men and beasts.

Threshing was the large dramatic episode of our year, and after that the summer seemed to draw its breath. Old Settlers' Day, in August and at Potomac, never equaled the Fourth, lacking firecrackers and fireworks. The reminiscences of township pioneers, always old and seldom eloquent, could not rouse us as the Fourth's national patriotism had done. The wheel of the seasons turned quietly through burnt, brown, and yellow days into fall and the earliest crisp nights.

As my brothers and I went to school from the first of September to the first of June, I was a spectator not an actor in the main work of the farm during those months. Fall, winter, and spring meant to me, outside of school and play, only morning and evening chores: milking, lugging in fuel, running errands, helping my mother in the house. I remember little about cornhusking—shucking corn the farmers called it—except the sound of the men getting their horses out of the barn before daylight, the thud of ears thrown against the bumpboard, the ring of scoop-shovels as they unloaded at the corncrib. Corn-shelling was to threshing what Old Settlers' Day was to the Fourth of July—not unlike it, but a paler copy. About winter I remember best the horses, with shaggy coats, stamping in cold stalls, the cows shaking their stanchions and sending out vaporous breath, the sheep in their sheds crowding and snuffling and bleating—these and the English sparrows which fluttered in the lantern light when we went at night to stable or barn or shed, to kill the pests and save their heads for the bounty of two cents apiece which the township treasurer paid. I remember Christmas as a mysterious, spendthrift month, and do not remember Easter at all. The spring ploughing comes back to me as the smell of straight furrows of black earth and the sight of birds following the plough to pick up worms and grubs. But once or twice in the spring, at sheep-shearing, I stayed out of school for a day or two, to tie up the fleeces as they came greasy and stinking from the shearing-floor, and to trample them into the enormous burlap bags in which they went off to the railroad and factory.

I appear to tell of one year though there were ten, and such different years as those I lived through when I was a small child and when I was as tall and almost as strong as any man. But one year was as much alike another as the seasons and the crops which in annual rotation ruled our lives. If we were never bored, however tired, it was because we were always busy. Remote from the world at large, we did not realize it. No radio and no movies let the world in upon us, and no telephone, till the last year, brought even our neighbors close. The automobile had not yet enlarged the radius of the farmer's life from four or five miles to forty or fifty. Except to go to school or church and to visit a few relatives, my brothers and I left the farm hardly a dozen times a year.

Our liveliest interruptions were the too rare visits of my mother's brothers. The twins, Uncle Warren and Uncle Wallace, went from college to be Columbian Guards at the World's Fair, and came back with fine tales. Then they had something—I never knew what—to do with railroads, and brought us news as rousing as if they had been sailors off at sea. Afterwards they followed our older Uncle Clinton and Uncle Mark to the Indian Territory, about which, when any of the four returned, we heard of Choctaws, Chickasaws, Creeks, Cherokees, Osages, railroads, ranches, hunting, cowboys, booms, and a coming country. Tall, lean, brown, bachelors and Democrats, smelling of strong tobacco, talking casually of towns and distances, they were like windows in our plain walls.

And there was reading. I can barely remember when I could not read, and except in the most crowded seasons I read hours a day. Few current books ever reached Hope. The first book I remember owning was Green's history of England, in five volumes, which I won as a prize at school when I was nine. Its chapters on the dim Anglo-Saxons stand up in my memory like old photographs. Hawthorne with his New England was less real, and Plutarch with his Greeks and Romans. We had the works of Scott, Dickens, Thackeray, Mark Twain. Like everybody else in Hope, we had Ben-Hur, which most people read as if it were part of the Apocrypha, and two or three volumes of James Whitcomb Riley, who belonged to Indiana but might have been writing about us. We had Gibbon, in whom I dipped. We had Shakespeare, whose poems I read before his plays, Oliver Wendell Holmes, whose humorous verses tickled my father to tears, and Whittier—but no Poe or Whitman, no Tennyson or Browning. I remember crying, at five or six, over the story of Evangeline which my mother read me. When I was older I preferred the legends of Hiawatha, then the only mythology I knew. I read Fenimore Cooper and Irving, Pilgrim's Progress and Robinson Crusoe and Gulliver's Travels and the Last Days of Pompeii and Little Women and Quo Vadis. After I had discovered that I could order books by mail from Chicago, I bought books for all my birthday or Christmas presents to my family—always books I had not read myself. We all read.

We read greedily and uncritically. A book was a book, and it was interesting or it was not. We liked Dickens and Mark Twain best, and David Copperfield and Huckleberry Finn

best of all. After my father's youngest brother committed
suicide in Cincinnati, my brothers and I remembered that
when, shortly before, he was staying with us he had read
Huckleberry Finn and had not laughed once. We thought
that this somehow explained the tragedy. If we had no new
books to read, we read old ones again. From my father's medical books, which I read more than I let on, I learned a great
deal about anatomy. I made little of the Compleat Angler
which my grandfather, angler himself, took for a kind of
hand-book, though he often disagreed with it. He called
Walton an old codger, but I doubt that he knew or cared
when Walton lived. None of us knew or cared about literary
chronology. Books for us were like stars, all apparently the
same distance away, yet some brighter than others. Reading
was simply experience otherwise denied us. We traveled without leaving Hope. When later we did leave, life was not so
strange as we expected. Books had enlarged the village.

8

IF, REMEMBERING, I make out life at Hope as a cool pastoral,
I misrepresent it. There was the weather. Between its almost
equatorial summers and its almost arctic winters Illinois has
a range of temperature to be found in few quarters of the
earth. In July or August the thermometer might stand for
hours a day at 110 in the shade. After such days the swelter-
ing nights of corn-growing weather brought no real relief.
Men lay on top of unbearable sheets and horses sweat at midnight. It might be 30 below zero in January or February,
when the cold came down like a clamp, and the roads froze

in iron ruts. Such cold seldom lasted long, but was followed by sudden thaws, as trying as the next fierce spells of cold again. I wonder, now, at the fortitude with which we bore these extremes. It was the fortitude of ignorance. We barely knew that elsewhere the seasons could be easier. We no more thought of going south for the winter or north for the summer than if we were still in the eighteenth century, when the United States chose Washington to be its capital. Because we did not realize that we might suffer less from weather, we could not realize how much we suffered, and so perhaps suffered less.

After Spoon River became famous, my brother Mark once asked me if Hope, from which he went away at six, had been at all like that infested village. I recalled some dark or furtive story that I, still a boy, had picked up about every household in the neighborhood.

One Sunday night a farmer was murdered on his way home from church—not our church—but the one just south of us. A scared rider came for my father, who the next morning brought fatal news. The farmer had quarreled with two of his hired men. They had armed themselves, waylaid him and his wife, and, when he whipped his horses past them, had fired and killed him. The county sheriff arrested them and took them off to Danville, where they were hanged. We heard stories of their insolent bravado in the jail. One of them was said to wear a piece of rope around his neck, to toughen it. The other told a visitor that he had a new job for the fall: he was going to stretch hemp. In their native Kentucky they might have had ballads made and sung about them. Hope had no ballad-makers. The crime was remembered in prose.

Two farmers in Hope had a feud over a bad fence and

roving stock. They did not speak when they met on the road, and usually avoided each other. But one day when one of them was in the blacksmith shop, the other came in, angry and vicious. Without a word he grabbed a spare wagon-spoke and attacked. The first, throwing up his arm, was struck with the end of the club on a fleshy muscle which tore like a rag. A great red-whiskered man, he came staggering and bawling to my father's office to have the ugly three-cornered tear sewed up. Nobody did anything about the assault. The victim was unpopular, the victor feared. That so small a man had won a fight and that so large a man had blubbered made the affair ridiculous.

Feuds, it is true, seldom lasted. They sank to grudges and died out, without actions to keep them alive. One of the farmers had a grudge against my father, because the farmer's son had died of some sickness which my father had been unable to cure. I heard only vaguely of the one-sided grudge, and never saw any outward signs of it. My grandfather, years before, had disputed with his nearest neighbor over the boundary line between their farms. Each of them had planted his hedge where he thought it ought to be, leaving a long strip of waste land which in time had grown up to a matted tangle of weeds and bushes. Called a devil's lane, it stood there as a stubborn memorial, meaning nothing. My grandfather and his neighbor, as old men, were civil enough, and one of the neighbor's daughters was my mother's closest friend. When, writing my first novel, I tried to work into it these two grudges, I found them the dry seed of a kind of drama alien to this community.

Violence at Hope was likely to be swift and savage. A furious man might beat a balky horse with a pitchfork or a trace-chain. Fathers might punish their sons with blacksnake whips. There were brutal husbands, though public feeling was all against them, and if their wives left them, the wives got the sympathy. But interference in private matters came slowly if it ever came. Some of the farmhouses, we knew, were inviolate castles where evil things went on.

The scandals outnumbered the crimes and misdemeanors. A woman in the village, whose husband was a drover and often away from home, drifted into loose habits. Men visited her at night, and laughed about it at the village store. Whether or not she deserved her bad name from the first, she had it and was damned. The preacher one year set himself to save her, and he was damned too, and dismissed as certainly a fool and probably a lecher. Every one talked, nobody told her husband. At last he found out when she had a child which he was sure could not be his. Divorced, she left for Danville to practice a trade. There she prospered, opened a disorderly house, and made her bad name conspicuous. For years she must have had a wider renown than any woman or man who had ever come from Hope.

Adultery in the village was so rare that I heard of no other instance of it, except that some of the rougher married men went disreputably to Danville. Circumstances at home made it almost impossible for a married woman ever to be alone with any man except her husband. On the prairie a call in the daytime was certain to be noticed, and the waking hours of the night were brief and domestic. Wives had few opportunities to stray, and, I think, fewer impulses. Married young, mothers soon, and generally overworked, they had neither strength nor leisure for adultery. I imagine that their sexual experience was curt and unimaginative. When they hinted at it, as they seldom did, they called it, revealingly, family duty. The married women fixed the sexual code of Hope,

and the married men had to fall in with it. So did the unmarried women with respect to married men. Without
women adultery could not thrive.

Fornication was not uncommon. Young men and women
did their courting without chaperons, much of it in long
drives on dark nights. When this led to hasty marriages and
babies born six or seven months afterwards, it caused talk
and reproach that gradually ceased if the offenders settled
down and behaved themselves. Only the censorious and the
humorous remembered such things long. Fornication that
did not lead to marriage roused grave scandal. If a man
seduced—ruined—a girl, and deserted her, her outraged
father might drive her from the house. This seemed old-
fashioned. In most cases she remained at home, outcast, till
she married some other man who was not important enough
to be fastidious. As she was punished more than her first
lover, she was blamed more. "It's for the man to ask, and for
the woman to say no," the blunt saying ran. The seducer's
fault need not prevent his early marriage to some more prudent girl. Fornication at Hope, at least as I heard of it, was
always serious or desperate with fear of conception, never
light or merry. Women held to strict responsibility did not
play at love.

The comedy of sex appeared in obscenity. On a farm like
ours, even small boys could not overlook the hot deeds of
potent rams, roosters, and gobblers, could not fail to get at
the reason for them, and could not help making comparisons
between them and human conduct. Boys of ten knew all
that most of them would ever know about the theory and
science of reproduction, and were more than ready for experience to teach them how to feel about it. Desire did not
surprise them. They had gone to school in the barn. The barn

was the men's house, where women seldom came, and where on rainy days the hired men joked. Mothers might speak of love as if it were always the sacred way to motherhood, and fathers as if it were a pleasing, harmless motive in the business of marriage. But there was still, boys knew, something unaccounted for: the rank impulse that rose in them like sap, salty and acute, agitating them. Into this the hired men, talking, let a crude light that seemed to answer morbid questions. When the hired men laughed, broad and lewd, the sultry air was stirred and the tension eased. Foul and false as it often was, their obscenity quieted while it excited us. It enlivened a passion which without them might have been too sentimental or too tragic. If obscenity was comedy, it was realism too.

The pioneer time had seen hard drinkers in Hope, but in the last years of the century liquor could not be bought within twenty miles and seldom reached us, though a few men went on sprees to Danville. Gambling was heard of only in men who speculated in grain on the Chicago Board of Trade, and invariably lost their money. The other vices of Hope were the greed which drove whole families to senseless toil, the avarice which denied them satisfactions they might as well have had, the cruelty which came both from anger and from stupidity. Hope was, I repeat, a microcosm.

9

OUR last night at Hope we spent not in the farmhouse but in the village house where I had been born. The neighbors who were our best friends had invited us there because our own goods were packed and loaded, ready to leave at day-light. As I was to drive one of the wagons, I got up while it was still dark, and walked across the fields, to feed and harness my team.

Still dark, the night was beginning to break up. In the close, high silence I could almost hear the rumble of the dawn. The first birds fussed. Roosters crew. A dog barked. Walking, I seemed to feel rather than see, over my shoulder, a faint light lessening the stars. I looked back and saw the horizon pale and then flush. Thin rays from the sun broke through and touched the sky above it. My mood rose with the light, as if the sun were in me. I had been heavy and relaxed with sleep, full of night. Walking alone between night and day, and both of them somehow inside me, I expanded with a tingling, melting ecstasy, as if my bones were water and my flesh were air. The earth under me, the sky over me, had pulse and breath, and my own pulse and breath moved with them. I could hear my heart.

The horses were stirring in the barn, but the house was empty and quiet. I stopped for a moment and looked at them, at the cold white fences and the shadowy trees. There was no reflection in my mood, only boundless sensation. What I felt, now, was not the general night and day, earth and sky, but the farm itself, and the familiar ways of living there. On every rod of land I had worked or played, and I could have found my way blindfold anywhere. The farm was in me. I had eaten it as food. I had been sheltered by house and barn and tree, in every weather. The animals were hardly less kin to me than my family. My hands knew all the tools. If I had thought, I must have known that I was not merely leaving the farm but was being uprooted. Some of it would come with me. Some of me would stay behind. The filaments of habit and memory which bound me were tougher than I had ever realized. Even in my dissolving ecstasy I felt the pain of separation and half-foresaw a long homesickness.

The mood passed and left only my will, eager to go from the too-familiar farm and village to the unknown, promising town. I harnessed and hitched up the mules and waited for Guy to join me. Then we climbed on top of beds and chairs and tables for the slow, dusty drive.

Town

IF HOPE had been an idyl, Urbana was a comedy. The comedy began the first Sunday. At Hope we had always gone to church, not because we were devout but because everybody went and because on Sunday there was nothing else to do. Old people who called the church the meeting-house gave it its true name. In Urbana we went, that first Sunday, by a familiar instinct. It seemed the natural way to get acquainted.

I can only guess how the experience struck the others. We never talked about it. But I saw in a few minutes that what we found was not what I wanted. The preacher was as tire-some as he had been at Hope, where I had heard him before. The music was dreary. Worst of all, the younger members of the congregation looked, I thought, rustic: lumpish boys and savorless girls. My disappointment turned quickly to rebel-lion. I had not, during my last months at Hope, been restless for anything like this. Obscure as my ambition was, and crudely as it asserted itself in a young snobbishness, I knew that I demanded something quite different. In similar cir-cumstances, now, I should realize I was bored. Then I hardly understood the word, and not at all the dangers of boredom to a lively mind. I did not know that, having outgrown a pastoral, I could not bear to live it over again, or any aspect of it, in another and less suitable place. I only felt a need for change, as dumbly as a wild animal in the migrating season.

It would take a long story to tell of all that came from this disappointment and rebellion, which I think my brothers also felt from the first, though I may have infected them. Soon we were outspoken in our dislike. Whatever our reasons, our argument was that the new friends we were making at school did not go to the church of our first Sunday. At Hope we had not had one set of friends for Sundays and another for week-days. It would be disagreeable here. We insisted on going to some church our school friends went to. My father did not care, but my mother was troubled. The congregation I thought rustic had welcomed us, and they assumed that we would join them. To leave after a few Sundays would be a snub which my mother thought would be dreadful. I suspect she was nearly as much disappointed as any of us. If she was, she would never have admitted it, even to herself. That would have seemed to her conscience to be a kind of disloyalty to our old life: a change of heart with a change of scene. Her impulse would have been to stay on at almost any cost. The cost she could not meet was the clamorous discontent of her sons. She yielded, and we decided on another church.

The minister of the first church called on my mother and accused us of turning from simple virtue to worldliness. Few accusations could have hurt her as that must have. I remember her flushed face and unhappy eyes. But she held out to the last, as she would have held out for the sake of the boys against overwhelming waters or consuming fires. Later, she hit upon the excuse that she had always preferred the doctrine of the church which we selected.

The episode belongs to comedy, for there was little to choose between the two churches. A church could not mean to us in Urbana what it had meant in Hope, where it had

stood up in our lives as visible as the steeple, as audible as the
bell, across the prairie. Life in town had other centers. My
brothers and I went willingly to church and Sunday school
in Urbana as long as we enjoyed meeting other children
there, and then more and more unwillingly till about the
time we were old enough for college. All of us were cheerful
unbelievers by sixteen or seventeen, with brief worry and no
regret. Guy once said that though he had tried to pray he
had always found it like trying to telephone and not being
able to reach the operator. My mother was deeply distressed
by such heathenism. She thought of churchgoing and goodness as cause and effect, the effect unlikely if not impossible
without the cause. But I could never see that any of us was
either better or worse for going to church or better or worse
for giving up the habit.

2

THE shift in our attitude toward church must have been the
same as thousands of American families were then going
through. With us it was the first step in a larger process.

At Hope we had lived in easy touch with an entire community, a parish with one church, a district with one school,
a social group with a single occupation. Our society had been
almost classless. I remember an argument I had with one of
the hired men, who said I was rich. I denied it. "Well," he
said, "anyway, your dad is. He's as rich as an old Jew."
When I told about this at home, I could see that while my
father was tickled my mother was disturbed. However the
people of Hope might want to prosper, they knew that to do

it was to run the risk of being thought, somehow, eccentric.
The knowledge came less from a dogma of equality, though
they held that also, than from a feeling of fraternity, a sense
of neighborliness. Extremes in wealth or poverty, in opinions or emotions, in vices or even in virtues, unsettled the
balance of averages. A man who was a good neighbor had to
be more or less like his neighbors. The community might be
large enough for private temperaments, but not for separate
classes.

In Urbana we found, if not quite separate classes, fairly
distinct groups. The first was the townspeople, the families
of official, professional, and business men who had most of
them been born there, as had the fathers of some of them.
The second was the families of retired farmers who had not
yet been made over into townspeople. The third was the
workers, some with families and some not, in the railroad
yards. The fourth was the teachers and students of the University of Illinois: this last group as numerous as all the
others put together. We did not at once distinguish these
groups, or perhaps realize that groups existed. But we could
not help being soon aware of little conflicts and incompati-
bilities in manners which divided the new society into which
we had come.

Most of the retired farmers had selected Urbana to retire
to, as we had, because of the University. They brought a
good deal of the farm with them: a horse or two, a cow,
chickens. They were likely to go on wearing country clothes
and almost certain to go on keeping country hours. Men got
up at daylight to tend their animals or work in their gardens,
to walk after a heavy breakfast to the post office for the mail
which the postman would have brought in an hour or so,
and to sit all morning, in warm weather, shirt-sleeved on

their front porches. They were often homesick for their farms and logy from not having enough to do. Their wives had too much: the same meals to cook as ever, and still more sweeping, dusting, washing, ironing than on the farm. They drudged while their husbands rusted and their children adapted themselves as rapidly as possible to the town.

We did not think of ourselves as retired farmers at all. My father was a doctor who had moved his office to Urbana, to practice medicine there while he went on farming at Hope. But neither did we think of ourselves as townspeople. We were a self-sufficient family for whom the town of Urbana was a stopping-place between the farm and the University. Uprooted from a community in which we had been absorbed, my brothers and I never took root, but lived detached, like Americans.

The family itself began, unconsciously, to split up. My father remained at Hope through our first Urbana winter, partly because he wanted to round out a full twenty years in his first practice. I entered the high school, Guy and Frank and Mark a grade school in another part of town. Instead of going every day, as at Hope, to be taught in one room by one teacher along with all our friends, we now scattered to different teachers, different friends. Within a few months my brothers were almost strangers to me. Except for Frank and Mark, who had started to school in the same class and stayed together to the end of college, my brothers were equally strangers to each other. We ate and slept in the same house and acknowledged the authority of the same parents. Against hostile outsiders we would have united quickly enough, if there had been any. But, left to ourselves, we took our own ways in brotherly independence. I know next to nothing about what the others did or thought or felt during the eight

years I lived in Urbana. We became acquainted only after
we were men.

As the oldest of them, I had to head the conflict with our
parents which sprang out of the change from village to town.
It began, I think, in the second or third week in high school
when I was elected president of my class. The election surprised me. I had supposed that high school would be more
formidable and resistant to a newcomer. This might have
been at Hope, where I had been used to little offices. But I
was pleased, too. Being president made me feel at home with
boys and girls who had lived in Urbana all their lives.
Among them I must not be rustic, whatever my father and
mother might be. They thought football dangerous. They
regarded dancing as frivolous, and my mother—not my father
—believed it was probably immoral. Almost nobody had ever
danced at Hope since the pioneer time. She could not help
remembering the old prairie rowdyism from which her generation had turned in disgust.

As to football I was so obstreperous that they had to yield,
though neither of them would ever see me play. Their solici-
tude seemed to me absurd, even when I came home with a
sprained knee or a wrenched neck or a lip which my teeth
had cut through. I never understood how they felt until I
saw my own daughter schooling her hunter over a jump in
a rough field—saw her and realized how absurd, if not insulting, my disquiet seemed to her.

Dancing was the subject of a long debate. I wanted less
to dance than to win an argument: to make my mother
admit that she had been wrong and give her willing permission. Reason must prevail. Guy, a little later, paid no
attention to her prejudice but went ahead and did as he
pleased. His disobedience and silence of course troubled her

less than my obedience and frankness. Unreason suffers more from reasoning than from opposition or defeat. But I suffered too. In all my life I have never felt such humiliation as when, at high school parties, the others danced and I could not. Since it would have humiliated me still more to acknowledge that I was not allowed to, I never acknowledged it. Instead I made up excuses, which I hoped would sound funny, about how awkward I was, and what a kindness it was to the girls that I did not dance with them, and why I looked with mature scorn on such childish games. Nobody believed me. My refusal was taken as some kind of singularity. My friends would have let it go at that, but I could not. I was by nature a whole boy wanting to live a whole life in a whole community. Dancing became a symbol, something that marked the pattern and set the rhythm of the town, distinguishing it from the plainer and slower village. Not to be free to do this one thing was to feel shut out from everything. Feeling shut out, I was too proud to compromise. After three or four experiences I stayed away from every gathering of my new friends where there would be dancing.

This did not last long. Time does for unreason what reasoning cannot do, and my mother in the end not only permitted me but urged me to dance. I had won my point. My younger brothers, as they grew older, had the benefit of my rebellion. Frank and Paul played football on later high school teams, and all of them danced, as naturally as natives. The conflict in the family ceased to be between village manners and town manners, and settled into the perennial conflict between parents and children.

There seems to me to have been as little reason for it in our family as in any I have ever heard of. My father and mother were affectionate and as indulgent as they thought they dared be, and my father was humorous. When, in a savage resentment against one of his teachers, Paul swore that he would leave school, my father said: "I tell you what you do. You go to your room and write out the story of what happened. Then put it away and read it after a while." Paul did not begin the document. But affection, indulgence, and humor alike are powerless against the instinct of children to rebel. It is as essential to their minds and wills as exercise to their bodies. If they have no reasons for it they invent them, like nations bound on war. It is hard to imagine families limp enough to be always at peace. Wherever there is character there will be conflict. The best that parents and children can hope for is that the wounds of their conflict may not be too deep or too lasting.

My own wound from my conflict and my withdrawal from the gayer society of the high school showed itself in solitary habits in which I took a morose, romantic pleasure. I used to say, and believe, that this chapter of my youth determined the course of my whole life: turning me from an absorbed participant in whatever went on around me into a self-conscious spectator. I am now as sure as I am sure of anything that nothing but physical constraint could have kept me, in any society or circumstances, from becoming a scholar and a writer. Actually I have not been a spectator, except to all the phases of politics. In profession and business I have never been bewildered or incompetent, and I have, to put the thing precisely, earned more money than I ever dreamed of as a boy. But if I was to be a scholar and a writer, I had at some time to set about it, saving for a special purpose the needed hours a day which might have been sunk in the general life of the community. I should have seized on some other occasion, if not on this, and should have found a picturesque excuse. Morose and romantic sentiments are fine company in the most studious solitude.

3

I REMEMBER when, soon after we moved to Urbana, I first exposed in words a secret which, until I spoke, I had hardly known I cherished.

"Have you ever thought, Carl," my mother said to me, "what you are going to do when you get big?" She meant when I should be a man. I was already a lank six feet tall.

"Oh, I don't know. Maybe I'll be a writer."

These are not the words we might have used, but the exact words we did use. They are as clear to me now as they were then. Her question had startled and excited me. My answer came without my willing it, almost without my meaning it, as if I had suddenly stumbled on it in my mind. I saw it there and heard it on my lips at the same time. Who can tell which is first, the idea or the word?

Perhaps the idea had been less in my mind than in my mother's. "I have always thought," she said, "that it would be wonderful to write romances."

I remember thinking that romances seemed an old-fashioned term for what I meant, which was novels. But no matter about terms. I had made an enormous discovery, of something I was quickly aware had been waiting to be discovered, evident enough if I had noticed it. Of course I wanted to be a writer. I would be a writer. From that day I never had any other ambition.

My ambition was as blind as if I had set my heart on a

trip through lonely space to the moon. I had never seen a writer or, so far as I knew, anybody who had ever seen one. Some of the professors in the University had written books, but I had never heard of them, and I should not have cared if I had. In my world a book, unless otherwise described, was still a novel. Even the poetry I had read had been chiefly stories. To write would be to tell stories. I had no theories or principles about that. It never occurred to me that in writing a book I could imagine myself over the obstacles which hindered me in actual life, or could get even with persons who angered me, or could bring new light or fresh beauty into existence. I wanted to write stories because I liked to read them and had lived a good part of most of my days in a stream of narrative. If I became a writer I could go on living in that pleasant stream.

Nor did it occur to me to take anybody into my confidence. My ambition for three or four years was the quietest of obsessions, an instinct that grew as if it fed itself. The first writing I did outside of school was comments on the books I read, usually one a day. I did not know that such things as book reviews had been written before, but I hit without guessing it upon what was to be for me a useful road to journalism. I wrote dozens of little dry, priggish essays—notes, rather—on good books and bad books, not too sure which were which. Though I was not a critic, I wrote criticism, by instinct or by accident. Instinct and accident are hard to tell apart.

What I wrote in school I did not consider writing at all, except once, when I had been asked to turn a passage from the Lady of the Lake into prose. To my surprise I found that the words I was using had become pliant and living, and that I could, it seemed to me, bend and fit them to the sense of the original, which I thought I had bettered. If I had had anybody to talk with about this, and had been willing to talk, I might have enjoyed it, like any other writer. But the high school in Urbana had nothing resembling an intellectual life. The only artist in it was Chic Sale, already a comedian, whom we thought less funny than his younger brother. Chic left high school after a year to work in the railroad yards. We heard he made the men laugh so much in the machine shop that he had to be transferred to the paint shop, where he would not be dangerous to hands operating swift machines.

I did not mind having no intellectual life in common with my friends. My secret made me feel important and superior, and it gave a kind of direction to all I did. But I did not think always, or perhaps very often, about it. Though the dim future might be intellectual, the present was animal and social.

4

THE summer before I was seventeen I went to the Indian Territory, where one of my uncles was now commandant of a Choctaw military school. A good many men from Vermilion County had gone to the Territory, and like other colonists they helped each other while they were helping themselves. My uncle, who had got his post through his Illinois connections, appointed me to run a kind of canteen at a summer school, held at the academy, for the teachers of the Choctaw nation. My daily duties were light but long. I drove into Hartshorne in the morning for ice cream, soft drinks, candy, and tobacco, and had to be on hand at the store till night selling them. My profits paid the expenses of my trip.

I found time to become acquainted with several young Indians, winter students of the academy, who were at the summer session. One of them was the son of the Choctaw governor, another was already a Choctaw politician. I had expected them to be more Indian than they were, or than I perceived. They seemed to me like white boys of about my own age. We hunted, rode horseback, and played baseball together, and they went with me when I tramped over the mountains looking for tarantulas, scorpions, centipedes, and strange insects for my cyanide bottle. For a month or so I was an entomologist, because my own school had required me to make a collection as the price of leaving before the close of the term. But I was not an anthropologist, any more than the young Indians were. They taught me a few Choctaw words, told me a few Choctaw legends, which I thought thin and dry. Only once did one of them, the politician, show what I considered the true Indian character. He declaimed the old address of Spartacus to the gladiators with forest eloquence. Or so it struck me then. Orator of a defeated and insulted race, as I heard between his lines, he threw back at the victors his lofty challenge. Not till later did I reflect that he was a politician, and that I too knew the address of Spartacus by heart.

Most Urbana boys of high school age made some journey or other, generally to the west or south, less often to the east, and came back with stories of their adventures. A very few of the townspeople spent summers on the Great Lakes or winters in Florida, and a larger number took trips—as they called it—now and then to see the country—particularly

California. The workers at the railroad yards might drift from job to job, and the professors at the University leave town for long vacations. But Urbana as a whole did little traveling. Automobiles, good roads, and cheap gasoline had not yet produced their lively race of casual, informal nomads. Mexico and even Canada seemed as remote as Europe.

My father had bought another farm only three hours away at a horse's gait, and we went there in summer. The boys could be useful and could be more easily kept out of town mischief. Incidentally we were kept out of such summer sports as tennis and golf. I never played either and have always been indifferent to both. But from the first days in spring when it was warm enough for the track team to go out of doors, to the last of November, when the football season ended on Thanksgiving Day, I seldom stopped thinking about the school sports I did play. When in my final year at school I found myself beginning to be bored by these too, I could not help feeling guilty. Within another year I had rid my mind of that, and have never since had anything to do with any sport, except as occasional spectator. I am fond of doing work with my hands, cutting down a tree or building a stone wall, but I rarely take exercise as such. When I see men, not boys, making a virtue of exercise I wonder what is wrong with their bodies that they have to do so much for them. But this is partly the arrogance of health. For thirty-four years (I write on my fiftieth birthday) I have never had to spend a whole day in bed.

The social life of Urbana was more complicated than that of Hope, but was still simple. All the children entered the public schools at six. There were no kindergartens and no private schools. Boys and girls together, they made their way through the grades, the brighter sometimes skipping a grade,

the duller sometimes having to repeat. Only the incorrigibles
dropped out before the end of the eighth grade. After that a
few of the boys and fewer of the girls went to work or stayed
at home to help their parents. The rest left their several
grade schools for the town's single high school. Each later
year saw a sharp decrease in the numbers of the classes. A
good many sons of retired farmers returned to their fathers'
farms, sons of railroad men got jobs at the yards, sons of
business men were put into business. More girls than boys
remained in high school until graduation, but more boys than
girls went on to college, almost invariably to the University,
which was so near as to seem a part of the town. Urbana
students could live at home, and tuition was free. Since the
cost was low, going to college was largely a matter of personal choice. Most students from Urbana thought of themselves rather as citizens of the town than as members of the
University. When they had had as much college as they
wanted, they reverted to Urbana.

Those who were academic in their tastes might be absorbed
in the University. Those who were restless and ambitious
might hunt their fortunes elsewhere. The majority found
careers and futures at hand. There was employment of some
sort for everybody who looked for it. Enterprising boys
would already have done odd jobs out of school hours to
earn pocket money. I picked strawberries on a truck farm,
went from back door to back door in the early morning to
take orders for a grocer, helped roof a house with slate, and
with Guy ran a hay-baler. Any kind of paid work was reputable, although boys were embarrassed if they were seen doing,
as chores around their own house, work which they thought
menial. When they became men they settled down in their
callings and as a rule did not change again. But the steadiest

man had been a jack-of-all-trades, and he was seldom at a loss in emergencies.

Men were likely to be married young to girls with whom they had gone to school. Such marriages of familiarity turned out much the same as the marriages of novelty, in which a man married a girl whom he had just met or who was so young that he had not till recently been aware of her as a woman. Few men or women married their first sweethearts. Boys and girls in school fell about annually in love, and long before marriage went through, in a tentative rehearsal which was also an experience, the shy delights and moody torments of their state and age. Their affairs were usually innocent, except that most of the girls permitted, and no doubt enjoyed, some of the free caresses for which all of the boys were eager. The ordinary boy while in high school had an unromantic initiation into sex at the hands of some easy girl or loose women, but he hardly looked for anything of the kind from the girls of his own group. A schoolgirl who was not pure— as the phrase called her—was notorious. Love and lust were sharply distinguished, as in all communities which reflect, and consequently know, little about either. I observed happy and unhappy marriages in Urbana, but never a great or tragic love.

Once married, young people adapted themselves quickly to the established life. The sons and daughters of prosperous parents were expected to live on their own earnings. This was partly a fiction, for they might receive both help and credit, but in practice they started more or less even with their poorer contemporaries. All but the shiftless or the sickly saved money to buy a house to live in. To live in a rented house was to feel half homeless. Any further savings not needed in the development of the family business, if there

was one, went commonly into other houses, farms, or mortgages on real estate. Urbana was agricultural not industrial
or financial in its interests. The banks invested some of their
money in bonds or stocks, but private citizens hardly thought
of such things before the purchase of Liberty bonds became a
patriotic duty. In the typical Urbana household the prime
charge against income and savings was the education of the
children. That achieved, the parents lived more easily. In old
age they set store by being independent of their children, as
they themselves in youth had been independent of their parents. Everybody believed in independence and everybody, in
those years, believed not only that he had it but that he had
won it by his own efforts. Hard times came and hard times
went, but they were so much weather. If they were explained
at all, it was when Republicans blamed them on the Democrats. The Democrats had no answers but Bryan's. The Socialists in Urbana were hardly a name. The old America
lived on in Urbana by custom and instinct, not by thought.

Everywhere men think only when they are forced to by
the pressure of life, and most men only when it is difficult
for them to make a living. In Urbana it was not too difficult,
any more than it was on the farms near by—or on farms or
in small towns throughout the United States in the opening
years of the century. The Americans who were still farmers
or small-townspeople lived by a settled and accepted pattern
of existence. They might never have heard of the social contract, but they had known the thing in the mutual assistance
of the pioneer time. They might never have heard of capi-
talism by name, but they were all capitalists to the extent
that they could and did work, save money, buy property, and
hold a stake in the social enterprise. People who did not,
appeared to be people who would not, idle and negligible.

Far more than half of all Americans in 1903, the year I left high school for college, took this classic pattern for granted and could scarcely imagine any other. It seemed American and eternal.

James Stephens once said to me: "Do you know the rock on which the Roman Empire split? The Irish language. Do you know the rock on which the modern world will split? The Irish language." I suppose no economic system can be as stubborn as an ancient tongue, and of course none is eternal. But the classic American pattern was more than American: it was what immigrants from many races had crossed the ocean to create out of long desires. In its pure form, among all the brutal and greedy exceptions to it, it has been a national, a racial, a human passion. The passions yield slowly to reasons, even to interests. I am never surprised, like some of my friends who grew up in industrial centers or in cities, that the older America persists. No newer America yet equals it in strength of custom or instinct.

University

From September 1903, when I entered Illinois as a freshman, to June 1911, when I took the degree of doctor of philosophy at Columbia, and then for five years more as a teacher at Columbia, I was in the University as I might have been in the Army or the Navy. While there appear to be many universities in the United States, they are in a sense all one, more or less distinct parts of a uniform system. The students who stream through them, the raw materials of the university process, furnish the spectacle. Behind that goes on the tranquil life of the permanent communities. I have often wondered why no novelist has realized that he could find as much comedy in American universities as Trollope found in his English cathedrals.

It did not occur to me, at eighteen, that the University of Illinois was only twice as old as I. Ivy already covered the buildings which rose out of smooth lawns among quiet trees. The University had been there as far back as I could remember, and I did not look farther. Antiquity is relative. If this had been Harvard or Paris I should now and then have thought of its past, as I later did at Columbia and Oxford, but it would not have touched my present very deeply. Illinois had a past which was long enough to have given the community a set of customs by which teachers and students lived. That was enough for the present. New students accepted these young customs as quickly as if they had been ages old.

Living at home, I was never absorbed in the life of the University, at least of the undergraduates. If anything absorbed me, for the first few months, it was athletics. The gymnasium rather than my fraternity was my club. Then, random in the library, I discovered Marlowe, and the glory of great verse changed my world as if mountains had sprung up out of the prairie.

All that was aching and inarticulate in me seemed to find a voice in him. Here was a poet who did not make me feel that he was older and wiser than I, only that he had words of light and fire for my cloudy thoughts and smoky feelings. I followed the course of his dramas almost without noticing what happened or what his characters were like, hearing his words as so much music. It was really an ear I found in him, not a voice. I wrote no plays in verse, nor wanted to. But I began to read poetry, and for three or four years I suppose I read as much of it as any boy alive. If there had then been better living poets I should have read them. I read George Santayana and William Butler Yeats. I knew the Shropshire Lad by heart. I remember the stir that Theodore Roosevelt made over Edwin Arlington Robinson. But most of the poets I read were dead poets, moving for me in a past above time and not subject to it. I hardly thought of them as living in any special day or place. They existed for me, my landscape, my melodious winds. Their rhythms beat continually in my responsive pulse.

My desire to be a poet was partly a desire to belong to the company of poets, like D'Artagnan's to belong to the Musketeers. Desire alone cannot make a poet. I had an exact ear and an exacting taste, and I always knew that the poems I wrote were not good enough. I was so jealous for the honor of poets that I would let no mediocre poet come among them, even myself. But I went on hoping for a miracle, hoping that the poetic excitement which sometimes visited me, fitfully, briefly, would sooner or later stay till it had mastered me and freed me. I cast myself in the rôle of poet, and privately wore the uniform. Meanwhile I read not only poetry but also the lives of poets with a curiosity so intense and tireless that I was, so far as this would take me, a scholar before I knew it.

The black melancholy of young men has many apparent causes, but the many are really one: that the young men wish and will more than they can do. Outwardly I had little, as an undergraduate, to complain about. At the first meeting of the freshmen, held stealthily under a hedge out of reach of the sophomores, I was chosen captain of the color rush. I was asked at once to join a fraternity. My earliest contributions to the literary monthly were accepted, and I soon became assistant editor and then editor. Indifferent to academic standing, I yet won preliminary, final, and special honors. In my last year I was president of the honorary senior society, and at commencement I was class poet. Though I had less money in my pocket than I could have used, I had as much as I needed. I was two or three times in love, not once in vain. My visible life must have looked like a cheerful success. Inwardly I was often as dejected as if I had the most valid reasons. Reading great poets, I walked day and night in the shadow of excellence. My will demanded that I be excellent too. Because I could not be, I furiously scourged myself, arrogant ambition tormenting sensitive flesh and blood.

Though I knew everybody and went everywhere, I was self-conscious and self-centered. I opened myself to none of my new friends. Even to my one close friend, Glen Mullin,

whom I had met in high school and who I now found was
determined to be a painter, I was never quite outspoken.
But he was a reader too, particularly of Blake and Rabelais,
and the two of us were a small society, forever talking, in-
satiable and inexhaustible. He made drawings for the magazine which I edited and for which I wrote—once the entire
issue under several names—poems, stories, essays, transla-
tions. With him I was oblivious of the rest of the University.
I did not think about how much its schools of engineering
and agriculture were doing to civilize the state, so recently
frontier and prairie. I barely realized how many students
came from how far, from China and India, to study farming
in Urbana. One foreign student I had been told was the son
of a renowned poet, but I did not know the name of Rabindranath Tagore.

2

ON THE whole I was self-taught in a university which gave
me leisure and excuse to read. At the end of five years at
Illinois I knew most of the Greek and Latin writers, at least
the poets, in translation, a good many French and German
and a few Italian and Spanish in the original, some Scandinavian and Russian, and so nearly all the English and American that I think I have never since heard of one with whose
name and qualities I was not more or less familiar. I read
Middle and Old English, and even wrote verses in Anglo-
Saxon. Though while still in Urbana I translated Hebbel's
Judith, I was not a linguist. (Now when I have to speak German or French I do it badly.) Reading in a foreign language

seemed to me like making love in mittens. I read as a passionate experience or not at all, and I never then, or later, read the whole of a book that bored me. But I was hard to bore, I read fast, I could get quickly at what I wanted, and at twenty-one I was as much at home in a library as on a farm.

Except for my desire to be with poets I had no motive in my reading. It was simple instinct, like hunger or love. Curiosity is a major instinct, and it can drive men to endure hunger or put love aside. My curiosity was about the life-stories of the men and women whom I met in history or fiction. Inquisitive as a village gossip, feverish as an eavesdropper, I watched and studied all the ins and outs of their secret minds. I sometimes identified, always compared, myself with them. Levin in Anna Karenina was the man with whom I felt most in common, though I was not religious. Reading Havelock Ellis on the psychology of sex, I was troubled at the number of dark impulses with which, out of so little experience, I seemed to have so much acquaintance. Flutters of recognition ran along my nerves, healthy and fastidious as I was. Few life-stories bewildered me. My curiosity was too large for me to be surprised or intolerant. I accepted all I learned as evidence that the world was as rich as I demanded.

If I became something of a scholar while living a passion it was because I effortlessly and minutely remembered whatever I had read that interested me. Scholarship itself was not an end, and as an undergraduate I never thought about it. The nearest I came to thinking about it was in the feeling I arrived at in the year when I had Evarts Greene as my teacher in American history. His tall shyness touched me. A kind of courtliness—I can think of no other word—in his intellect moved me. Seeing and admiring the conscience with which he hunted for the truth and the justice with which he tried to make it clear, I felt that I had been helter-skelter and sluttish. Exactness in learning, I told myself, was as satisfying as in verse. Scrupulous truth was beautiful, careless error was ugly. Ugly and dirty. I told myself that it would be cheap and mean ever to pretend to know anything I was not sure of, or not to know anything I had had chance or reason to find out.

This austere principle—this fervid sentiment—I cherished with the least effect on my general opinions. I was a skeptic in religion but in nothing else. Utterly indifferent to politics and economics, I accepted the public structure of the pre-war world without a question. Though the muckrakers had made me realize that there was a great deal of corruption in office, I had a vague faith that democracy could be trusted to purge itself—just how I never bothered to think out. I took progress in human affairs for granted, a kind of perpetual motion. What I had seen in Illinois I supposed was the law of life everywhere. In the obscure past there had, of course, been barbarous disorder and tyranny and warfare, but the revolutions in France and America had rooted out such ancient wrongs. Blind to the nineteenth century, I thought of the race as having risen steadily to the twentieth and having finally settled itself in the way it would always go. Each generation would have better schooling and better manners than the one before it, along with better clothes, better houses, better roads, better tools and vehicles and machines. In Illinois the past was all around us, in the memories of old men. Every one of them talked about leaving the world a little better than he had found it. He assumed that he would and that any man could. Everybody looked forward to the increase of population and of wealth without any sense, that I ever saw, of any price to pay for them. I thought of the future as growing like an immortal tree. That is, I did not think at all. I got my general opinions from the air, like most undergraduates of my time.

The first critical mind I knew well was Stuart Sherman's. Sherman came to Urbana the year after I took my bachelor's degree. I had remained at Illinois, part graduate student and part teacher. He came with his doctor's degree from Harvard and the reputation of having written the best dissertation ever submitted to the English department there. Neither of these things impressed me, since I thought of them as academic and had no academic ambitions. I was teaching only because, undecided what to do next, I had been offered a minor post and a salary. Like half the college professors in the United States, I was a teacher by inertia. But Sherman lived, with his wife and baby, in the next street from ours, and he and I happened one day to walk together to the campus. I have often wondered what it was he said that made me suddenly see him with new eyes. I cannot remember, though I see him still: broad, strong, a little stooped and sallow, with his habitual smile that was almost a sneer. But I do remember the uprush of my spirit in that moment when it seemed to me that an electric charge of understanding passed between us.

During the rest of that winter and the spring which followed I haunted him and his house like a talking shadow. Night after night I stayed late and later in his study, knowing I should go but unable to reach the end of what there was to say or ask. Talking with him about the books we had read, which I had read for the stories and the music, he also for the ideas, was for me like reading them again.

And talking itself, after my long reserve, was liberation and transport.

I must often have bored him. Four years older than I, he had in those four years studied far beyond me, been married, had a child, and established himself in a profession. Having outgrown, he thought, his romantic strain, he was then busy disciplining himself to maturity and reason, on the model of Dr. Johnson. He had been romantic about the decadents of the end of the century, and I was still romantic about nature and man as seen by Wordsworth and Whitman. I seemed to Sherman expansive, credulous, and patriotic. And he could not help being amused at the passion with which I put forth ideas which he had probably held four years back but had since discarded. When he ridiculed me for holding them he was paying himself off for having held them.

One night I had been running on in a spate of confidences. He leaned back, stretched out his legs, took his pipe out of his mouth, and said:

"You talk platitudes like an angel."

It was like being hit by a block of ice. I was too sick to argue. But from that night I was never again quite so ready to pour out my opinions without thinking whether they were as new to my audience as to me.

Another time, when some question of fact had come up and I had been too full and eager with information, he said:

"I hate your damned omniscience."

Instantly I too hated, not my omniscience, of course, but my ardent habit of seeming to have it, of making a guess at the point at issue and then going on to something related to it which I did know. This was a trick I then frequently played, and have never altogether cured myself of. But ever since he spoke I have known it for a trick, and been ashamed of it.

And my poems. He too had written poems, many of them in exquisite verse-forms imported from France, most of them sad and sleek. He read me what he thought the best, and then insisted that I read him the poems I owned I had written.

I did it, and it was the hardest thing I had ever done. Having painfully sorted and typed those I thought my best, I invited him to my study, with its dormer window and shadowy corners, and read him the secrets. He lay on the couch and listened without a word. As I read, I knew they were not good enough. If only they were! If only I were a brilliant poet, young and unknown, now surprisingly discovered! Though I knew better, I could not help imagining the miracle. The miracle did not come. The more I read the surer I was that I was right. They were not good enough. Even if he thought they were, he would be wrong. And I could tell he did not. My voice sounded dead to me, hearing with his ears as well as mine. I did not want to go on, and I wanted still less to stop and face his verdict.

I finished and forced myself to look at him.

"Well, Bard," he said, "what are you going to do to make a living?"

His oblique comment made me laugh and we hardly discussed the poems. Instead, he urged me to study for my doctor's degree, as he had done, and become a teacher. Doing that, a man could live by literature while living with it. I had naturally thought of this before. I could think of nothing else for which I was fitted. Writing, I knew, would not support me, and I needed a profession. Teaching was no worse than any other. It meant two or three years more of graduate study, during which I might still change my plans. But I would study at Columbia, not at Harvard. Columbia was in New York.

3

MY FATHER liked my class poem when he heard me read it at commencement, and that summer, when I was living alone in the big house on the farm at Villa Grove, he guessed that I was writing more poetry. One day he said, shy and embarrassed:

"You can have all the time you want to dream here."

It was his way of telling me his sympathy for what must have seemed to him my strange desire. I was too much embarrassed to talk about it. It is hard now to know why. For of all the fathers I have heard about he gave his sons the freest hand in choosing their careers. No doubt he would have been pleased if one of us had become a doctor or, probably, a lawyer. But he claimed no right to tell us what to do. I remember only one thing he ever said to me when I was making up my mind. Toward the end of my last undergraduate year I had the choice, for the year to follow, between teaching college classes at a very small salary or teaching preparatory classes at more than twice as much. Since in either case I should have about the same amount of time for my graduate studies, I wondered if I should not let the matter of salary decide, though I preferred college teaching.

"Why, you little fool," my father said, "you can't afford to make money at your age."

Yet he was in those years, with five sons in school or college, always under stress for money. Like the other farmer-capitalists of the time and place, he bought land on mortgage, worked it for interest, taxes, expenses, and amortization, and expected to sell it for a higher price at a profit. As the price of land in Illinois had been rising for fifty years, this was possible for energetic, optimistic men, in spite of the annual hazard of crops and weather. But such men, thinking of how much the land would finally bring, had a way of forgetting how much they still owed on it, and considered themselves richer than they were. Although we lived simply, we lived, in a sense, on what we were to have, and put off paying for it. Private debt to my father was no different from national debt—it merely provided funds. He neglected his practice as much as his patients would let him. He was absorbed in the farms, in country banks he had organized at Collison and Royal, near Hope, and, a little later, in still more speculative ventures. His optimism strengthened to a kind of obsession.

At Hope men of fifty were thought old, and my father had intended to live more easily after that age. But in Urbana he felt no loss of energy in himself as he approached his birthday. An editorial in a magazine—Facing the World at Fifty —precipitated his opinions. Alps on Alps arose. He had only begun to fight. Fifty a few weeks before my commencement, my father was actually more romantic than I, with all my poetry. We might have matched vision with vision, if I had understood him.

I did not. With the green hardness of youth I thought him insensitive. We sometimes clashed—or rather, I flung out at him, angry, and then furious at his laughing, affectionate good humor. It was a conflict less between us two than between me and the family in which, for twenty-three years by the time I left it, I had lived too long not to be restless. With nothing but love for any of its members, I had outgrown the thing itself, and I was cramped for want of room and exercise. I wanted to live alone, with my own hours and habits, without any household.

I left Urbana on a train that went late at night. Looking forward to that last evening, I thought how dramatic the occasion could be, if we were as a family not so disappointing. No sense of ritual. A humor that grinned away the grand style whenever it threatened to show itself. Any other family, I thought, would make a ceremony when its eldest son set out to make his fortunes. Mine I was sure would not.

Supper was very quiet. Guy, now a student in architecture at the University, seemed to pay no attention to the event. Frank and Mark, both in high school, kept staring at me with their bright brown eyes. Paul, only nine, sat close beside me, fidgeting and crowding. My mother ate nothing. My father self-consciously cleared his throat.

As soon as the meal was ended, Guy got his hat. Of all of us he was the most firm about avoiding scenes.

"I'm sorry. I have to go down the street. I guess—" and his voice trailed off in a sound of apology without words.

We shook hands, and both tried to be matter-of-fact.

The evening dragged. Paul, though he was to stay up for the train, went to sleep in a chair in the library. Frank and Mark had half a dozen scuffles. My mother disappeared. My father and I talked, neither of us saying a single thing that was on his mind.

I went to look for my mother. She was lying on a sofa in her bedroom, without a light. When I came near I found she was sobbing. I did not ask her why, but stooped to whisper to her. She suddenly threw her arms around me with the strength of an emotion I had never seen in her or anybody. Her sobs seemed to me to rise from some frightening deeps I did not know.

"You are the first to go away," she said. "They will all go away."

I could not comfort her. When I had to leave I felt that I was tearing myself like a tree from her breast.

Paul woke up, sleepy but clamorous about going to the station. On the platform, Frank and Mark tussled over my baggage. My father laughed at them. The train came, noisy in the night.

I shook hands solemnly with my father, who looked as if he would like to say something, many things. But he only straightened his neck, pulling in his chin in a shy way he had, and said goodby. Frank and Mark were excited. Paul put up his small face to be kissed.

I got into the train so unstrung and dissolved that after a time I could almost feel my frayed nerves slowly knit together.

4

NEW YORK thirty years ago was not for America what it has since become. To Urbana, a thousand miles away, Wall Street was an ogre conspiring against the whole country, Tammany an ogre plotting at home. But they were only ogres—a giant and a tiger—and they belonged to folk-lore. The life of the Four Hundred—as Illinois still called it—seemed as far away as the life of similar Romans under Nero, as far away as the dark streets of New York's underworld. Broadway and its theater were remote, though most successful plays came sooner or later to Urbana or the neighboring Champaign. (Before the College Widow came, shivering freshmen from the fraternities stood in line all night to be there when the box-office opened.) New York was still less a city of men and women than a symbol. The Sunday papers, the newsreels, and the radio had not yet familiarized the rest of America with New York sights and sounds. Those national gossips the columnists had not yet learned how to sell New York's interminable secrets to America's innumerable ears.

But then as now an American did not have to know much about New York to be drawn to it. The instinct that draws a young provincial to his capital may be hardly more than a human tropism. I had no desire to become rich and fashionable. I thought about the theater as little as about the underworld. My scholarship at Columbia was only something to take me to New York, like my railway ticket. The University would be my hotel while I explored the town. In September 1908 I had had no experience of cities, except one or two unsatisfying visits to Chicago. Yet since I was old enough to consider it at all I had never had any doubt that I would go to New York. I did not think about it and decide. I seemed already to have made up my mind when the idea occurred to me. It was, somehow, as if though not native to New York, I was natural to it, and the accident of my being born in a distant village made no difference. I was conscious of a wish to live where books were written and published, but this simple motive was lost in the urgency of a general instinct. Life would be large and free in New York, and I must go there to find out what largeness and freedom were.

I chose the longest route, to Cincinnati and far out of my way down through Virginia and up by Washington, and I rode the whole distance in day coaches—to travel the most miles and see the most people for my money. For the cost of a sleeping car I could buy a dozen books.

Travelers often puzzle me with their sharp impressions and memories, and I suspect them of thinking up later what they claim they saw at first. I traveled to New York in an excited fog, and I remember nothing but a park in Cincinnati, where I waited between trains, and the high shoulders of unidentified mountains rolling past in the dark. Nor did the excitement clear when I left the train and from the ferry looked across the Hudson at the shining city.

Could that be the smell of salt water? Were those seagulls, with their harsh cries and hard, cold feet? The river was busy with boats of all shapes and sizes, moving up and down, back and forth, in and out. The river was loud with hooting whistles and jangling bells. Beyond the river the city sprang up and towered above the rock of Manhattan. Solid as the rock, and yet built by men and full of them. Men living in houses of steel and stone. The men: were they steel and stone too? The roar of the city was more than human. Yet the mist lay soft on its jagged pinnacles, and the September sun was sweet.

I must have watched the ferryboat rub into the slip, must have jostled with the crowd through the dock to the street, must have ordered my trunk sent to the University. I must have, but I do not remember. I do not remember one thing I saw or heard or smelled in my first minute in New York. Then I saw a street car swinging and grinding around a circle. In a daze I asked questions and was told, impatiently, that in this car I could go crosstown to Madison Square and the Subway.

Sweating, I climbed the steps with my heavy suitcase, and, since there was no vacant seat, planted myself about the middle of the car. There, I thought, the bag would be out of the way of the passengers using either door. The car started with a jerk, and a man fell over the bag. He glared at me, muttering. Others laughed, I suppose at both of us. I took all the laughter to myself, hot and wet and limp with shame. As we jolted along, stopping at every avenue, it seemed to me that angry men and giggling women stumbled over my bag in a procession. Those who sat still took it as a farce. Wherever I looked, I caught amused glances, just turning away. One very well-dressed man stared insolently at me and spoke, I could half-hear, disgustedly to the very well-dressed woman beside him. This helped me, for it made me angry. But for that I would have got out and walked, carrying the bag.

When at Madison Square I did get out I could not at first see the Subway entrance. A little man with a face like a rat was instantly at my side, grabbing my suitcase.

"Looking for the Subway, sir? Yes, sir, right this way, sir. That's what I'm here for, sir, to show strangers to the Subway. Right this way."

Before I could think of a reason for not letting him have the bag he had it, scuttling down the stairs, more like a rat than ever. I kept at his heels, expecting him to slip at any second into his hole with my bag, and hating myself for my slow wits. He had no chance to get away from me—if he ever meant to. At the ticket gate he stopped.

"Right here, sir. Five cents for the ticket. Where do you want to go, sir? Columbia University? Take a Broadway train, sir. You can't miss it. Yes, sir."

Though I had never in my life tipped anybody but a Pullman porter, I guessed that this called for a tip, and I gave the rat a dime. Rat eyes looked from the handful of change to my flushed face.

"Beg pardon, sir, they generally give us a quarter. Yes, sir, that's the regular charge, a quarter. Yes, sir."

I apologized and gave him a quarter. He thanked me, briefly now, and scuttled away with both coins.

I had heard enough about the Subway to be prepared for it, and I took the thunder underground for granted. Columbia at first sight seemed strange, with its formal yews and poplars instead of forest trees, its paved courts wider than its lawns, and the tall city close around it. But there were runners on the cinder track in South Field, and men with green bags who were unmistakably professors. One university was like another. I knew universities.

That afternoon I spent hunting for a furnished room in the neighborhood and found one barely larger than my bed at home. The landlady—faded, fussy, Southern—was uncertain whether she wanted a student for a lodger. Deciding for her, I decided for myself. Then, alone in my new room, I lay down for a relaxed moment to plan my first evening in New York.

The first night of a young man in a strange city: as stirring as a battle, as delightful as a bride. Young men come ready for adventure. They have only to put out their hands. Dangers lurk around corners. Girls smile, walking slowly and peeping back. Luck looks for young men in cities. They find money, they make friends. A hint given, a chance taken, and life begins. On a farm, in a village, at a university a young man might live a hundred years and see nothing, do nothing. But in a city—in New York—the night was alive and waiting. What should I do first? What should I do? What——

What I did was fall asleep, worn out with travel and excitement, and sleep till late next morning.

The sun shone on the early afternoon when I went by Subway to Astor Place and walked wondering and elated to Washington Square to take the bus up Fifth Avenue. I sat on the open top, in a front seat, staring and hoping no one would notice that I was. We swung under the Arch. The Avenue lay long and straight before us. I know it was not as jammed as it is now any fine afternoon. There must have been more horses than motors. The men and women must have worn the clothes which in pictures now look outlandish. They did not look outlandish then. I was aware of countless motors. The traffic, vehicles and pedestrians, streamed, swarmed, swirled, shuffled. The bus nosed and butted its way through the traffic.

Again I suspect travelers. My ride that afternoon comes back to me, not as a series of impressions, one after another, but as a thousand simultaneous shocks that went on like tom-toms beating at my senses. The only clear images that have stayed in my memory are the Flatiron Building and St. Patrick's. The rest is chaos and tumult. Two infinite parades, endlessly meeting and endlessly slipping past without a sign. Sidewalks crowded, spilling over at the cross-walks. Insolent, assured faces everywhere. Voices, when I could overhear them, speaking unfamiliar languages. Now and then a colorless tramp slinking with his eyes down—and nobody noticing him. Poverty lost in the multitude of riches. Unbelievable riches. Imperious men and their golden women. And all the men and women, if not rich, then knowing. They moved along Fifth Avenue as through a great bazaar. Acres of brazen signs invited them. Through acres of glass they could see the bazaar's treasures. Come in and buy, rich and knowing men and women. Take the world home with you for a price.

If the street and the crowds, the carriages and automobiles, were like drums to my nerves, the shop windows were like needles. I had never wanted to be rich, I had had no desire for intricate possessions. But the treasures of this bazaar were set out with the tempting skill of devils. They created desires. Desire pressed so close to desire in me, one giving way so soon to another, that I almost at once was tired, like a child under a skyful of moons. But I did not want them, I did not want them. If I did, what could it matter? I could never have them. I did not know the uses of some of the things I wanted yet did not want. I did not know even their names.

I did not know even their names. What most stung and deadened me was the terrible confusion of ignorance, asked to learn too much too fast. If I could have said confidently to myself: That rug comes from Turkestan: or, The silver mirror over the ebony console—I like that: or, I wonder what tinted blonde will get the sapphire: or, No such coat without a massacre among the minks: or if, observing further, I could have said: The architect of that house owes half his commission to the Florentines: or, After all, a Rolls-Royce is a Rolls-Royce: or, The man in the brown tweeds looks as if he were off for Long Island: or, The shopping center will soon be north of Twenty-third Street: if I could have said these things casually to myself I should have wanted little more. I needed less to own than to know. Unless I could know I could have no sense of commanding either this enormous universe or myself. I could not, in my mind, choose and reject and so keep my stature. Here in Fifth Avenue meaningless objects and desires overwhelmed me, like a mob of people without faces. Lost in them, I seemed to grow smaller and smaller, weaker and weaker, till I too was meaningless.

Confusion rose around me and poured over me. I could not escape any more than I could master it. Still the drums, still the needles. Streets and streets to go, miles and miles, eternities and eternities. My mind could not help me by thinking. It too was panic, spun in a vortex of sensations. There is no reason in a nightmare. Over and over I said to myself: This is New York, where I thought life would be large and free. This is New York, and I am a stranger in a nightmare.

Now, thirty years later, when I ride along a Fifth Avenue so much more splendid than it was then, and find it so familiar and natural that I may see few things which particularly strike me, it is like remembering an old dream to remember that half-hour when the mountains of the city fell on me, and covered me, and I was suffocated with the dread conviction that the city was forever beyond my strength, losing sight of my real need, which was to understand, and not realizing that it takes time to understand, or that to understand is to possess.

But I remember that I was still in the nightmare when I suddenly felt the wind from the Hudson blowing on me as the bus swayed and rumbled along Riverside Drive. There was the river, there was the sun. I saw two or three good horses on the bridle-path, with riders who were, I thought, less easy in their saddles than I would be. Some of my self-esteem came back. But I returned to Columbia like a monk to his monastery.

5

Beware of drama, that short cut to history. A dramatist could make a whole life turn on a panic nightmare. But this is history. The nightmare passed like any other and never came back. During the few days before the university session opened I tirelessly, excitedly wandered the streets, most of all at night and often in parts of the town which I only later learned were dangerous. In Urbana there had been no night life. Here were Broadway and the Bowery. At my first play, the Man from Home, I told the man beside me that I was from the same part of the country as the hero, and he told me about the Sunday amusements of New York. On the Bowery I talked with a panhandler, to his profit, not so much because I believed his story as because he was the first person I had ever heard use the word bloke. The contrast between poverty and riches oppressed me dreadfully for a time, but I got used to it, as to the eternal pavements. I was never so homesick as, writing home, I said I was. New York gave me elation and privacy, and I had a gift for living alone.

At the end of a semester I moved from my furnished room to one of the residence halls.

The life of a graduate student is nearly as monastic as if he were at West Point or Annapolis. President Butler with commencement rhetoric once called Columbia the greatest and most influential university in the world. In law, penology, and some of the applied sciences the University did affect the world of action, and textbooks written by its teachers were studied everywhere. But most of its public influence, like that of any university, was indirect and hard to trace. The direct, traceable part was upon the thousands of students trained at Columbia to be teachers. Most of them would go back to their native sections and be lost in the wilderness of elementary schools. A few would be teachers in other universities. These few were the chief concern of the graduate departments at Columbia. They were apprentices to the masters of the guild. They listened to lectures, learned the tricks of research in seminars, and wrote laborious dissertations on the most specialized themes. Not yet sure, as students, where they would be appointed to teach, they already talked university shop and thought of themselves as belonging to the permanent university system.

I never thought of myself as belonging to any such system. When I found that graduate study in the department of English and Comparative Literature at Columbia meant merely the study of literary history and was almost pure antiquarianism, I did not object or complain. Though this was inertia it was not docility. Rather, it was arrogance. I would do lightly what was required of me and save my strength for doing otherwise as I chose. I wanted to know more than I did about ballad and epic and Dante and Chaucer and the Elizabethan drama and the life and times of Defoe and the Romantic movement and the modern stage. Things more important to me I would learn in my own way.

I thought I was moving easily in the academic system without yielding to it. For my dissertation I chose to write, not the customary monograph, but a biography of Thomas Love Peacock. My formal reason for the choice was that Peacock, friend of Shelley, father-in-law of George Meredith, and himself the author of lively satirical novels, deserved a sounder place in literary history than he had, and that a study of his life would be a contribution to knowledge. My actual reason was that, having happened to read something about him in Urbana, I had read most of his books and been amused by them, and, thinking occasionally about them later, had wondered by what processes of the mind he had outgrown conventional verse and had come to write original prose. Disinterested scholarship less than private curiosity set me to work. I wanted to find out, if I could, how another writer had done what I now thought I should like to do. The academic system gave me a free hand. A fellowship supported me in part. The committee in charge of my dissertation left me alone. When I had written as much of the book as I could write in New York I went to London, to the British Museum and to Peacock's granddaughter, who told me what she remembered. I had no difficulty in finding a London publisher for the book. Once more at Columbia, I submitted a manuscript to the committee without telling them that the biography was already in type in London. Any corrections they made I disregarded, certain that if they ever looked into the printed book they would by that time have forgotten the manuscript.

Yet independent as I thought I was, I had been touched and colored by the system. Except for it I should never, I think, have written a literary biography for my first book, never have confined myself so closely to English literature, never have crammed my memory with the academic litter I took to my doctor's examination. Except for it, I am sure, I should never have felt the tightening in my brain—I could feel it plainly —which went on while I made myself more and more a specialist. By nature I was a scholar of the ranging kind, erudite when excited, but always incurably passionate. I became a specialist only as much as passion could make me. But, like most members of an academic community, I fell into the way of small passions for small things. I saw most of the past in the light of literary history, and most of the present in its shadow.

In literature there was not, between 1908 and 1911, much of a present to see. Bernard Shaw and H. G. Wells had already agitated many minds and had convinced some, and John Galsworthy and G. K. Chesterton were beginning to be talked about. But in America there was Paul Elmer More and no H. L. Mencken, only James Gibbons Huneker. Stephen Crane and Frank Norris had died too young and Theodore

Dreiser had been suppressed. Willa Cather was barely, and James Branch Cabell wrongly, known. The reputation of Edwin Arlington Robinson was as obscure as most readers found his poems. Still no Robert Frost, no Vachel Lindsay, no Edgar Lee Masters, no Carl Sandburg, no Edna St. Vincent Millay nor Elinor Wylie, no Amy Lowell and only preliminary grumblings about free verse. Mark Twain and William Dean Howells and Henry James had already settled into being classics, and Edith Wharton and Hamlin Garland seemed to be succeeding them. No Sinclair Lewis yet, nor Van Wyck Brooks, nor Ludwig Lewisohn. John Reed was an undergraduate at Harvard, Randolph Bourne at Columbia.

Graduate students seldom thought of their contemporaries in literature. Brander Matthews knew a great deal about the living theater, and William Peterfield Trent, my favorite teacher and the noblest man I ever knew, was by temper a philosophical statesman as much as a scholar of the most exacting erudition. But even their students could view literature as a museum, full of orderly exhibits, ticketed, secure, and dead. And when, in the summer of 1910, I went with Stuart Sherman for our first visit to Europe, I went, as he did too, as if we were exploring a museum's older, longer, cooler, darker corridors.

6

THE hills of Ireland were purple when we first saw them, then green, and then silver in the moonlight, as we passed by on our way to Scotland. I could not sleep all night, and the next morning I thought Greenock was beautiful. In Glasgow one day, and that Sunday, we saw only the University and the galleries, and hurried off for Gourock and the Crinan Canal to Oban. From Oban, in a pitching boat, we visited the Cave of Fingal at Staffa and landed on the holy island of Iona, for the sake less of St. Columba, who lived here, than of Macbeth, who may have been buried here. Scottish kings, Scandinavian kings, in a row of stony tombs, and two young Americans trying to believe in them. On the mainland were Ballachulish, where James Stewart of the Glens was hanged for the murder of Colin Campbell, and Glencoe of the massacre. Scott and Stevenson were more than guidebooks to us. Scott and Stevenson were the country we were traveling through, and the landscape was there chiefly to confirm them. Johnson and Boswell had made a tour to the Hebrides. To tease Sherman for his Johnsonisms I began what I called the Pseudo-Boswell, a journal sometimes written down but more often orally improvised, in which I parodied my eagerness and his bullying.

We left the Caledonian Canal between Oban and Inverness to climb Ben Nevis for the sunset and, four hours later, the sunrise, but what most delighted us was our first cuckoo, calling across a valley: a cuckoo out of a poem, it seemed. Which was real, poem or bird? Inverness for us was Culloden Moor and stories of the battle. In Aberdeen we wondered on a Saturday night how so many people could be so merry and so ugly, and we listened to orators talking in the market place against Rome, the royal family, and Roosevelt. But we looked most at old churches, old bridges, and the tomb of John Barbour, whom the sexton of St. Machar's called the first Scottish poet. Then to Edinburgh by train, talking the whole way with a young parson from Lilybank who had been a student of George Saintsbury and who was surprised to learn that Americans had heard of William Butler Yeats.

Edinburgh was a museum which had the originals of works of art we had seen only in reproduction. Edinburgh was a library of which we had read the books and now studied the manuscripts. We stayed there for two weeks, up to our eyes in history. The monuments were alive, not the men and women who walked the streets. Mary of Scotland, in Holyrood, was more real to us than the pretty and graceful girl who kept our rooms. Boswell and Burns, Scott and Carlyle were almost the only men we talked to—except the mechanic from whom we bought bicycles and who tried to sell us an aeroplane. We went for a day to Hawthornden, where William Drummond had had Ben Jonson for his guest.

Patriotically on the Fourth of July, with all the British Isles waiting for news of the Jeffries-Johnson fight ("Do ye fancy the black mon?" the boots asked me), we set off on our bicycles for Oxford. Melrose and Abbotsford and Selkirk for Scott. Along the Yarrow and through the Ettrick Hills remembering Wordsworth and the Ettrick Shepherd. Dumfries for Burns. Ecclefechan for Carlyle. Gretna Green for runaways. Cockermouth and Keswick, the Falls of Lodore, the Druid Circle, Skiddaw and Helvellyn, Grasmere, Rydal Water, Windermere, and Ambleside for the Lake Poets. By train through unpoetical counties to Nuneaton, then again on bicycles to Coventry for George Eliot and Lady Godiva. Kenilworth for Scott again, and Warwick and Stratford for Shakespeare. Not Eden nor Utopia could have stirred us as Stratford did—Stratford with its stodgy memorials and goggling tourists. These we did not see. We saw Shakespeare.

Oxford for Addison, Johnson, Gibbon, Shelley, Arnold, Pater—and Max Beerbohm. We spent ten days there, drifting around the colleges, rowing on the river, walking through lanes and meadows, hunting for books in richer bookshops than either of us had ever seen. We had been buying books all the way from Glasgow, reading them, and sending them ahead to London. Now, having sold our bicycles, we gave ourselves up to vacation idleness. In Oxford I wrote what turned out to be my last verses for many years:

> As idle as the winds are we
> And idly sigh and sing and say:
> There is no labor but in play,
> We laugh at labor that we see.
>
> Yet are we idle in our glee,
> Nor frolic madly as we may.
> As idle as the winds are we
> And idly sigh and sing and say:
>
> Where we are may no labor be
> Nor twilight weary of the day.
> The idlest is the wisest way
> And labor only folly's fee.
> As idle as the winds are we.

Writing these languid verses roused me. In a day or two I was as active as ever, and we went voracious to London, our museum of museums. It was dull in August, I suppose, and all who could manage it were out of town, and streets were being repaired almost as if this were America. It was not dull to us. Here are the names I find in my diary for the first few days: Oxford Street, Holborn, Newgate, the Bank of England, Trafalgar Monument, the Strand, Fleet Street, Ludgate Circus, the Victoria Embankment, Waterloo Bridge, Charing Cross Road, the British Museum, the manuscript of Beowulf, St. Paul's Cathedral, Hyde Park, the Houses of Parliament, Westminster Bridge, Westminster Abbey, the Poets' Corner. We knew the names. Now we saw the things. We saw the King and Queen on their way to the London Hospital. We listened to the orators in Hyde Park. The great, troubling city closed comfortably around us. Its history was less visible in its face than Edinburgh's had been, and we were not in such a hurry as we had been in Scotland, but the present was there, for us, chiefly to prove that the past had been. We met, or tried to meet, no living Englishman.

After four weeks Sherman had to leave for America. Restless and footloose, I went to Holland early in September. The first of my line, so far as I know, to go back for nine generations, I had nothing Dutch about me but my name, did not speak the language, and read it only by analogy with English and German. But I could feel Dutch as I never could feel English. Tired of English food, I rejoiced in my first Dutch breakfast in Rotterdam—and then walked along the Hoogstraat to the site of Erasmus's birthplace. Again history had me by the willing throat. I followed the trail of Dutch painting to Amsterdam, where I spent the whole of my twenty-fifth birthday in the Ryks Museum.

The nearest I came to the Dutch present was the nineteenth century as it still persisted in Apeldoorn. An old Dutch gentleman lived there, Hendrik Ankersmit, who years before had run away to America, had in some way become acquainted with my Grandfather Butz, had lived with him on the farm at Hope, before I was born, and had kept up the long acquaintance. He invited me to Apeldoorn for a week in a house like a pleasant fort beside a sleepy canal. At mealtimes we saw the boats go by, higher than our windows. Two sisters lived with him, another in her own house not far away, and his brother an invalid doctor in another house, and a brother-in-law a retired teacher in lodgings. These six, none of them under seventy, made up a whole society like the persons of a quiet Dutch novel. In the evenings we played whist at one house or another, and every day Mynheer Ankersmit took me sightseeing or told me about Apeldoorn or asked me about Hope. On bicycles we covered miles of roads through landscapes like those I had thought unreal when I saw them painted in The Hague and Amsterdam. We walked through the grounds of the royal palace Het Loo, as small and neat as if it had been made for children. We went out one morning to see the Queen and her Consort, with the little princess, leave the palace in the rain to go to Amsterdam, where the King and Queen of the Belgians were coming to visit them. This was the first time the little princess, still a baby, had ever left the house where she was born. The burghers stared politely from under their umbrellas and walked home talking with a kind of amused affection about the court. My host said bluntly that the courtiers were not important: they were too poor. I did not realize how much this one remark had to tell me about the Dutch, that race of realists who have made themselves rich by peace not poor by war and glory. I was busy thinking how quaint the Dutch were.

Still thinking about quaintness, I am afraid, I went on from Apeldoorn to Nuremberg and Munich, by way of Dresden, where I saw one of the earliest Zeppelins. I watched the dirigible, hating some Saxon officers, helmeted and horsehaired, who crowded civilians off the sidewalk. The Zeppelin meant nothing to me except that the Germans were an inventive people, with a taste for fantasy. Look at their absurd atavistic respect for soldiers. The saber-scars I had just seen on those arrogant faces reminded me of the warpaint of Red Indians. Strange that such childish notions should survive among a people so orderly, so scientific, so civilized, so devoted to all the arts. I found less of this nonsense in Nuremberg, which was a Germany I knew better: the Germany of Hans Sachs and Albrecht Dürer, the Germany of picture postcards. Munich was all beer and paintings and the Oktoberfest with its peasant costumes. Oberammergau was the Passion Play, like the miracle plays I had read in English, only longer. Stuttgart and Mannheim for Schiller, whom I had never cared much for. Heidelberg for the University. Down the Rhine— the storied Rhine I would then have called it—to Cologne, where the Cathedral stood up out of the mist before we could see the city. At the door of the Cathedral itself a soldier, who had just come out, helped himself to a cigar that some wor- shiper had left on a convenient ledge. "Good touch for Heine" I wrote in my diary. And so back to Rotterdam and London again.

The rest of my stay was sullenly industrious. I worked all day at the British Museum, rewriting my book on Peacock, walked then for hours through the winter streets, and spent most of my evenings in solitary reading. "Same old pro- gram," ran one entry in my diary: "work, walk, wallow." Yet though I was often dejected I seldom realized that I was lonely. There were diversions. I made visits to Oxford, to work at the Bodleian, play with students, and gossip with dons. I spent an antiquarian week-end in Canterbury. At Christmas I went with a group of young Americans to Paris. We looked for monuments and museums there too, but we dined in hilarious restaurants, went to the Opera and the Folies Bergères, and lived mostly at night. In all my life I had never been so gay.

There were diversions in London. In November the suf- fragettes had a great demonstration in Parliament Square. I watched a score or so deliberately slapping policemen and being temperately arrested. My sympathies were with the women and against the hoodlums who jostled them. In January Winston Churchill used an army or so to dig his anarchists out of Houndsditch. I got as near as the battle-lines would let me, and debated with other young Americans whether it would take six or a dozen New York policemen to capture the offenders. The general elections that fall struck me as lively but unintelligible, though I had been on the side of Lloyd George as against the House of Lords. History-hunting as I was, I never had any use for conservative England in modern politics.

I came back to New York in January with English clothes and hundreds of English books, but with no sentimental hankering for England. Nothing had disgusted me so much as the Anglophile Americans of London and Oxford. I was an American, and I have never forgiven any Englishman who thought he was paying me a compliment by telling me I did not seem like an American to him.

7

AN AUTOBIOGRAPHER never knows quite what account he is giving of himself. Historian of acts of which he was the actor, he is still inside the self which remembers. No man, with the help of whatever mirrors, can know how he really looks to other men. Nor can he be sure how he sounds to them. Let him tell the plainest truth in the plainest way, he cannot know what else he may imply without suspecting it. Often he must wonder what the plain truth is. His memory has been quietly working his past over, and when he goes back to such unchanged evidence as letters and diaries he finds the story different from that he has come to remember. The man who remembers is not the man who did what the record shows. The man who was is now as strange to the man who is as the man who is would be to the man who was. Two men—a dozen men—with the same name, and the latest man in the series expected to make one story of them, while he too is changing day by day, and changing all the more swiftly because he is trying to stand still long enough to understand and communicate their history, called his. Is there a truth about what was? Or is there no truth except what is remembered? I have tried to tell the true story of my youth, yet I cannot be sure how far I have done that, or what I may at the same time have been unconsciously revealing about the child on his faraway farm, the boy in his little town, the young man at his universities and on his travels.

I had the feeling, that first winter and spring at Columbia, of cheerfully settling into harness after too much running into too many pastures. Teaching itself was tame, but it was pleasant to be at work, to earn the money I lived on, and to move in a society. Though I should have preferred some kind of journalism, I knew absolutely nothing about it. Columbia offered me work without my looking for it, at a salary I should not have been able to get elsewhere. And Columbia was in New York, where I wanted to live and write. Scholarship had seduced me, I used to say—not understanding then that seducers can seduce only when the seduced are undecided and half-willing.

For no better reasons than these I fell into the hospitable backwater of the University system. Time seemed to stand still there, in the last years before the war, and to wait on learning. Some of the teachers grew into deans or chairmen of departments, and buzzed and managed as if this were any practical enterprise. Some of the others slumped into increasing idleness, sometimes elegant, more often colorless. These liked to say that they put all their strength into their teaching, but they were not the best teachers. The best teachers, as a rule, were the men who gave their students only the time they could spare from their own work as scholars. Their students valued them the more for this fruitful brevity, and could tell the difference between living knowledge, perhaps new that day to the teacher, and old information read monotonously from old notes. But even the scholars who stayed alive were likely to work most at big monographs on little subjects. Original research they called it. What mattered was that the facts they found had not been known before, not that they were worth knowing. Some other specialist might sooner or later make use of them. The specialists in all the universities wrote for one another, with the patience of mound builders, for mysterious ends. They supposed, when they thought about it, that all their facts might at last be gathered into some great synthesis. But there was time for that. There was time for everything. Time stretched out before them into a smooth eternity of peace.

There must have been among them at least a few men who knew enough history to know that this happy breathing-spell could hardly last forever. If there were, their knowledge did not touch the general opinion. Columbia with its scholars, like Hope with its farmers or Urbana with its townspeople, had the short memory of mortal men. The habit of peace had come to seem the order of life. Peace had lasted for Americans ever since the close of the Civil War: the war with Spain had been a flutter in the newspapers, and so had England's long war in South Africa. Almost everybody at Columbia had been in Europe, and almost nobody guessed that a war was at hand. War in a museum! And if there should be one, as in a comic opera, it could not touch America. America was done with all that. This was the New World. Good men believed in peace as they believed in the law of gravitation, taking it for granted and not expecting to be put to any serious test.

Scholars could lay out large projects in the faith that unreason and violence would not interrupt them. I rode two horses: in the summers I wrote novels, none good, none published, and in the winters I turned scholar again. There was no history of American literature on a scale above that of a textbook. I planned one, to be written by many specialists and edited by Sherman, John Erskine my colleague at Columbia, and me. Before we had gone far a publisher asked Professor Trent to edit a Cambridge History of American Literature to go with his English Literature. Knowing of my plan, he brought us into the venture. His masterly design was its foundation. On that, as the most interested and the youngest of the editors, I did the work of building the book: outlining the chapters in detail, explaining them to the specialists, bringing the material together, fitting the parts into the total scheme, reading the endless proofs, seeing the volumes through the press. Planned before the war, it was a pre-war history of pre-war literature, and it remains that. But there was so much unreason and violence to interrupt that the last of the four volumes did not appear till 1921, when I had been five years away from the University and thought of myself as belonging to the new post-war age.

8

WHEN my grandmother was seventy-six she fell and broke her thigh. After six months in bed, when the bone had knit, she got up and learned to walk. She fell and broke it again. Six months more, and again she was walking. She and my grandfather decided to go back with me at the end of a summer and see New York for the first time.

What really delighted her most was the kitchen at Mount Vernon—Martha Washington's kitchen. "We had a fireplace like that in Indiana when I was a little girl," my grandmother said. "I learned to cook over an open fire." New York did not daunt her, even the threatening trucks when she crossed the street, heavy on my arm. "You ought to be old enough by this time," she said to my grandfather, "not to be afraid of a team." We looked at the city from the top of the Woolworth building and steamed round the island on a sight-seeing boat. We went to the Hippodrome and to the theater. We saw cathedrals and Columbia. My grandmother never once flagged in this adventure. She was doing a life's traveling in two weeks. Her Indian silence left her now and then, and she talked things I had not supposed she thought. One evening at dinner, when my grandfather had been moralizing, she teased him about a young man whom she had known before she knew him and whom she might have married except for her parents.

He was uncertain and possibly afraid in the city, which tired him. What pleased him most was a two-day excursion, alone, to Hope, New Jersey, and the farm where he had been born. He bought two barrels of apples there and sent them to my small apartment. "The best apples in the world," he said, "bar none." He liked to sit in the parks and strike up acquaintances. He bustled us out to eat a picnic lunch, conspicuous, on Riverside Drive. He did not know that it was conspicuous and would not have cared if he had.

I took him to a convocation at the University. Something that President Butler said so roused my grandfather that he whispered to me: "I'm going to give them my Indian warwhoop"—and he drew in his breath. I knew what his warwhoop was. Nobody who had heard it could ever forget it. I do not know quite how I stopped him. If he had been at his best I could not have done it. He would have whooped without warning me, and the steel girders in the roof would have rung, and the caps and gowns would have shuddered, and a stately decorum would have died. At the time I was in terror. Now I am half-sorry he did not have his way without my academic interference. If my grandfather and President Butler had met after the explosion they would have liked each other. And one Columbia convocation would still be remembered.

II SECOND WORLD: POST-WAR

War
Journalism
Literature

War

However the war came politically, it came morally as an unexpected ghastly wound. First the shock and the stunned numbness. In my diary for all of the ominous June of 1914 and for all of July except the last two days, there is not the least reference to what was going on. Then for 30 July: "The thought in my mind from morning till night was the thought of a general European war. The cataclysm has laid a hand on every soul I met today." After the shock, incredulity. This could not be happening to the world I knew. Then the horror of pain, the gradual sense that it must somehow be borne, the long endurance, fevers that rose and fell in the blood, relief, and dragging recovery. But the wound had done its damage. The first day of the war was the end of an illusion by which my contemporaries had lived. This was not a world of humane and reasonable order finally arrived at. This was a world in which anything still might happen.

Politically the war was in Europe for three years, but morally it was in America too. Americans sat in the gallery of that monstrous drama. From the outset most of them saw it as melodrama: black villains and white heroes, deliberate evil and outraged good, unprovoked assault and honorable self-defense. From the outset most Americans hissed and applauded. But this was more than stage melodrama. Actual men were actually dying. The dark smell of blood reached the gallery. American nerves responded with passions stronger than the theater ever calls for.

I am not talking about the bankers who wanted to make loans, or the traders who wanted to make money, or the editors who wanted to get new readers, or the preachers who brayed to their gods, or the professors who turned orators, or the orators who remained what they were. I am talking about the run of Americans whose interests were touched only by the higher cost of living and who had nothing to do with the war but fight its battles. At first they were cool enough. One of my students at Columbia told me he was not going to bother himself about the war just now, but would wait till it was over and then read a short history of it. He was later drafted and went overseas. Americans could not stay cool. War has a higher temperature than peace. It affects sensitive onlookers. They take sides in spite of themselves and grow passionate. They wonder if they can, as human beings, decently do nothing. They begin to feel guilty because they are safe, and to despise themselves. The hasty and headstrong and cocksure among them bawl for action. The nozzles of the bankers and traders and editors and ministers and professors and orators play upon the people. Perhaps the people never really want war. I do not believe that a popular vote of Americans would have been in favor of our entering this war. But the people do not know what to do until the decision has been made for them. Then the drums tell them and they follow, too feverish to hold back.

I knew almost nobody who was wise during the war. I was not. On the day after the Lusitania was sunk I wrote in my diary: "Thorndike has a kind of Rooseveltian idea as to the need of war, sooner or later. And I am by no means sure we can avoid it. But what shall I do with my reason if it comes?

What with my pride of balance and judgment? How can I hate a nation where I have merely laughed at its bad manners and bad learning? I think I could easier die." I was never ready for war, and I welcomed each delaying note from the White House. The delay seemed good for its own sake. When in doubt, do nothing. Yet my aversion was mere instinct. I did not want to kill or to be killed. I did not want to be involved in any madness that must always see white or black. I was bewildered by the fury of the war. I did not even guess how much of what we were told about the origin and conduct of the war was lies. Skeptical by temper, I still could not help being stirred by tales which I did not seriously believe. Again and again I found myself, horrified, half-sunk in a pit of hatred for the Germans, half-willing to sink and be lost in a frenzy without thought or judgment. Because I did not wholly sink I was called pro-German by an occasional witch-hunter. (The witch-hunters were subtle. Let a doubt cross your mind while they raved, and they could feel it.) But I was neither very prudent nor very reckless, because I had no clear logic in my actions. I lived by the stubborn instinct of those men who do not make wars but who survive them and pay for them.

The wisest man I knew during the war was my great teacher, Professor Trent, a scholar who was a prophet too. He had been in Europe in the summer of 1914. When he came back, his friends expected him to join them in the gallery of the melodrama. He did not. He already saw the conflict as most sensible men were to see it twenty years later: not as a simple melodrama with its moral all over its face but as the outcome of a hundred years of greed and aggression and stupidity. He was in the predicament of any prophet. To his

short-sighted friends his long-sight seemed wrong-headed-
ness. They did not see what he saw. Why should he? In the
passion of the times they condemned him. One of them said
to me: "Trent has sinned the sin against the Holy Ghost."
No man, so far as I know, ever dared to say such things to
him, the kind, fierce, gray Virginian lion. But he got insulting letters. Eyes wavered and dropped when he came near.
He must have felt silences and imagined talk behind his
back. Friends fell away. It cannot have been pleasant to him
to find himself sought by professional pro-Germans who
misunderstood him as thoroughly as his old friends did. I
suppose he suffered everything a prophet can suffer when the
pack turns against him—everything but violence and death.
Professor Trent had to endure more cunning tortures. He
could barely finish, and could not publish, his life of Defoe.
One of the monuments of American learning exists only in
manuscript.

Though I loved him, and looked upon him as a second
father, I was far from realizing how wise he was. Often he
struck me as intemperate. Yet even then I knew his rages
were noble—no less noble for being witty. "Yes," he said one
day, "the English are surely the strongest people in the world.
Millions of Englishmen every day resist what must be the
irresistible temptation to hang themselves." I laughed, like
everybody to whom I have ever quoted the remark. But I
was often troubled for him. Once, when he had had a vicious
letter from a publisher, and John Erskine and I were trying
to keep the peace between them, I wrote in my diary: "What
is come to the world, when youth must be impartial and cool
and hold age back from the lash and saber?" Not always
agreeing with Professor Trent, I held my tongue, though

afraid my silences might sound to him like those of the friends who condemned him. I did not know how to tell him how I felt. The tongues of young men are tied when they most want to speak: to speak of affection and loyalty and devotion and veneration. When the young men are old enough to speak, as I do here, they sadly wonder if it may not be too late.

All over the country there were, I now realize, men who were opposed to the war on grounds well reasoned out. I barely realized it at the time. No hero either for the war or against it, I kept to myself my instinctive aversion to any war, my belief that this was Europe's war not ours, and my worried sense that the crusade was only a stampede. Historians had made me believe—or at least assume—that in the worst times there would be strong men with clear aims. Now I began to think that the men in power were no stronger and no clearer than men in general. Events had got out of reasonable hands and were running away in unpredictable directions. The war was an epidemic. My generation thought it had learned the secrets of this old disease and mastered it. Now the plague had returned with fresh virulence. It was as if smallpox had suddenly struck alike at the vaccinated and the unvaccinated. Millions died and doctors went mad. Even those who neither died nor went mad moved about in a terrible excitement. I could not avoid quick pulses and jumping nerves. Bands played, flags waved, uniforms filled the streets, young men left their natural affairs for camp and trench, women were heroic or hysterical, old men staying at home told how they wished they could go. Terse bulletins from the front were swollen by the papers to alarming or consoling pages. I had bloodthirsty thoughts and spoke bloodthirsty words when the intermittent fevers came. The war was epidemic, and the epidemic was delirium.

2

YET the war in fact did not come very close to me. It touched me most through my two youngest brothers. Mark was twenty-three in June 1917. He had taken his first degree at Illinois three years before, had studied a further year with Sherman and had written his book on Thoreau published a year later, and had followed me to Columbia. There he had done his work for his doctor's degree and had almost finished his study of Dryden's poetry. In all my teaching I never enjoyed anything so much as the seminar I gave with Professor Trent the year Mark and his friend Joseph Wood Krutch from Tennessee were among our students. In all my supervision of research I never took such pride in anything as in Mark's work on Dryden. "The essay owes much to my brother, Carl Van Doren," he said in his acknowledgment, "whose idea it largely was and whose immense resources of encouragement were always at my command." I had suggested that Mark, who was a poet facing an age of confusion, should study the course taken by some earlier poet who, facing a similar age, had got through it and become serene and powerful. We hit on Dryden together. Mark wrote the book alone. What he undertook may have been for him more or less like what my undertaking with Peacock was for me, but the two books had nothing in common, and Mark's was better than mine. He was the first of my brothers whom I had known well as a man, and I knew that he was the most gifted and charming of us all, as Guy was the most humorous, Frank the handsomest, and Paul—already at eighteen—the most shrewd and worldly.

Mark was the first to go to war, or toward it. Apparently frank, actually impenetrable, he gave me no real understanding of his state of mind, though I could be sure he hated war and had no crusading illusions. With what seemed to me a kind of disgusted fatalism he refused either to enlist or to protest, and let the draft take him in September to Camp Dodge, at Des Moines, where he worked for his commission. I went out that winter to surprise him with a few hours' visit, and I still see him as he came toward me in his straining uniform, fine-boned in heavy harness, stuttering when he spoke. We talked all the hours I was there, but I never found out what he thought about the war—never found out or needed to. After he got his commission he was sent to Camp Pike, at Little Rock, and served monotonously till after the Armistice.

Paul at the end of a year at Illinois quietly enlisted in the Marine Corps, had his training with the Thirteenth Regiment—along with tough marines recalled from Haiti—at Parris Island off the coast of South Carolina, crossed the Atlantic to Brest, spent months guarding German prisoners near Bordeaux, and came back to New York in August 1919 suave and silent. He limped as we hunted through town for food that could make him forget rations. A sailor with a truck had driven it into a group of marines and given Paul's spine an injury that left him limping for months.

Bloodless history, and mild reading now. Then all the days and nights were anxious. My mother, hating war but fatalistic, said that she could stand it as well as any mother. Once she said something that startled me by what it revealed: "If the young men are killed, who will be the fathers of our children?" It sounded to me less like my mother speaking than like all women asking out of a deep racial preoccupation. My mother, herself now a grandmother, began to look more and more like my grandmother, with her Indian silence. My father could not believe that the boys had to go. Food would win the war. Well, let them be farmers and raise food. When he was finally convinced that Mark must go and Paul would, he had met what I think was the first defeat his will had ever had. It took a world war to beat him down.

Little as I wanted a hand in any war, I could never get rid of a guilty sense that I should go instead of Mark and Paul and leave them at their studies. We had called them the little boys at home, and I was the oldest, and had felt responsibility for all my brothers. Here was a responsibility I could not take. Guiltily, wretchedly, absurdly, I wrote a letter to each of them every day he was in the service. It may have embarrassed them, and it did not relieve me. But those were the days of the war, and strange infections were in the air.

Except for the tedium of a wasted year apiece, Mark and Paul paid no more for the extravagant war than any of us. Guy, graduating in architecture at Illinois in 1910, had followed my uncles to Oklahoma—their Indian Territory—and had established himself in Muskogee in boom times. Married while I was in London, to Verla McCray who had been born near Hope but whom he had met only after her father and mother had retired to Danville as ours had to Urbana, Guy had a daughter by the time the Muskogee boom collapsed. (I conclude that women, young or old, cannot be spoiled by too much love, or Mary would have been lost before she could walk, with so many uncles to whom by merely being a little girl she was a miracle. She was not spoiled. There is no such thing as too much love for a woman to assimilate and thrive on—only wrong kinds of love.) But for the war Guy would possibly never have gone off to Detroit, prosperous with war, to enter the complex of that industrial world which rode so high, fell so far. Frank, who had studied agriculture at the university, settled on the farm at Villa Grove, and was married to Grace Gay of Rockport, across the state near Quincy. By 1920 he had begun to pay, as he has paid ever since, for the war-madness of the farmers—which he did not share while it was raging, and was drawn into only because my father was.

My father was the war's worst victim. Go to war, young men, and protect your fathers. Between fifty and sixty he had increased his optimistic ventures: besides his farms and banks, an electric railway, and an addition to the town of Urbana, with a park in the center and building lots for sale. The electric railway had come too late. Cheap motor cars and hard roads doomed it. My father would not believe this or give up. Let a man hold out and hang on, and he was bound to win. This was America. Look at real estate. It had always been rising in value. It would go on rising. He poured money into pavements and sidewalks and planting and assessments. When the war came, and the price of land rushed upward, he could not see that this was abnormal and temporary. At last his long faith was justified. "You will never see the time again," he told me, "when the price of Illinois land will be less than five hundred dollars an acre." He would have a fortune to leave each of his sons. Instead of selling his land, at war prices, paying off his debts, and living easily, he bought more land, more land. This was Eldorado. He somehow contrived to feel certain both that the war would last a little while and let Mark and Paul come back unharmed, and that the war would last forever and keep prices up. For two years he exulted, justified. Then in 1920 that short, flushed chapter ended. The price of land went down and down. Men could not sell land for the amount of their mortgages. Men could not sell land at all. They could not raise enough grain or livestock, at the new prices, to pay interest and taxes. In that panic confusion my father still did not doubt that America was Eldorado. Hold out. Hang on. He had seen hard times before. All experience showed—but his experience betrayed him. He was like leviathan thrown by a tidal wave on dry land and still sure he could save himself by swimming. One world had shaped my father, and the war had lifted him up and set him down in another.

3

THE war was a wound, but of course it did not always hurt or ache. The mind can mysteriously go about its business for hours, as if nothing were wrong, burying its trouble in some limbo of the memory, and feeling the pain only when at intervals it rises and runs along the nerves till they throb again. Men can stand more pain than they think. I have often looked at men at work, when I knew that they were privately unhappy almost to despair, and have wondered that they could behave so much like the happy men beside them. I have myself worked as well on days when I thought I could not face the night as on days when I could scarcely wait for it.

My instinctive life went on as if there had been no war. Married in August 1912 to Irita Bradford of Tallahassee, I lived professorially near the Columbia campus. For the summers we discovered Cornwall, the greenest town in New England, near Litchfield, Connecticut. Since 1915 the town has become known for the writers who live there in summer. Mark has a farm in Cornwall Hollow, Lewis Gannett another on Cream Hill, and for several years Krutch had one near Cornwall Center. Henry Canby declared that when I was editing the Literary Guild and Irita the Books supplement of the Herald Tribune from Cream Hill, and he was editing the Saturday Review and the Book-of-the-Month Club from Yelping Hill, and Mark was literary editor and Krutch dramatic critic of the Nation: that then Cornwall touched the literary taste of all America. What was more important, I thought, certain Cornwall sights and sounds, trees and flowers and animals, barnyards and tumbled houses were being caught by some of Mark's poems in a crystal immortality. But in 1915 the town was a cool green wilderness. Most of the land was owned by families that had settled there two hundred years before. The names on the tombstones were the same as those on the mailboxes. The town of Cornwall, they told me, had voted against ratifying the Constitution of the United States. Satisfied with their hills and forests, its people saw no need for being united with anything larger than Connecticut. They accepted Hartford, where they had representatives in the legislature. They accepted Yale: some of the farms in Cornwall belonged to Yale College. For the rest of the world, Cornwall had been, and was, as independent as Hope when I lived there.

This conservatism charmed me, perhaps because Cornwall was a kind of rural museum. There I saw my first scythe and cradle—as my grandfather had told me about them. I watched oxen at work—and remembered my grandfather. There were no hard roads in the north part of Cornwall and only one automobile. When we had to go further than we could comfortably walk we drove horses. We bought a house, formerly the parsonage, which had no heat but from one fireplace and no plumbing but a pump in the kitchen. The house sat in the shade like a hen hovering its chickens—in the shade of eight elms. The lawn sloped, velvet, down to the ragged road. Across the road was the garden where I raised the vegetables we ate. A mile along the road was Cream Hill Lake, where we swam every afternoon. Writing, gardening, swimming made up my day. In the evening we heard the frogs in the marsh and saw the fireflies over the meadow. On clear nights the stars were silver splashes on the sky. Those stars, I knew, were elsewhere looking down on the brutal, valiant war. But here in Cornwall there was no war.

No war in 1915. Later the war came even there, and young men went away. Summer visitors appeared, more and more of them. Asphalt ran up and down the hills and wound along the valleys. Visitors brought automobiles, and farmers bought them. Some of the farmers gave up half their summers to working for the visitors. But for the eight years we lived at Threeways, the old parsonage, Cornwall was still a green hiding-place. My daughters—Anne, born in 1915, Margaret in 1917, and Barbara in 1920—have never spent, or wanted to spend, a summer anywhere but there. Until Barbara was three she thought that Cornwall and country meant the same thing, and as soon as she got out of the city pointed to the fields and said: "Cornwall."

In 1916 I resigned from Columbia to become Headmaster of the Brearley School in New York. Nobody knew or cared less than I about the secondary education of fashionable girls. Though the Brearley was one of the best, as well as most fashionable, of schools, I had never even heard its name. My New York was its scholars. I lived as far from Park Avenue as if I had been in Urbana. But since teaching was only a trade for me, not a passion, I did not mind leaving a university where I was assistant professor for a school where I would be head. The invitation utterly surprised me, and pleased me—still more Professor Trent's belief that running a school would be easy for a person of my disposition. I did not recognize myself at all in the person he thought I was. I thought I was passionate and yet slow in action. But it took me only four or five days to make up my mind to this revolution. Still, I kept one graduate class in American literature at Columbia—kept it and met the class Friday afternoons for fourteen years.

Ever since I left for Europe in June 1910 I had put down a daily record of all I did and much of what I thought and felt. (There are eleven volumes for those six years, but the way I wrote is more remote than the things I did, and I have been willing to quote only a few words from it in these maturer memoirs.) Months after I went to the Brearley I first noticed that the diary had lapsed. The last entry was for the day the school opened in October 1916. The young man who had written so fully about himself no longer existed, and I was not really interested in his successor.

The Brearley was the only uncongenial work I have ever had or tried to do. The four hundred girls, from six to eighteen, were delightful. The forty women teachers, though inclined to be suspicious of me as a man, and younger than most of them, were friendly enough. The directors, though inclined to nag and fuss, out of the best thinkable intentions, were generally enlightened. I had an expert assistant principal who spared me the technical drudgery of administration. Still I did not like it, and after a year gave up hoping I ever could. I could not stand the other headmasters I met: most of them either childish or snobbish. They seemed to me uncertain whether they were bishops or butlers. I resented my status with the parents, who about equally feared and snubbed me, and so I never felt at home along Park Avenue. I found it as dull as Hope had been my last year. And I discovered that in this world, though often so shining and so varied, there were only the same kinds of people as I had known in Hope and Urbana. Money and smartness do not clearly distinguish one society from another. It takes intellect to do that.

The trouble lay less in the school, no doubt, than in me. I simply had no taste for endless wrangling and scheming and plotting, and I had no taste for them because I did not care how most of the arguments came out. I could not think of them as living issues. What if Elsie was habitually late? What if Abby did slip out the back door and go to the next street for ice cream? What if Anne and Sylvia did play truant to see and hear the visiting Archbishop of York? What if there was a crisis in this or that department? What if nine-tenths of the teachers were jealous of one of them? What if some mother did think the lunches not sufficient? What if, even, there were complaints that too many of the girls were now preparing for college instead of getting ready for their debúts? The directors had picked the wrong headmaster and I had taken the wrong post.

But I learned something about how affairs are managed, anywhere. A school is the same as a nation. At first I felt like an organist, sitting at strange keys, not sure, if he pressed this or that one, what pipe would respond or where it was. It was a long while before I got used to unexpected reverberations in unexpected quarters. It was longer before I learned how much authority my mere position gave and how careful I must be about using it. And I could never be reconciled to the little objections—not the large objections, generally reasonable—which were brought against my painstaking management. Let a governor have enough intelligence to know what the best interests of the governed are, as I tried to have, and let him have enough goodwill to desire nothing else, as I had, and he will find that a large part of his energy must still go into explaining why he does what he does, to people who ask without listening and hear without trusting. All government, except tyranny, is a form of education.

When, at the end of my second year at the Brearley, I told the directors I would not go on beyond the three years for which we had a contract, I did not know what I should do next. But I was as lucky then as I have usually been. Oswald Garrison Villard, whose daughter was in the school, invited me to become literary editor of the Nation. The reason he gave me was that he thought highly of some reviews I had written for the paper. I have always thought it was, rather, that once when he had asked me if his daughter might leave school before the end of the term, I had refused. I had been wondering at the time if the school ought not now and then to make some exceptions to its strict rule in such cases. He probably thought that I showed character.

Journalism

HERE is a letter dated 25 December 1921 which came to me, as literary editor, from Pascal D'Angelo, then an unknown Italian laborer in Brooklyn, who had entered the contest for a prize the Nation was to give for the best poem submitted between Thanksgiving and Christmas:

"In sending my poems I would like to send a little autobiographical sketch that may interest you. This is the first prize contest I have ever participated in and I therefore entertain very little hope. Because I am a pick and shovel man, I have never studied in English in any school. I have learned all by myself. So mistakes are not too difficult for me to make especially the grammatical ones. I hope you consider all this and beside I hope you could see where I am living with your own eyes, then you will realize all my sacrifices. I am explaining myself in words but they cannot vividly illustrate my present and past suffering. I am striving to raise myself from the Hades of ignorance to the light of recognition, where I can express the living protest of my fellow-toilers. Please now is the moment that I can have an immediate recognition and you are the man of the hour that can lift me out of these burning flames of ignorance. If you give the prize to a man who is already well known you are not helping him much, because his works are accepted by the publishers. But I am without a name, without a literary friend that can introduce me and without money to buy a name as many of the writers of [have] already done. So if I am worthy of being helped, why not help me? You might give the prize to someone who spends its money in cabaret, beer saloons, and many other places. While I with $100 prize if given to me I can live 4 months without work at the same time I write, more—my works will be accepted because of the prize I have won. Then, is then when I am lifted out to light—to light. Please pierce me not with the black flaming sword of rejection, please no! no!"

Hundreds of manuscripts had reached the office during the last week of the contest, and it took some time to acknowledge them. The impatient hungry poet could not wait. The day after New Year he wrote again. Here is his original letter, not yet revised for its later publication:

"I have submitted three poems 'For The Nation's poetry prize' within the established period as described in the columns of 'The Nation'. Not having heard anything from your editorial office, I would be obliged if you could inform me on the matter.

"I hope you will consider them from a view-point that they have been written by one who is an ignorant pick and shovel man who has never studied English. If there are not too many mistakes I must warmly thank those people who have been kind enough to point out the grammatical errors. I am one who is struggling through the blinding black flames of ignorance, to bring his message before the public—before you. You are dedicated to defend the immense cause of the oppressed. This letter is the cry of a soul stranded on the shores of darkness looking for light—a light that will point out the path of recognition. Where I can work and help myself. I am not deserting the legions of toil to refuge myself in the literary world. No! No! I only want to explain the wrath of their mistreat. No! I seek no refuge! I am a worker, a pick and shovel man—what I want is an outlet to express what I can do beside working. Yes. To express all the sorrows of those who cower under the yoke of doom.

"I suffer. And there are no words that can fitly represent my living sufferings. No! no words. Even the picture loses its mute eloquence before this scene. I suffer: for an ideal, for freedom, for truth, that is denied by millions, but not by the souls who have the responsibility of being human. Yesterday, New Year's Day, I only had 5 cents worth of bananas and a loaf of stale bread, for food. And today: a half quarter of milk and a loaf of stale bread. All for the love of an ideal. Not having sufficient bed clothes for a stoveless room like mine, I must use my overcoat as a blanket at night and as a wrinkled coat during the day. The room is damp—and my books are becoming mouldered. And I too am beginning to feel the effects of it. But what can I do? Without a pick and shovel job and without a just recognition! And besides, the landlady has notified me to leave her room not later than January 10, 1922. She may have someone who can pay a little more than me. So I must go where another room can be found. Perhaps it will cost more than this. How can I afford it? Without work and without recognition that will allow me to work!

"Please consider my condition and the quality of the work I submit. Then say if I can be helped without expense on your part. You can do. Then do something for me. Even in this horrible condition I am not asking for a financial help. I am not asking for pity, nor am I asking for an impossibility. I am only asking for a simple thing—a thing which you are giving away free. While you are giving it away free, why not see where this thing can help the most?

I am not coveting the prize because of the money. No! But because it will give me recognition, a thing I cannot do without. If it's given to me, in this helpless state I can go around to all the Editors, and say I have been awarded 'The Nation's poetry prize.' When I say that, they will hear me—they will consider my works—they will begin to accept them. Then dominated by an impulse of encouragement I will write: a novel, two, 3—who knows how many! But how can I go on now, without an introduction of this kind? They don't hear me. If I ask them to see my manuscript they say they are busy, or else they let me leave some poems and then they put them hatching oblivion in an obscure corner of their editorialo-cratic drawers. When a certain time they might accidentally happen to see my poems they glance at the name, and see it's an unknown one. Then return them without reading them. What do they know what I have written? Must it continue like this forever? That is why I am asking this help from you. If it's a help without expenses why not help me? Makes no difference to whom it is given, it does not the same help that gives to me! Because there is no writer in this condition, and can present the same quality of work. Then let this prize break those horrible barriers before me, and open a new world of hope! Let this prize (even if an honorary one) come like a bridge of light between me and a waiting future. Let me free! Let me free! free like the thought of love that haunts millions minds. If it's without expenses on your side then give, give me an opportunity. You are the man of the hour! This is the moment when for nothing you can give me all. When for nothing you can put me into a place where I can work hard and make enough money to have a musical education. For I want to compose music. And yet I do not know the difference between one note and another.

What bars me from doing so? When I know music then I can glorify the immense cause of the many. Then I can vilify the horrible injustice of the vile few! Then give me! give me an opportunity and see what I can do! Oh! please! hear me I am telling the truth, and yet who knows it? Only me. And who believes me? Then let my soul break out of its chrysalis of ignorance and fly toward the flower of hope, like a rich butterfly winged with a thousand thoughts. Remember! what I want is a help without expenses: the honor of the prize. Please hear me! who can see these weights of duty that crush down and yet I cannot perform. I am not a spendthrift. $100 will last me four months. I am not asking for an impossibility. Let me see what I can do. O! please let the strength of this prize lift me, and place me on the pulpit of light. Where I too can narrate what the Nature-made orator has to say in me!"

"When night comes," he said in his autobiographical sketch, "and we all quit work, the thuds of the pick and the jingling of the shovel are not heard any more. All my day's labors are gone, forever. But if I write a line of poetry my work is not lost, my line is still there—it can be read by you today and can be read by another tomorrow. But my pick and shovel works can be read neither by you today nor by another tomorrow. If I should bring you to all the above mentioned places [where he had worked building roads] you wouldn't be able to understand all the works I was forced to do while I was there. But if I show you a manuscript written even before that time you can see my works of a year or two or any amount of years right in front of your eyes and appreciate its value. But how can you see my other works when they have vanished? So I yearn for an opportunity to see what I can ambitiously accomplish before the clutches of senility make me their unpardonable victim. Also before all the sufferings, colds, wets, dampness, and rheumatism begin to harm me in the not a distant future, having all these other evils to overcome besides misery and ignorance."

I sent for him and he came to see me, in his wrinkled overcoat that had no buttons and hung on him like a horse's blanket. Through his torn trousers I could see a bare knee, that winter day. He gave me a hard expressionless hand, awkwardly and timidly. He looked like dozens of Italian laborers I had seen standing beside chaotic roads—and I suddenly thought that men like him had built the ruthless highways of the Caesars. But he was taller than most such men and his eyes were nearly level with mine. Eyes as soft as an animal's, with an occasional flash of eager fire. His eyes were the only evidence that he was a poet. Nothing that he said reminded me of his letters or his poems. Monosyllabically shy, he answered my questions, but said no more. It was like talking to some ragged peasant messenger who brought poems without knowing what they were.

His poems did not seem to me good enough to win the prize, but I bought two of them and paid him at once. In my Nation column, The Roving Critic, I wrote an article about him. Recognition came as fast as he had said it would. Other editors bought other poems and printed them. Friends of poetry sent offers of money and clothing. Mary Austin said she would give him a typewriter. Newspapers took up his story and made it a week's wonder. The Italian-language press celebrated him. I could not see that these things affected him at all, though when next he came to see me he was more warmly dressed. He could have a job, he told me, as editor on an Italian paper, but he preferred to be a poet in English.

He was writing his autobiography. I helped him a little with that, and wrote an introduction when it appeared, late in 1924, as Pascal D'Angelo: Son of Italy. In the meantime he went on working with his hands, in a Brooklyn cemetery. After the autobiography he dropped out of sight again and lived obscure until the papers in 1932, learning that he was dead, remembered the story of his short renown.

He would probably have been a poet of one book in any circumstances. It has been guessed that he was not even that: that he only ran errands for some knowing writer who used this trick to hoax an editor. I find it easier to believe that Pascal D'Angelo the poet existed than that he was invented. Who invented him, the letters—I have them still—with their cry for help, the poems, the convincing and moving autobiography? A man clever enough to invent them would have kept on writing. Pascal D'Angelo might have stopped. "All my day's labors are gone, forever. But if I write a line of poetry my work is not lost." Perhaps his book, seeming to him monument enough, quieted his passion. Other men, in the grip of that ancient instinct, get children, build houses and temples, establish fortunes or empires. Pascal D'Angelo taught himself to write and wrote a single book. "If you killed all the horses in the world," John Erskine once said, "there would be no more horses. But if you killed all the poets, there would be as many poets as ever in the next generation."

2

BEFORE the war the Nation had been as conservative as it could find reasons for being. By the end of 1921 it was offering an annual prize for poetry, in the new manner, and a pick and shovel man could say to it: "You are dedicated to defend the immense cause of the oppressed." Pre-war had given way to post-war.

The old Nation, though less conservative than the universities, got most of its reviewers from them. The last three editors had all been professors in their time. Paul Elmer More, orthodox among journalists, was close in temper as in friendship to Irving Babbitt, then heretical among professors. More made special use of Stuart Sherman, whose assaults on Dreiser and Mencken and George Moore put Sherman first among academic critics and gave him a general hearing before any other critic of his years had won it. In those days the way for a young man to rise fast was to agree with his elders. He could seem wise at once, comforting them in their settled judgments. Sherman had more than the usual old head on young shoulders. He had wit and comic force and eloquence. In a university beside professors who did not even read the newer writers whom he drubbed, he looked bold and venturesome. Had he not denounced the unimaginative study of literature in the graduate schools? More had learned about Sherman from Babbitt, Sherman's favorite teacher at Harvard. The elder who had remained a professor commended the young man to the elder who had become a journalist. All his life Sherman was more or less divided between the two careers, but he did his best work, in Urbana, for the old Nation. His final two years as journalist were not long enough to make him over. He was the last of the professors.

I must be on guard against a possible illusion. When I say that about the time of the war the professors lost their authority in criticism to the journalists, it may mean only that

I, changing from one profession to another, had lost touch with the universities and lived in a different world. But I do not believe that I confuse what happened to me with what happened to literary opinion in general. Brander Matthews and William Lyon Phelps did cease to be the Castor and Pollux, if not the Scylla and Charybdis, of critical America, yielding in influence to Mencken and Nathan and Heywood Broun, to Ludwig Lewisohn and Van Wyck Brooks. Once I heard Agnes Repplier say that the new critics made her remember William Dean Howells and Henry James, then young, riding their high horses of realism over all they thought romantic. History, she said, repeats itself in strange disguises.

The Nation under Paul Elmer More had been in effect a weekly literary supplement of the Evening Post, and its prestige had come rather from its reviews of books than from its comments on public affairs. When Villard, owner of the Post, sold it in 1918, he detached and kept the Nation, which he thought of, under his editorship, as a weekly newspaper of liberal opinion. Villard was never, so far as I could see, interested in literature itself, only in literature as a form of argument in behalf of virtue and justice. His private tastes ran to the simple and sentimental, and he was often mystified as well as troubled by the poets and dramatists and novelists and critics of the twenties. He had a strong sense of piety toward the old Nation, which his father had owned and his uncle edited. He wanted to lose none of its critical prestige—even wished, I sometimes thought, that the new Nation could be conservative in literature, radical in politics, and hardly saw why it could not be both at the same time, as he was. But he gave me as free a hand as if he had held, with me, that a new book has the same right to exist as a new baby.

Those old subscribers who immediately cried out that the Nation had become un-American can have had no native memory. Villard was as American as the Hudson or the Merrimac. His vigilant defense of the Negro minority went back to his grandfather William Lloyd Garrison, and his defense of all minorities was in keeping with it. His insistence on civil liberties might have come from Thomas Jefferson, and indirectly did. Villard's hatred of war and his opposition to imperialism had been shared by many of the best Americans, though he knew more about the army and the navy than any other peace-lover. He believed in free trade, like the Democrats. Like the Republicans, he was by nature paternalistic toward labor. He found it hard not to think of the Nation staff as working for him, loyal through him to his—and of course their—ideas. He knew little about economics and almost everything about politics. If he had stayed at his earlier post in Washington he might have been the best Washington correspondent the country ever had. In most respects a typical American, he had one quality in which he surpassed the majority of Americans and the majority of men anywhere. That was what he called moral indignation. It was not always reasonable and was sometimes, it seemed to me, a passion for unpopular causes only because they were unpopular. He had to feel he was in the minority to feel he was right. But there could be no question that Villard's moral indignation gave the Nation its power. Like a bull of virtue he charged at every vice.

What the most reactionary newspapers now say about the treaty of Versailles seemed near to treason when the Nation said it as soon as the treaty reached the public: that it was

iniquity and madness perpetuating grievances as bad as any
that the war had been fought over. The Nation made war
on the peace-makers who had made no peace. It made war
at home on all who tried to keep the war alive. It demanded
the release of political prisoners, the return of alien property, the repeal of emergency acts, the restoration of civil
liberties. The war was over. Let the peace be better. Nobody
on the Nation staff, during the years 1919-1922 when I was
with it, had any very clear vision of the economic read-
justment which was going on throughout the world. One
or two were members of the Socialist party. The rest were
simply liberals, if they still could bear the name, or frankly
radicals. I never saw much difference between them. They
watched Russia and wanted the United States to recognize
the Soviet government. They thought the Allies could and
should pay their war-debts if they had enough money to go
on maintaining and increasing armaments. They sympathized, in American affairs, with strikers as against owners, with the people as against officials. But they neither
expected nor desired a revolution in America. The war had
interrupted and disturbed, not overthrown, the national order. Bring order back again. But bring with it liberty and
truth or it would not be worth having. The right of free
assembly, the freedom of the press, of talking, and of teaching: on these the Nation never compromised. They were
good in themselves, without reference to their visible effects.
Truth could come out of them alone, and without truth
there could be no liberty.

So, for those three years and later, the Nation ransacked
the news of the world for events and issues that most newspapers disregarded or misrepresented or misunderstood. It
studied and exposed the signs which it thought pointed to

other wars. It brought to light the sly or bungling methods of imperialism, particularly of the United States in Latin America. It published details of economic exploitation. It never missed a chance to report violations of civil liberty, or racial discriminations, or the insolences of persons in authority. This was the newspaper of a passionate minority clamoring for justice. No doubt, forever nipping and goading, it often seemed tiresome and bad-tempered. The staff, gay enough as individuals, now and then became self-conscious and decided there must be less doom and more humor in the paper. Not much came of this, and the readers seldom cared. What doubled and trebled and quadrupled the circulation was the bitter truths which the Nation offered to a public surfeited with the sweet lies they had been told during the war.

3

In one of my Roving Critic columns I tried to define the fourth dimension in criticism which the book reviewers of the new Nation looked for:

"Criticism ordinarily asks about literature one of three questions: 'Is it good?' 'Is it true?' 'Is it beautiful?' Each of these questions, of course, permits the widest range in the critic. He may be so simple as to think a given work is not good when it fails to emphasize some truism or when it violates the sort of poetic justice which children in the nursery are mistaught to expect; he may be so complex as to demand from literature the subtlest casuistries concerning moral problems; he may be so perverse as to wince at the first symptom of any plain contrast between good and evil. If it be the true which exercises him, he may sink so low as to be worried over this or that surface error in his author—such as an anachronism or a blunder in botany or mechanics; he may rise so high as to discuss on an equal plane with a great authority the difficult questions what the nature of truth may be or whether there is after all any such thing as truth. Or, holding beauty uppermost in his mind, he may at the one extreme peck at a masterpiece because it departs from some traditional form or at the other extreme may view it under the light of an eternity of beauty and feel satisfied if he can perceive and identify the masterpiece's peculiar reflection. Yet wide as these ranges are, they can all be reduced to three questions and they mark what may be called the three dimensions of criticism.

"There is, however, a fourth dimension—to continue the analogy—which comes into the account when a critic asks about literature: 'Is it alive?' In a sense this query includes all the others and in a sense it transcends them.

"Odysseus is not good: he is adulterous and crafty; Faust is not good: he sells his soul for the sake of forbidden power; Gargantua is not good: he buffets and tumbles the decencies in all directions; Henry V is not good: he wastes his youth and wages unjust war; Huckleberry Finn is not good: he is a thief and a liar. The heroes, the demigods, the gods themselves occasionally step aside from the paths into which men counsel one another; there are at least as many stories about gorgeous courtesans as about faithful wives. It is not the 'goodness' of all such literature but the vividness that gives it its perennial impact. Better a lively rogue than a deadly saint.

"To a different extent the same thing appears when truthfulness is concerned. There is a vitality which lies back both of naturalism and of romance and which communicates itself through books as dissimilar, say, as Madame Bovary and The Faerie Queene—one of them the most fastidious document and one of them the most spacious dream. The gods of Homer are not real; the history of Virgil will not bear scrutiny; Dante wanders in a maze of superstition; Shakespeare lets his plots take him almost where they like; the machinery of a folk-tale is good enough for Goethe, as it was for the author of the Book of Job. How many cosmogonies, Bernard Shaw points out, have gone to the dust heap in spite of an accuracy superior to that which keeps Genesis alive through cynical centuries! The looser Molière is in the long run no less convincing that the tighter Ibsen. Swift and Voltaire and Lucian, twitting their worlds for their follies, dare every extravagance of invention without serious penalty. Ariosto with his whimsical paladins and Scott with his stately aristocrats and Dickens with his hearty democratic caricatures and Dostoevsky with his tortured souls—to find a common denominator of truth among them is so hard that the critics who attempt it are likely to end in partisanship for this or that one and to assign the others to a station outside the approved class. Yet an author may be killed a dozen times with the charge of untruthfulness and still live.

"And concerning beauty the disagreement of the doctors is unending and unendable. Whitman is now called beautiful and now called ugly; so are Browning, and Hugo, and Tolstoi, and Nietzsche, and Lope de Vega, and Leopardi, and Catullus, and Aristophanes. Moreover, by any æsthetic standard which the judgment can arrive at, any one of these authors is sometimes beautiful and sometimes not. Nor does it finally matter, as it did not finally matter that Socrates had a thick body and a pug-face. The case of Socrates illustrates the whole argument. Was he good? There was so great a difference on this point among the critics of his time that the majority of them, translating their conclusion into action, put him to death as dangerous to the state. Was what he taught the truth? It is of course not easy to disentangle the actual Socrates from the more or less polemic versions of him which Xenophon and Plato furnish, but it seems clear that he had his share of unscientific notions and individual prejudices and mistaken doctrines. Was he beautiful? He confused Greek orthodoxy by being so uncomely and yet so great. But whatever his shortcomings in these regards, no one ever doubted that he was alive—alive in body and mind and character, alive in war and peace and friendship and controversy, alive in bed or at table. Life was concentrated in him; life spoke out of him.

"So with literature, which collects, transmutes, and utters life. It may represent the good, may speak the truth, may use the modes of beauty—any one or all of these things. Call the good the bow which lends the power; call the truth the string which fixes the direction; call the beautiful the arrow which wings and stings. But there is still the arm in which the true life of the process lies. Or, to change the figure, one of those gods who in the mythologies model men out of clay may have good clay and a true purpose and may shape his figure beautifully; but there is still the indispensable task of breathing the breath of life into it before it will wake and go its own course and continue its breed to other generations. Life is obviously what makes the difference between good literature and dead literature.

"The critic who is aware of this fourth dimension of the art he studies saves himself the effort which critics less aware contrive to squander in trying to explain their art in terms of three dimensions. He knows that life began before there were such things as good and evil; that it surges through both of them; that it will probably outlast any particular conception of either one or the other: he knows that it is not the moral of so naïve a tale as Uncle Tom's Cabin which makes it moving but the life which was breathed into it by a fiery passion. He knows that the amount of truth in poetry need not always be great and often indeed is much exaggerated; that a ruthless hand can find heaps of theological slag in Milton and corners full of metaphysical cobwebs in Plato and glittering excrescences of platitude in Shakespeare: he knows that these poets now live most in those parts of their work in the creating of which they were most alive. He knows that a powerful imagination may beget life even upon ugliness: he knows it because he has felt the vibrations of reality in Browning's cranky grotesques and in Whitman's long-drawn categories and in Rabelais's great dung-cart piled high with every variety of insolence and wisdom. Not goodness alone nor truth alone nor beauty alone nor all of them in one of their rare fusions can be said to make a great literature, though these are the tools of that hard trade. Great literature may be known by the sign that it communicates the sense of the vividness of life. And it communicates it because its creators were alive with it at the moment of creation.

"There are many kinds of literature because there are many kinds of life. Pope felt one kind and Wordsworth another and Poe another—and so on and so on. There are no universal poets, not even Homer and Shakespeare. Nor, of course, are there any universal critics, not even Lessing and Sainte-Beuve. Neither creator nor critic can make himself universal by barely taking thought about it; he *is* what he *lives*. The measure of the creator is the amount of life he puts into his work. The measure of the critic is the amount of life he finds there."

4

READING this now, I wonder at the academic parade of great names which I brought into what was to be a kind of program for a weekly review of current books. I wonder still more at the vagueness of my fourth dimension. What did it really mean to insist that a book must be alive? How could you tell whether it was or not? These questions I did not answer, and I still cannot answer them. What is alive to one reader may be dead to another. But I do know how I had come to this way of thinking about books, along with the whole decade that gave America a new age of its literature.

Like other specialists—like the professors—I had learned to read with a part of myself. I would sometimes read to find out how men had thought and felt long ago, or how different writers had dealt with the same matters, or how fashions of speech had changed with habits of life, or how bare facts had been molded to poetic shapes, or how new ideas or idioms had been welcomed or rejected: to find out these and many things that specialists in literature hunt for. I had read for information, for vanity, for a living. But for a dozen years, by 1920, I had seldom read with the lust for experience which had taken me through so many books when I was a boy. That is, I had not read with mind fully awake and emotions generously engaged: I had not read as a whole man.

By 1920 I was nearly done with my long work on the history of past American literature and had reached the present, which flowed in a stream of new books across my desk at the Nation. These new books, coming close as only contemporary books can come to any reader, were alive for me with a fresh vitality. I had grown up in a time when there had been few contemporary books to stir the air, and so I had learned to read not close to books but at a distance, as with classics. I had one standard for old established books, another for the new and ambitious. But the books new to the earliest twenties, with their ambition and vitality, called for a single standard. Spoon River Anthology, North of Boston, The Man Against the Sky, Sister Carrie (now revived after long neglect), My Antonia, Jurgen, Main Street, The Education of Henry Adams: these in 1920 had already a classic look. As I could not help measuring them by older books, so I could not help measuring older books by them. My mind went back and forth in search of a common denominator to understand them by. I hit upon one and called it the fourth dimension. If this was partly academic, it was partly strategic too—a bridge between two ages. There was a strong conservative resistance to the new books, especially to those which made up what was called the New Poetry. The public read them but doubted that, being exciting, they could be lasting, as the books the public had read in school were said to be. Sister Carrie was surely not good, Jurgen not true, Spoon River Anthology not beautiful. So the public said, or asked. The professional critics, who might have guided lay readers in making up their minds, were either violent on one side or the other or else learned and indecisive. The Nation was learned but it would not, I resolved, be indecisive. It would take the side of life, old or new.

Almost at once young writers turned to the Nation as to a critical friend. Sinclair Lewis in November 1920 wrote me

from Washington about my review of Main Street in the
Evening Post and another in the Nation which he thought
might be mine though it was actually Ludwig Lewisohn's:

"Yes, I have, I suppose, a responsibility; at least I'm going
to act as though I had one. Already I am planning a second
novel of the same general sort as Main Street, though utterly
different in detail. It is, this time, the story not of a Carol but
of an Average Business Man, a Tired Business Man, not in a
Gopher Prairie but in a city of three or four hundred thousand
people (equally Minneapolis or Seattle or Rochester or Atlanta) with its enormous industrial power, its Little Theater
and Master of the Fox Hounds and lively country club, and
its overwhelming, menacing heresy hunt, its narrow-eyed
(and damned capable) crushing of anything threatening its
commercial oligarchy. I hope to keep it as far as may be from
all 'propaganda'; I hope to make that man live—that man
whom we have heard, in the Pullman smoker, ponderously
lecturing on oil stock, the beauty of Lake Louise, the imper-
tinence of George the porter, and the excellence of his 1918
Buick which is so much better a model than the 1919——

"All this you have brought on yourself by your interest! I
want very eagerly to talk of novel-writing in general, of this
next novel in very particular, with you. . . . It is, frankly, a
hell of a job: first earning a living by nimble dives into the
Saturday Evening Post, then realizing all the enormous and
strident phenomena of a Detroit, then selecting, coordinating,
crystallizing. There are not, in America, many to whom one
may run wailing with problems, as one might, I fancy, in
England. (There, perhaps, there are too many, and Beresford
and Swinnerton destroy, not develop, each other.) Hence you
have brought on yourself—a responsibility, to quote you!"

I do not know whether Lewis talked with Lewisohn about

this first outline of Babbitt, but many writers did turn to him. He too had left a university, Ohio, for journalism, as dramatic critic for the Nation. Night after night he went patiently to the theater, enduring bad and mediocre entertainments for the sake of an occasional play worth writing about in his weekly notice. Almost every week he wrote a review of a book, generally a novel. He was no less a journalist for being a scholar and an artist. Hardly any excellence eluded him, though he did not care for Jurgen. The copy sent to him for review was lost, and the Nation missed a chance to speak out for the book before it was prosecuted. But Lewisohn was as alert as a hawk, seeing better because he lived naturally in the upper air. He touched nothing that he did not elevate. In a play by Eugene O'Neill or Susan Glaspell or many a less thoughtful dramatist he would unfailingly discover some idea, some issue, and enlarge it as with a microscope. Even if the thing were small in itself, and he had to say so, he could mount it, somehow, in a setting of greatness, and a clear light would fall on it, and it would be seen to belong in the company of eternal ideas, immortal issues. Or if he had been watching only the chorus at the Follies he might come away full of the image of countless perennial girls who had once delighted the princes of Babylon and now delighted the magnates of Pittsburgh, always with the same bright fixed smiles and fine flesh, with the rhythm of merry feet, with laughing hints and gay temptations.

Lewisohn recently asked me why, after his novels, so many people still remember his criticism. The plays he noticed have left the stage. The novels he reviewed have been forgotten or established. Plays or novels, lost or living, they are beyond the need of his individual opinions. But a good critic survives his journalistic moment by a merit that is in himself, not merely in his subject. Lewisohn's merit lay in his power to enlarge and elevate the matters before him until they were matters before everybody. Disciplined by learning, his mind kept a Goethean serenity when he wrote about literature, however passionate his emotions. In his novels he seemed to me to be writing out of emotions that were relatively new to him, and not quite mastered. A disciplined mind outlives the emotions that besiege it. When Lewisohn wrote Expression in America his mind seemed free and masterful again. And readers realized that what they had always valued most in him was his lucid mind, whether now in his ripest book or long ago in his weekly journalism.

In 1920 Mark and Krutch came back from a year of traveling fellowships in Europe, and joined the Nation's staff of reviewers, not as editors with salaries but as regular contributors. Mark took the poetry I did not review myself, and Krutch the novels for which Lewisohn had no time. The responsibility for the department was in my hands, but we were all four so close that we were in practice a committee. This is the only literary group I have ever belonged to, or any of the others. That three of us were doctors of philosophy from Columbia and Lewisohn had all but completed the work for his degree there was the least thing we had in common. We were held together by a shared passion for literature as an art so interwoven with life that neither could be understood without the other. This passion set the tone of criticism in the new Nation and has marked it ever since. After Lewisohn left for Europe and I for the Century, Krutch was dramatic critic and Mark literary editor and later Krutch was both.

From the old Nation I inherited many conservative reviewers, whom Villard hoped I could keep. As tactfully as possible, but as rapidly, I stopped using them except for books about which they had special knowledge. Specialists, I found, are more likely to be radical than conservative when they are at home. And specialists would take pains with their reviews. I had only, as a rule, when a new book was announced, to think of some specialist who would have to read it, offer him the book and the Nation's small fee for his opinion, and then wait. The review would come and other editors would envy. I asked more than special knowledge. No matter how learned reviewers might be, they must be lively too. For every dull specialist in any subject there was somewhere a rival of more spirit. And if I had to use a dull reviewer he might be made to seem almost animated when enough of his original review had been cut out and thrown away.

But of course what really mattered to the new Nation was the new imaginative and critical literature of the twenties. Older readers were astounded to find a sketch by Dreiser in pages that had been hostile to him. Mencken became a contributing editor—an honorary post which meant less that he sympathized with the Nation's causes than that he liked a fight and was willing to lend his name to it. This was a symptom of the times. The Nation had turned from Sherman to Mencken. The professors had been beaten by the journalists. Suddenly the age was irreverent, contemptuous of the pre-war world and rebellious toward the dead hand which still lay across the present. The age was outspoken, claiming for its books the right to be as free as literature had been in all the centuries but the Anglo-Saxon nineteenth. The age was young, or thought it was. The Younger Generation assumed its name and suspected its elders who had not known how to avoid the war. What good was age if it had no wisdom? Youth had life. To be alive at all, when so many men had lately died, was a kind of triumph. The more life the better. Let nature thrive and prosper.

Now that the writers of the early twenties are all middle-aged, or dead, and some of them have lost their novelty and urgency, and some have come to be taken for granted, it is possible to forget, even for those who can remember, the days when new poets and new dramatists and new novelists and new critics seemed to come in gusts, singing, satirizing, speculating, telling stories: a fresh literature in a fresh language. I knew the history of American literature as few persons have ever had the need to know it, and I knew that this was unlike anything that had happened before. Boston in the middle of the past century had come nearest to it. But that was a quiet concert of chamber music compared with the full, varied, and sometimes discordant orchestra of literary New York. Mencken's burly voice, hooting. The tom-toms of the Emperor Jones throbbing in Macdougal Street. Lawyers wrangling over Jurgen, and the public taking sides. Debates about Main Street, whether villages were or were not what Sinclair Lewis said: Look at Spoon River. Babbitt becoming a byword. Scott Fitzgerald with his new fashions in heroes and heroines: What was the Younger Generation coming to? Eliot and the Waste Land, for worshipers and parodists. Copies of Ulysses slipped through the customs and passed from eager hand to bad. Edwin Arlington Robinson gravely, profoundly revisiting Camelot. Robert Frost bringing me a poem for the Nation all the way from Vermont, and the two of us sitting through lunch at the Century Club and the whole afternoon, talking about farming. Innumerable young women wondering what it would be like to be like Edna St. Vincent Millay, if she were like her poems. Elinor Wylie arriving from Washington, to be poet and queen of poets in Manhattan. Mark Twain

rising to another stature with his posthumous books and becoming a touchstone for criticism. Remember the war: Three
Soldiers, The Enormous Room, What Price Glory? Poor Randolph Bourne, poor John Reed! This Simian World. The past
recaptured and revalued in Wells's Outline of History and
van Loon's Story of Mankind, which Charles Beard told me
he thought was better. The expatriates leaving America with
large gestures to live in Paris, where they could be free. Other
Americans staying at home to free America. Every American
his own Columbus.

All this the critical committee of the Nation viewed with
such detachment as it could have while it was itself a part
of what went on. Lewisohn wrote Up Stream, a beautiful and
troubling book by a foreign-born American who, for once,
was not complacent about how quickly he had changed his
native colors for red, white, and blue, not flattering toward
the civilization which had tried to make him what he was not.
Krutch undertook, a little later, to go back of what to an
earlier generation had seemed the mystery of Poe and to find
there nothing much more mysterious than nervous disorders
familiar to psychology: as if a chemist should explain what
the alchemists had called inexplicable. Mark began to write
his country poems, as fresh as the grass which creeps back
where the plough has torn the earth and left it bare. I wound
up the long affair of the Cambridge History, published in
The American Novel the first history of that literary form,
and in Contemporary American Novelists the first systematic
study of post-war literature. Mencken wrote me from Baltimore, when parts of this book had appeared in the Nation,
that he hoped I would not leave out two novelists whom he
thought highly of: Willa Cather and James Branch Cabell.

Too few readers knew about them, he thought. The new literature was still a forest with no paths cut through it.

Trying to define what seemed to me the strongest impulse back of what the American imagination was just then doing, I named it the Revolt from the Village. America had become urban and industrial without realizing it, and its memory had gone on cherishing and celebrating the village as the home of all the virtues. "The village," I wrote, "had seemed too cosy a microcosm to be disturbed. There it lay in the mind's eye, neat, compact, organized, traditional: the white church with tapering spire, the sober schoolhouse, the smithy of the ringing anvil, the corner grocery, the cluster of friendly houses; the venerable parson, the wise physician, the canny squire, the grasping landlord softened or outwitted in the end; the village belle, gossip, atheist, idiot; jovial fathers, gentle mothers, merry children; cool parlors, shining kitchens, spacious barns, lavish gardens, fragrant summer dawns, and comfortable winter evenings." But life had disturbed it, if it ever existed, and literature was catching up with life. Spoon River, Winesburg, Gopher Prairie had broken a pattern and had challenged a past. Let Americans live now and know how they were living.

Behind the most balanced criticism there is a person as well as a critic. I was divided in this conflict between old village and new city. I remembered Hope with affection and I had not been made unhappy by anything Urbana had ever done to me. The revolt, I thought, was partly revenge for early irritations. Dullness had come to be the villain, as sin had once been. Melodrama still lived. I did not think that much would be gained by hating the provinces in New York. In the warmth of my argument I talked about Main Street and about Sinclair Lewis, whose earlier books I hardly knew about. In

October 1921 he wrote me, from Italy, a letter which belongs to literary history.

5

"I HAVE just been reading with the greatest interest your Re- volt from the Village—as indeed I have read with such in- terest all the articles in the series.

"It is my supposition that you will publish these articles in book form, or use them as the basis for a book. If you do, the book will be taken as authority by a large number of people. Therefore I wish strenuously to suggest corrections in the con- sideration of myself in the article. Were it not for this book- future, I should not comment on them.

"In the first place, I am not, in any slightest degree, nor have I ever been, influenced by Mr. Masters, greatly though I admire him: yet this you state as a definite (and important) fact—for example in 'it seems a notable achievement for a temper like Mr. Masters's to have drawn such a character [marginal note: *i.e.* S. L.'s] into its serious wake.' I very defi- nitely began to plan Main Street just after my sophomore year in college, in 1905—sixteen years ago, and ten years before Spoon River was published; I planned it in a form funda- mentally like that in which, after many false starts, it finally appeared. Second, I have never really read Spoon River even to this day! Four years ago a friend used to read me certain of his favorite poems from Spoon River. I was enchanted by them—but the idiot, like so many disciples, so overread and overpraised that I have not even yet quite recovered enough to sit down with the book. Hence I know only the ten or twelve characterizations he was always reading; and because they were so few I have always thought of them as quite detached pictures of personalities with no especial relation to any small town or any revolt against a small town.

"I have seen three or four quite complete and convincing proofs that I took Main Street almost bodily from Madame Bovary. This seems improbable to me, as I had written half of Main Street before I chanced to read Bovary. But certainly I do not think I could have taken it both from Bovary and Spoon River.

"And I rather question (though here I am only guessing) that you are equally wrong about the influence of Masters on Zona Gale, and possibly even on Sherwood Anderson. Of course Masters, Gale, Anderson, myself, a hundred others, are all influenced in various ways by the same spirit of the times, by the same environment, and the same reactions against that environment. But this is always a commonplace of literary biography; it is no more unusual than the same influences acting on Keats, Shelley, and Coleridge; or on Bennett, Wells, and a number of others.

"My second complaint is (to me) more serious. I wonder if you realize that you present me as a damnably shabby figure jerked by chance into a freakish best-selling? 'Before Main Street,' you say, 'Mr. Lewis had belonged to the smarter set among American novelists, writing much bright, colloquial, amusing chatter to be read by those who travel through books at the brisk pace of vaudeville.' This clown, yea even he, could be influenced by the great Masters to turn to decent work! I resent that—after the eighteen [footnote: 18 since the first thing I had published; 22 since I definitely began to write] arduous years I have spent in, first, learning my craft to some degree and, second, becoming able, without total starvation, to begin to practise it!

"I have written 'amusing chatter,' yes, and a good deal of it—as Arnold Bennett, H. G. Wells, and even, in some of her short stories, Edith Wharton have done. And some of that same amusing and *colloquial* chatter was, essentially, just as serious a presentation of human affairs as anything in Main Street. Ponderosity is not necessarily the distinguishing feature of veracity.

"But I have also written three novels which are in no sense amusing chatter. They are all bad, for various reasons, but they are none of them vaudeville. Have you read any of them? I doubt it. Certainly if you had read The Job, you would not have been quite so cheerfully sweeping. Let me sum them up: Our Mr. Wrenn, my first novel, published in 1914; a rather Kipps- or Wheels of Chance-like study of a little boarding-house man for whom I felt the greatest tenderness. The Trail of the Hawk, a novel very bad in its thin surface of realism, yet as honestly worked out as it could be at the time. Finally, The Job, the story of a quite dull stenographer which, far from being vaudeville, was too somber, too lugubrious. It had some small attention—for example a full-page review by Francis Hackett in New Republic, another by Floyd Dell in Masses, a half-page review by Edgett in the Transcript. Its sales were almost nothing, and it took me three more years before I was ready, mentally and financially, to take off the year required to write Main Street.

"And even in my magazine stories (yes, even in the serial Free Air, of which you were thinking when you wrote that objectionable sentence) I have steadily sought to work out a means of doing as honest work as the powerful negations of the magazine editors would permit. Out of perhaps fifty stories in Saturday Evening Post, Century, Harper's, and so on, I doubt if more than ten could with the slightest justice be classed as 'brisk and amusing chatter.' (For examples, see The Willow Walk, reprinted in E. J. O'Brien's Best Short Stories of 1918; or a story called Young Man Axelbrod published in the Century, probably some time late in 1916; or a story with the bad editor-given title The Scarlet Sign published in the Metropolitan some time in 1917: a story fully as bright and brisk and amusing as Dostoevsky; or He Loved His Country, the story of the German-American who loved, and went on loving, both Germany and America, published in Everybody's some time in 1916; or the sardonic Mother, rejected by the Sat Even Post because it was so impolite to mother-love, and published in Hearst's—God knows why!— in 1918; or The Enchanted Hour, published in the Sat Even Post in August 1919 and telling the case of a man who, at 45, discovers he has done none of the fine ardent things he desired as a boy; or A Woman by Candlelight, The Whisperer, or Things, published in the Saturday Evening Post and each giving as unvaudevillistic a picture, with as unchattering a style, as anything in Main Street—or in Moon-Calf!)

"But especially I want you to read The Job, if you are going to publish these articles in book form. And you might glance at some of the others. And then I want you to think with considerable care about each word you wrote regarding me.

"Mind you, I should—could—have nothing to say if you reported that everything I have written, including Main Street, is bad, very bad, ill-written, clumsily conceived. Of that I cannot judge. But that I have for all these eighteen years since I first published a magazine article (I was eighteen then) been an only too serious workman, working definitely toward something which, I hope, I am now just beginning to get; that I most certainly have not been just a Smart Chatterer whose conversion by Mr. Masters is almost miraculous; this I do insist.

"I am very sorry that you have so presented me to the Nation readers—the Nation being the one particular American periodical which I like best, and the only one which I have been reading regularly here in Europe. I am very sorry. I wish there were some way of your correcting it—if you find me not a liar in the preceding statement of what I regard as facts. And certainly if it comes to a book, I hope you will change it. . . And why not in the Nation?

"I am, at thirty-six, at the beginning of my work as a writer. Certain praises of Main Street at last give me the hope that eventually my work will veritably count. Of my work as a whole, no one has ever really written—except yourself —and you present me to the considerable number of readers of Main Street who may, perhaps, wish to know something about me, as the shoddiest of charlatans reformed by chance. And you do this, you sum me up, without having taken the trouble to read such novels of mine as The Job, or such short stories as Things and The Willow Walk and The Scarlet Sign and He Loved His Country. I *know* you could not have read them; for however bad they are, however insufficient, however amateurish, however much the hypnotic influence of magazine-writing may have caused the writer to fall into that careful omission of 'dangerous subjects' which produces sterility, yet certainly not one of these, or the others mentioned, is 'bright amusing chatter to be read by those who travel through books at the brisk pace of vaudeville.'

"I have, so far as I can remember, written only six letters to critics and journalists whom I do not know personally regarding the thousands of reviews and comments, favorable and unfavorable, on Main Street. (This is the seventh, and one of the earlier six was a letter to you regarding your review in the N. Y. Evening Post.) Of the six, four were notes of thanks; and only two were protests—one regarding one of the innumerable insulting statements Mrs. Dawson has made regarding my book, my personal taste, my appearance, my social position, my morals, and my manner of lecturing, in the New York Globe. The second was regarding an editorial in an Indianapolis newspaper which asserted (in Tarkington's own town) that I had ridiculed Booth Tarkington, when I had done precisely the opposite. I have passed without notice some hundreds of long and short announcements that I am a liar, a fool, and illiterate, and God knows what all, because they come from people who do not matter. But you do, and your work does, and—behold!

"Finally, since I have made this so long, may I just query (but much less certainly since this is a matter of opinion rather than fact) your theory, as expressed now both in the N. Y. Evening Post and in the Nation, that I hate all dull people, that is, unintelligent people; and that therefore I am forever barred from the class of the Fieldings and Balzacs and Tolstois (I use your own selection of people by whom you prove my deficiencies). In Main Street, I certainly do love all of the following people, none of whom could be classed as anything but 'dull' (using your own sense of dull as meaning lacking in conscious intelligence): Bea, Champ and Mrs. Perry, Sam and Mrs. Clark, Will Kennicott (dull about certain things though not all), Will's mother, and almost all of the farmer patients. And I love Carol who is dull about all the male world that interests Kennicott. And Guy Pollock who is of only a slight and dilettantish intelligence. And these are about the chief characters . . . But this I do not want to argue. It may be that you are quite right. But with the keen deep love I have for Bea in that book (for one example) I wonder if it is more than partially true. And I always wonder whether it is ever very valid, that frequent mode of critics of saying that Evelyn Scott isn't a great writer because she isn't as suave as Edith Wharton; or that Edith Wharton isn't worth a damn because she hasn't the learning of Anatole France; or that Anatole France is altogether hopeless because he has never written Shakespearean lyrics; or, to make the circle complete, that Shakespeare isn't much worth reading nowadays because he doesn't, like Evelyn Scott, write of America and today?

"So!"

Lewis was right. I had read only Free Air, and not all of that, among his earlier books. And he was right in feeling that I had been unjust. I corrected the essay before it became a chapter in my book. Since then we have been the closest friends, and the story of his youth is known to many people. But I know nothing which gives so clear an idea of what he had tried to do before Main Street and of what kind of man he was the year after, as this account he wrote himself.

6

I MET Edwin Arlington Robinson, whom I valued above all living poets. Joyce Kilmer had often talked to me about him, before the war at the Authors Club, but he was said to be a hermit and I knew nobody who knew him. Finally a bookseller introduced us and we dined at Halloran's. I remember that he noticed my eating only grilled mushrooms, while he ate, as usual, a steak. Which of us was the poet? He never forgot what I had eaten that night, and always recalled it at later meals, teasing me with a shy amusement at me for my mild appetite and at himself for his recollection of it. He was almost as shy as Pascal D'Angelo, I thought, and talked little, only about plain matters. With me, at least, he did not gossip, did not play with ideas, did not bring topics up, and did not say things which stuck in my mind in the very words he had used. He was not slow in apprehension, but he liked things said plainly to him. His subtlety was in his poetry.

"Please let me thank you," he wrote to me in May 1920 from Brooklyn, where he then lived, "for your most refreshing and intelligent notice of Lancelot in the current number of the Nation—and at the same time for your praise of the book. I am particularly grateful to you for not going out of your way to damn me for not doing what I never intended to do." Like an editor, I wrote back to him asking if he would review a new book by Thomas Hardy—and, of course, if he could not let me have a poem for the Nation. "I thank you for your letter of yesterday," he answered, "and for your suggestion in regard to Thomas Hardy's poems, but I am just now starting off for what looks like a summer of uninterrupted work and don't feel that there will possibly be time for anything else. Moreover, I am inclined to believe that the poetry-makers should stick to their trade and leave criticism to the others. I may change my mind, but that has been my attitude, in spite of a few lapses, for the past thirty years . . . Just now I have nothing in the way of verse to offer you, but hope to have something before very long."

He went that summer to Peterborough and wrote Avon's Harvest, but in October he had a poem for me, which he offered apologetically because it had been to another magazine and had been, after a good deal of palaver, rejected. "I am sending you the poem that caused all that commotion in the office of Collier's. I am still at a loss to detect its difficulties or its dangers, or to believe that the public is made up entirely of imbeciles. Of course you may not like it enough to use it, but that is another matter." What he sent was Mr. Flood's Party, one of the best of his short poems, and one of the simplest of them. I accepted it with joy, and every poem he ever let me see—though some of the Nation's editors wondered what they meant.

In December he wrote that he had nothing to submit to the Nation's prize contest. "I am all tangled up just now with a sort of metrical dime novel and an impending collected edition of my immortal works. I hope you may find yourself in a humor to review the book when it comes out—probably in September." And in January 1921 he spoke of something which had confused some of the readers of his metrical dime novel: "I supposed, by the way, that the knife would be enough to show that the other fellow was not drowned, but chose merely to let Avon think so. Maybe I had better add a few lines to the collected edition to make this entirely clear."

"I am writing to tell you," he said in a letter from Peterborough in August, "that it will give me great pleasure to ask them [his publishers] to send you my Collected Poems as soon as they are available, if you find that you will have an opportunity to review the book—which I should send to you in due time in any case. Without implying anything in the nature of a request, I hope sincerely that you may be able to 'do' the book, as you are one of the very few critics who understand me and what I am driving at." He was always generous with praise, like all men of ample natures, though he always praised in few words. And he was humorous about himself. In this same letter he referred to the evening, that past spring, when he had come to dinner at my apartment, near Columbia, and had got lost on the long way from Brooklyn and had been very late. "I still regret that I had to stir up your household to such an extent when I made a mess of finding it, and I am still at a loss to know how I made so gross a topographical blunder."

New York is a city of fitful friendships, and for some reason—for no reason, rather—I seldom saw Robinson again for half a dozen years. He spent his summers at Peterborough, at the MacDowell colony, his winters in New York, with stays in Boston in the spring and fall. These were the years of his almost annual long poems, which I could not publish in either the Nation or the Century, and I hesitated to approach him except as editor. But he sent me copies of his books and I reviewed them, though I had no chance to write at length about him.

Talking and writing are such different matters that I have often thought they should not both have to use words and so appear to be the same thing. Once in a while they are, as in Mencken, whose talk has not only the force of his written prose but even the variety and rousing imagery. While you listen to him you might believe you were reading, just as while you are reading you seem to be hearing his actual voice. Krutch talks even better than he writes. He catches each new idea on the wing and, even if it is new to him, thinks it out faster than he can speak, and so, when he comes to put it into words, gives the impression of having known it long enough to have got just the right words for it. And there is Robert Frost. One winter day when he was in town, we met at an apartment which Zona Gale had taken, or been lent, near Washington Square. She had so many guests that Frost and

I had to go into the kitchen where he was to read me a poem. I had never heard him read before. As he read, leaning against the cold stove, the sound of his voice for the first time explained his poetry to me. I had always, somehow, read the words as universal English, like any other poem's. But now I found they were Yankee words and without their true intonation had never said to me half what they meant. He writes only what he can hear himself speaking and is satisfied only when the written words have the tone and flavor of speech.

With Robinson the two modes had nothing in common, or did not seem to have. The profound rhythm of his poetry, its singing brevity, the exaggeration of his understatements did not touch his tongue. He appeared to be unable to speak out. He would say "Kipling's poetry is better than most people think" and then stop, without the expected argument or illustration. Put a volume of Kipling in his hands, and he would go through it, find the poems he liked best, and possibly read—not very well—fine passages. But that was all he would have to say. He would talk about places he had been to, but never describe them, or about persons he had known, but seldom characterize them. Asked whether he had had actual originals in mind for Captain Craig or Miniver Cheevy or Uncle Ananias or Richard Cory or John Evereldown or Leffingwell or Clavering or Tasker Norcross, he would answer frankly enough, and even mention names. But he would add little to what was in the poem. The poem was what he had had to say, and he had said it there. He seldom talked about his youth in Maine, or about Harvard, or about his early hardships. But he did say once: "They praise me for never doing anything but write poetry. I would always have taken a job if I had known how to get one and keep it." He had had the luck to be unhandy about the common work of men and so had had to stick to poetry. He knew, of course, that the MacDowell colony had really saved him. It had given him long quiet summers for work, a comfortable sociable existence, and the sense of being cherished and honored. But he would not have said such things because they would have made him seem to be saying that it was important for him to have been saved. He was completely modest about himself in speech, though he had the faith to be always himself. It was hard to get at his general opinions. He distrusted Soviet Russia: this was the only political opinion I ever heard him express. I think he was not religious, but he was sympathetic toward those who were, and he hinted at mystical experiences of his own. He appeared never to think of money, little as he had. Once when a friend was in sudden trouble, Robinson managed to raise a hundred dollars, nobody ever knew how, for he was supposed to be living on ten dollars a week. Ever since I read, in Merlin, his account of Vivian, I have known he must have been greatly in love, and there was talk of one or two women. It was said that his Arthurian poems had a personal basis, in that he had been Lancelot to some Guinevere married to some Arthur his friend. Of that of course he never spoke, and he never spoke of women or love at all, in my hearing, except in the most incidental way.

By the time I met him Robinson was already, within a small circle, a very famous man, and though he was seldom seen, nobody ever refused an invitation to go where he would be. The most brilliant and least maternal young women felt for him at sight a quick, adoring protective instinct. The cleverest young men listened to every word he said with an attention that caught all the implications his words might carry because they were his. His poems were already in their minds. I never saw him, in those first years of our acquaintance, except in the company of people much younger than he. I suppose he enjoyed the adoration and attention, but he gave nothing that looked like a sign of it. I have heard that he was at his best in his little flat in Brooklyn, where, with one or two guests, he cooked a steak himself. Away from home, where I saw him, he would always, barring accidents, arrive with the punctuality of a modest stranger, and would at first be able to say only perfunctory words. Tall, he did not seem as tall as he was, as if he were too shy to be. The most notable things about his face were his eyes, which hunted about the room as if looking for words but which were a little obscured by his glasses, and his sensitive mouth. It was a guarded mouth, with lips that puckered continually, most of all when he dissented from what he heard. He might not utter his dissent, but it was plain to anybody who read his lips. They seemed to keep out as much as they kept in. He liked good food, eating slowly. When I knew him he had given up almost all liquor, for his health. After dinner he would sit the whole evening, hardly moving, even his beautiful, long, expressive, unmuscular hands. He did not appear to mind if silences fell upon the conversation, for he did not need to talk, as some more nervous persons do. As he never wandered when he talked, neither did he when he listened, and I doubt that in all his life he ever interrupted another speaker.

I can only guess how he might have affected some one who did not know who he was and who could have judged him only by his few words. I always thought of him as a great poet who happened to occupy a house of flesh and blood in which he lived secretly. For the neighbors, talking to them, he had only simple prose. In his house he was all poet, making his poems in secret ways and sending them out to the world when they were done. Talking to him, you heard no actual words that gave away his secret. But now and then you would think you got a glimpse, as through a window, of the man he was, and then you knew he was a poet, and great.

7

WHEN we say we know that the world is changing we mean we have noticed that it has changed. We learn piecemeal through the senses and reflect only when perceptions force themselves on our minds. Then we shape some kind of image and compare it with the image already in our memory. If they are not alike we talk of change. Even this friendly spring which came so soon after the harsh winter of Illinois (where I write) had several intermediate days in which flesh had been relieved and nerves relaxed before the thought of spring was a thought. So with what was to be the post-war spring, though it was marked off by the armistice from the long winter of the war. It was a chaos of sensations before it took any form that we were conscious of. The first sensation was a wild joy that the killing had ended. But the second sensation was conflict. Now we could go back to the good days before the war: now we could run ahead to better days. Every man was divided between the two sentiments. So were men in general. The conservative majority in the United States made Harding President, and Coolidge. The minority had for its most articulate spokesmen the Younger Generation.

A few weeks ago I heard a young woman say that though she had been twenty in 1920 and had then lived gaily in New York, she had never moved in the heart of the Younger Generation but only near to it. She was the third person I had heard say the same thing in three years. They were right in thinking they had never quite belonged to the Younger Generation, wrong in thinking there had ever been one to belong to unmistakably. For the Younger Generation was nothing more than a generalization.

If it can now best be studied in the literature it produced, so could it then. Randolph Bourne was its philosopher, the earliest young thinker with a program, the soonest dead. He was an undergraduate in Columbia when I came back from Europe, his body misshapen, his mind straight and clear. I remember his reading his poem Sabotage before a literary society. Only a few of the undergraduates who heard it—this must have been 1912—thought the subject proper for a poem. Another of them read a blank-verse monologue in which a troubadour lamented times lamentably past. When Bourne declared in an article that nobody ever got a new idea after twenty-five, his elders at Columbia pointed out that he was twenty-five. When later he published, in the New Republic, satirical portraits which might have been of President Butler and John Erskine, most of the professors, who all read them, thought them in bad taste. Bourne, it was told, had said he could write only when he hated. One of the professors mentioned Pope, another crooked poet. John Dewey had been Bourne's teacher, the New Republic was his chief outlet. After they had found pragmatic reasons why the United States should go to war, Bourne, who had meant peace when he talked about it, was lost. The war killed him early, and he survives only as a pitiful small legend. But his History of a Literary Radical is the whole history of the thoughtful young men of his decade, and his scheme for a league of youth which was to rejuvenate the fallen age had in it all the Younger Generation's purposive if naïve faith.

If Bourne was its philosopher, John Reed was its hero, Edna St. Vincent Millay its lyric poet, Eugene O'Neill its dramatist, Sinclair Lewis its satirist, Van Wyck Brooks its critic. The Younger Generation respected Bourne but hardly knew him: he died too soon. Reed's league of youth was the Soviet government: this narrowed his influence with a generation which had few communists. But Edna Millay was a song and a flame, more daring and light-hearted about love than any woman had ever been in English verse. O'Neill was the Younger Generation's challenge to the American cult of the happy ending: strong meat for young nerves. Lewis laughed at sacred cows. Brooks argued that the older America had destroyed its artists, even the great Mark Twain, who had not dared to be himself.

All these had been heard by 1920. In that year the Younger Generation put on new colors. Scott Fitzgerald was younger still. He had gone off to war from college, like E. E. Cummings and John Dos Passos and Ernest Hemingway and Laurence Stallings and Edmund Wilson. But Fitzgerald was precocious, found his voice before any of his contemporaries, and was heard along with writers ten years older. The public did not distinguish the two ages. The name Younger Generation was fitted to whatever, in the early twenties, was rebellious, aspiring, experimental: to whatever was restless. Name-calling was not enough. The Younger Generation was personified in Fitzgerald's heroes and heroines. "Few things more significantly illustrate the moving tide of which the revolt from the village is a symptom than the presence of such unrest as this among these bright barbarians. The traditions which once might have governed them no longer hold. They break the patterns one by one and follow their wild desires. And as they play among the ruins of the old, they reason randomly about the new, laughing."

So it appeared in 1921. But even then it was plain that Fitzgerald was a romancer. Where in actual life are the young men and women all beautiful and witty, and all poets? They were not in the early twenties. Fitzgerald had created—had invented—his light and lively characters. He set a fashion. Not that there were many boys and girls who could be like those in his stories; that would have called for too much talent. Though nature may want to follow art, it seldom can. When observers tried to imagine or describe the Younger Generation, and found themselves limited in experience of it and faced by its contradictions, they took Fitzgerald's version for the truth and did not look beyond it. The moralists did not need to know more, or the sensationalists. They talked of the Younger Generation in one breath. The Beautiful and Damned. All the Sad Young Men. Baby Byrons.

Sherman, visiting in New York and Cornwall, studied my household with puzzled eyes.

"You and Carl see a great deal of your children, don't you?" he said to Irita.

"Why, yes, of course."

"You like being with them."

"Absurdly. But why shouldn't we? What are you driving at?"

"Well, I had supposed . . . you with a job . . . not much interested in such matters . . . The Younger Generation."

He had been reading, in Urbana, and had generalized, trying to put incompatibles together and wondering why they did not match.

There were two Younger Generations, one rebelling against old ideas, one against old manners.

Whoever tries to compare succeeding generations starts with the hopeless disadvantage that he belongs to one of them and cannot really know the other. I have heard parents boast that they knew all their children did or thought, and have seen the children look guilty, or embarrassed, or sly. I have had children tell me what they said was all about their parents, and have never believed them. Before parents can be parents they must have lived a good part of their lives. They remember their experience less as itself than as its consequences. But the children's experience is still itself, with its consequences to come. The two experiences are not the same and there is no common language for them. I loved danger, says the father, and it hurt me. The son says: I love danger. On both sides there is special pleading. The parents give advice which either justifies what they have done or else urges the children to do the same thing better, that the parents through them may have another chance at living. Do as I did. Avoid what I should have avoided. But the children do not want to justify or repeat or vary what has been done. With the pride of strength goes the sense of originality, or the illusion of it. Times have changed, father, and I must do what I do as I do it. The wisdom of neither is communicable to the other. All wisdom is incommunicable. When we say a man is wise we are saying only that what he says agrees with our own experience. So parents and children, with no common experience and no common language, must be largely strangers. Not till when they both are old, if the parents live so long, can they draw close together. Then it is too late to matter. And even then they are still separated by the impossibility of telling each other what happened while they were apart.

I am not sure that I know more about what goes on in the minds of my children, when I see them every day, than about what went on in the minds of my parents before I was born. I must guess in either case. But I have the impression that when my father and mother were young they accepted the authority of their elders not only because they were obliged to but because they did not challenge their elders' right to rule. I knew I grew up, though dissatisfied with individuals, taking such a right in general for granted. It gave life a logical pattern. Human beings had to live to maturity to find out how to live. Then they knew and could go on without further mishaps. If their children, still immature, went off in wrong directions, the parents called them back—if necessary, compelled them back. The line of life was a straight line drawn through the adults of the generations.

Suddenly, about 1920, this pattern no longer served. It had been fading for half a century and the war seemed to have rubbed it out. Down with authority. Up with instinct. Youth was as likely to be right as age. Youth, the Younger Generation held, was always right.

"Conservatism," a Nation editorial said, "is the element of death and radicalism is the element of life. The human tribe, struggling through the wilderness of the world, perpetuates itself by begetting and bearing its young, who, at first protected by bosom and counsel, eventually detach themselves and move toward the front while their parents gradually slip toward the rear and are left behind. The process is cruel but it is real; and it is irresistible. What other course, after all, is there to take? Who knows where we come from or where we are going to? If youth has now and then plunged blindly along blind roads, so has age wrought incalculable evil by inquisitions and oppressions aimed to check the march of mankind in its natural advance. Experience grows cynical and lags heavily back, scorning the impulse to create. Youth staggers under the burden of freeing itself, as if it were not enough to perform the hard tasks and fight the bitter battles which the old men of the tribe wish upon it. No wonder high hearts falter under their fate when they do not rebel; no wonder they grow old so soon and take up the immemorial complaint; no wonder the youth of any particular generation always does so little. It is right but it is in the minority."

I wrote this, I remember, with Anne, then four or five, sitting on my knee and pretending to write too. I had not thought much upon the subject. I had to write an editorial for the next day. I began to write and all the commonplaces of the time poured in upon me. The Younger Generation was in the air.

That youth was precious instinct, not raw trial and error: this was the basic doctrine of the early twenties. Randolph Bourne thought much about schools and about how youth, being educated, might not lose its natural creative force. The inquiring minds of the Younger Generation looked at the world from the side of revolutionary youth. Let generous instinct guide it rather than weary craft. What blunders had not fear and prudence made! Fear led to war between nations and classes. Prudence put and kept the management of affairs in hands that were already half-dead. Under the rule of fear and prudence life went on stiffening into rigidity. Life must be flexible and free or it would be unjust and dull. Life in America had been standardized till it was mere habit, the dry routine of middle age. Give youth and genius the reins. Or at least tolerate youth and genius, the saving ferment.

These were the simple tenets of the rebels against old ideas. The more dramatic rebels against old manners were what the public took to be the Younger Generation.

For their critic they had Mencken, who on most points was conservative. In a superficial time he believed in learning. He believed in civil order if men had to go back to aristocracy to get it. He believed in monogamy and industry and economy in private life. The expatriates only tickled him: he stayed at home and worked like any good citizen. But the rebels did not examine his ideas closely. They liked the strong beat of his satirical prose, hitting away at foolish heads. "Before the war, of which he says that he neither advised nor approved it," I wrote in 1923, "he was a useful conduit leading to the republic from Shaw and Nietzsche and Ibsen. The war played into his hands, it begins to look, as into those of hardly any other literary American. Heretofore, to change the figure, he had been but an interne in the hospital of his American kind, satisfied with an occasional run in the ambulance, an occasional appendix to cut out, an occasional skull to help trepan. Now he was suddenly invited to apply diagnosis, surgery, or the lethal chamber in such a range of cases as no native satirist had ever been allowed to practice on. He found hundreds of politicians palsied with incompetence, thousands of journalists and educators and preachers flatulent with prophecy, millions of patriots dropsical with sentimentalism. He found idealists who had delusions of grandeur, scholars who suffered from obsessions of hatred, business men who had been shell-shocked out of all self-control, women whose long-repressed instincts burst into frenzies of cruelty. He found, what seemed to him the source and cause of all these maladies, the plain people turned into a vast standard mass, now dumb and snuffling like a flock of sheep, now loud and savage like a pack of wolves. All the folly which overwhelmed him had, to his eyes, the symptoms of having risen from the body of democracy. No wonder, given his conception of life, that he should have laid aside his scalpel and taken to the jolly bludgeon as the only tool he needed. No wonder, given the consequences of the madness he observed, that he should finally have declared the worst result of the war to be the fact that so many Americans survived it."

What he had in common with the young rebels was not his special ideas but his general love of liberty. "The stupidity against which he wages his hilarious war is the stupidity which, unaware of its defects, has first sought to shackle the children of light. It is chiefly at sight of such attempts that his indignation rises and that he rushes forth armed with a bagpipe, a slapstick, a shillalah, a pitchfork, a butcher's cleaver, a Browning rifle, a lusty arm, and an undaunted heart. What fun, then! Seeing that the feast of fools still has its uses, he elects himself boy-bishop, gathers a horde of revelers about him, and burlesques the universe."

Beware of metaphor, which abridges the truth while it dramatizes it. The image of Mencken and the rebels as the boy-bishop and his revelers is only a composite picture, true at large but true of nothing in particular. The rebellion against old manners was merely a widespread unrest, with no focus but in literature. It was like the unrest of any young generation except that it was now easier than it would once have been for the restless young to learn how numerous they were, and so conspire. They read Main Street, in which restlessness was heroic, and This Side of Paradise, in which it was romantic. At home the old-fashioned family had broken up. The young could get into automobiles and almost at once be miles away. They could go to the movies and at once be worlds away. Dress and speech had become informal in the emergency of the war. The chaperon had disappeared. Boys leaving to be killed, it might be, had claimed the right to see their girls alone, and the sexes had drawn together in a common need and daring. After the war they were still not divided. The sexes would be comrades, they thought.

In the same year with Main Street and This Side of Paradise Edna Millay in Aria da Capo distilled in exquisite allegory the war and the mood which followed it. "The little play," I was writing three years later, "now dainty with artifice and now racy with slang and satire, opens with Columbine and Pierrot skylarking in their pretty fashion, using, however, words with two sharp edges to each of them. But they are driven from the stage by tragedy, which sets the friendly shepherds Thyrsis and Corydon to playing a scene in which they divide their mimic field with colored ribbons, which they call a wall, find one of them mimic water on his side and the other mimic jewels, move on to a conflict which they did not mean or want and which they see is hardly so much reality as senseless acting, and in the end kill each other across the barrier, dying in each other's arms. Back come Pierrot and Columbine to resume, only a little disturbed by the dead bodies lying under their feet, the happy farce. Love among the ruins! Butterflies above the battle! Such folly as had been acted by the nations, the play hints, belongs rather to the painted theater than to the solid earth. There is not enough wisdom to understand it; there are not enough tears to bewail it. It may be better to frolic and forget."

I warn against metaphor, but I see this history cannot dispense with poetry, which is history's essence. The early poems of Edna Millay are the essence of the Younger Generation. Ask the romantic Younger Generation what it demanded, and it answered: to be free. Ask it free for what, and it did not answer, but drove faster, drank more, made love oftener. When it came to the sterner time after 1929 it had to give up its habits or else seem like an elderly beau, amusing to the youngsters. The youngsters now condescend to the early twenties as to an age of amateurs.

8

THE Younger Generation believed that with it love in America had for the first time discovered it had a body.

It must be a long time since any human being has discovered anything about love which, however new to him, was not old to some one else. Whatever rapture of the mind, ecstasy of the flesh, quirk of the nerves the lover may cherish as his own, he can probably find it in an ancient Chinese poet or, if he is willing to talk about it, in a candid neighbor. The young, first feeling love, half think they have invented it, and are sure their elders cannot understand. They see their elders as parents not as lovers, and find it incredible or repugnant to think of them in love, ardent and agitated. Between two generations there is no topic so charily, so clumsily discussed as this. Neither speaker dares to cite his own experience and is afraid what he says may be taken as that. They speak in terms so general they mean nothing. As no one knows both generations, no one can unerringly compare them.

Certainly in this account of the Younger Generation's discovery, or belief in a discovery, I surmise as often as I know. I had grown up in a rustic, had lived in an academic, community. That pre-war world of mine had been greatly unlike my post-war world of Greenwich Village, and no doubt went on being. Time was not what made the difference. I had not merely gone ahead in time but had stepped aside in space, from one parallel world to another. I must not mistake the differences between New York and Hope or Urbana for differences between the Younger Generation and that preceding it. And yet I am convinced that love in America, about the time of the war, began to seem, which means to be, something different from what it had been before.

In all American history there had been no hero, real or imaginary, who was known particularly as a lover. No Nelson, no Parnell, of course no Louis XIV or Catherine the Great, no Dante and Beatrice, no Tristan and Isolde, no Manon. The heroes and heroines of the nation had lived vigorously apart, except when they were joined in reasonable wedlock, like George and Martha Washington. If there had been talk about the loves of conspicuous men, it had been scandal, as about Thomas Jefferson or Henry Ward Beecher or Warren Gamaliel Harding. Most Americans would have been startled to hear that Daniel Boone had a wife. The American poets had not made their loves into legends, though there were sentimental stories about Poe and the child he married, about Emily Dickinson and the man she did not marry. Whitman seemed a rowdy old bachelor, the other poets gray professors. American fiction had created no memorable lover besides Hester Prynne, expiating the sin of love. Rip Van Winkle was the runaway husband of a shrew, Leather-Stocking was wedded to the forest and eluded women. The dark, sultry lovers of Herman Melville were almost unknown in 1914. Mark Twain had written about love as if his hands were tied behind him. The characters of William Dean Howells and Henry James were sufficiently occupied with love, but their love was not passionate enough to be contagious. Frank Norris and Theodore Dreiser and Upton Sinclair had written with a more realistic warmth: Norris had died young, Dreiser had been long suppressed, and Sinclair had turned to other subjects. As to the run of novels in 1914, which must have been some kind of mirror to the time, a reader could never guess that their heroes felt desire or that their heroines ever would.

About 1924 I was talking with a pleasant, worried man of sixty who did his best to keep up with new books and plays. "I don't understand these novels," he said, "when they deal with love. The people seem to have such strange feelings and sensations. I don't believe it used to be like that. A young fellow would fall in love with a girl, and want to marry her. There might be difficulties, but he would wait and generally things would come out all right. That was all there was to it. But now the whole business is a fever. It doesn't seem natural to me."

He was a serious and intelligent man, though conventional, and I could not doubt that he was saying what he thought was true. Still, it could not be true of his whole generation. Desire was as old as love, and older, and had not come to America in 1917. A nation did not declare a state of desire as of war. I reflected that in the older novels the word lover meant suitor, not, as it had come to mean in the language of my day, possessor. An age of innocence, when there were only two orders of men, husbands and lovers, and no need to distinguish between the lovers who simply wooed and those who had already won? Human life was always more headstrong than that. But if enough people had thought as this man of sixty did, desire might have been less active in his youth than in the twenties of this century. There is usually a kind of wild reason in desire, limiting it to what seems not too impossible. It was easy enough to imagine lovers who, assuming that desire could and must not have its object yet, would put off thinking of it and so not let it get its greedy hold. It was easy to remember them—me, as a youth, among them. Desire in such circumstances was not so much repressed, and dangerous, as postponed, and stimulating.

The war changed the face of postponement. It might be forever. Young soldiers do not think often about death, but they think about it oftener than young civilians. Mark and Paul both noticed in the army that it was common for the younger men to feel horror at the prospect of being killed before they had known women. Their instincts demanded to be used while there was time. Love before death. To the instincts of men the instincts of women naturally responded. There were hurried marriages. There was love-making that the moon would never have seen but for the war. If a boy was ready to give his life, what could a girl refuse to give? This was the feverish logic of the feverish time. And when the short war was over, the older, simpler form of love, with its dualisms of mind and body, love and lust, romance and desire, could not soon come back. Spirit and flesh had discovered one another and would not be divided.

I suppose the same thing happened in the Civil War, but

that was not followed by a brilliant critical generation to rationalize the instinctive process. The twenties had a new philosophy of love—new to America—to support its impulses. Love need not be thought of as having two natures, one higher and one lower. It might be one, spirit informing flesh, flesh enriching spirit. If both were fused the mind might draw strength from the body and the body hold up its head in self-respect and joy. In any case, love was instinct, love was nature. Nothing unnatural had come in. The Younger Generation had found all this in itself, and would not cover it over and keep it down. It did not think that love was like pigs, to be penned. Love was life at its best. Release it.

Here, I think, is an epitome of all moral changes. New customs are not imported for new times but are brought up with the rise of instincts which the old times kept dormant. Men remake themselves from within themselves, whatever outer forces suggest and drive.

This renascence of the flesh in love was what most disturbed the elders in the twenties. They objected to the increase of drinking after prohibition had made liquor harder to get in public than at home. They objected to the noise and irresponsibility and hit-or-miss manners of the young. But they especially objected to what they thought the shameless ways of young women, exposing and adorning their persons like the trollops of an earlier day, drinking and smoking with young men at all hours, and saying what they thought. A shocked elder who had sat beside one of them at dinner told about her in words that were a classic for a season: "Why, she would talk about anything, and she wouldn't talk about anything else." His words showed as much about him as about her. He assumed that his anything could be only one thing: the last-mentionable theme of sex. It had become so notorious that even women knew about it.

At one point the two generations actually went to law over the new philosophy of love: in the proceedings against Dreiser's Genius and Cabell's Jurgen and various European books, all of which are now as freely circulated as readers choose. Lewd, lascivious, and obscene the guardians of the old philosophy called them. There was no prosecution of books for blasphemy or heresy, any more than for cruelty or stupidity, and none for sedition. The one thing that roused the older generation was candor about love and desire. If a book had that it was a dirty book: a nuisance and a menace. There could be no agreement between the two philosophies. Krutch said it was simple: such books should be permitted because some people liked to read them. The law is not as simple as good sense. The cases had to be taken up one by one, and judge or jury had to decide. The Younger Generation defended them all, the better with the worse, and went on writing freely about sex until the subject became tiresome. By that time the guardians of the old philosophy had temporarily lost hope. For the present, at least, American literature might be like any other good literature and deal with any matter it could find in life.

The release of love seemed to be rather a release of women than of men. Men had a tradition of desire. In the English-speaking countries for something like a hundred years reputable women had been supposed not to feel it. Whether they did or not, they had most of them accepted the fashion which identified chastity with coldness. The earlier feminists, demanding equality with men, had almost never demanded equality of desire. The feminists of the Younger Generation did. The period of the war had done more than the feminist argument. The absence of young men and the chance that they would not come back seemed to wake in women an instinctive agitation. No men, no mates, and sterile lives. Women need not be conscious of their instinct to be stirred by it. If, after the war, there had been a quick return to an old stability, the agitation might have passed. But the turmoil lasted, speech and manners became bolder, and more and more women, feeling free to feel desire, felt it.

They had a poet. "What sets Miss Millay's love poems apart from almost all those written in English by women," it seemed to me in 1923, "is the full pulse which, in spite of their gay impudence, beats through them. She does not speak in the name of forlorn maidens or of wives bereft, but in the name of women who dare to take love at the flood, if it offers, and who later, if it has passed, remember with exultation that they had what no coward could have had. Conscience does not trouble them, nor any serious division in their natures. No one of them weeps because she has been a wanton, no one of them because she has been betrayed. Rarely since Sappho has a woman voiced such delight in a lover's beauty as this:

> 'What's this of death, from you who never will die?
> Think you the wrist that fashioned you in clay,
> The thumb that set the hollow just that way
> In your full throat and lidded the long eye
> So roundly from the forehead, will let lie
> Broken, forgotten, under foot some day
> Your unimpeachable body, and so slay
> The work he had been most remembered by?'

Rarely since Sappho has a woman written as outspokenly as this:

'What lips my lips have kissed, and where, and why,
I have forgotten, and what arms have lain
Under my head till morning; but the rain
Is full of ghosts tonight, that tap and sigh
Upon the glass and listen for reply;
And in my heart there stirs a quiet pain
For unremembered lads that not again
Will turn to me at midnight with a cry.'

In passages like these Miss Millay has given body and ves-
ture to a sense of equality in love: to the demand of women
that they be allowed to enter the world of adventure and
experiment in love which men have long inhabited. But Miss
Millay does not, like any feminist, argue for that equality.
She takes it for granted, exhibits it in action, and turns it
into beauty."

If the guardians of the old philosophy were alert they
must have seen that here was implicit doctrine as dangerous
as any they tried to suppress. There cannot have been too
many women like the heroines of Edna Millay's poems. A
woman has to be in part a poet to be like a poet's heroine.
But early in the twenties it was plain that women, feeling
and acknowledging desire as a natural part of love, had become lovers of what seemed a new kind. The change was so
rapid that many men even of the Younger Generation stared.
Young husbands and lovers wondered what had become of
the traditional modesty they had heard about. Young women,
cheerfully dressing before unshaded windows, laughed at
men as the modest sex. When men and women swam together without clothes, as here and there they began to do,
the women were less self-conscious than the men, and sooner
naked. One girl, so timid before that she had made others
hesitant, unexpectedly emerged one day from her shapeless
feminist uniform, on a remote beach with a dozen friends,

so beautiful that they all applauded, though it was the convention, elaborately kept up, that no one should notice any one in particular. As chaste as ever, she became another person, pleased with herself because she had given pleasure.

Modesty in women, it appeared, was part instinct and part convention. The convention went like an old fashion. Discovering their own flesh, they seemed to have discovered it in general. It had been conventional for women, lagging in desire, to blame husbands or lovers for their impatience, and to resent it. Now they began to take it as tribute: a carnal compliment I heard one girl call it. Tributes are easy to tolerate and pleasant to respond to. Companions in work and play, men and women were companions in love—believing that this was new in the world's history, and excited by the sense of adventure. Since it was actually newer to the women, I think they outran the men, trying to catch up with them. I am sure I observed as much courting begun by women as by men, and I think more. It may be this had been always true, in sly ways, but now the ways were as frank and direct as the women knew how to make them. Power came up in women, as if America had tapped a new natural resource.

There was a good deal of waste. Some women seemed to me to run into love affairs on principle, without much love. I recall from the time a dozen women I then observed —and offer these anonymous but accurate statistics. Only one of the twelve, I am sure, never had a lover outside of marriage: I am so sure that I should not dare to ask her. Two others, whose first lovers became their husbands, had no later lovers. Of the remaining nine, every one had a lover or lovers before marriage or after it. Five of the nine, and probably seven, had known no men before their husbands. They were not different as to later lovers from the women who had married with more experience. Six of the twelve marriages ended in divorce. Five of the divorced women were married again, only one of them, I believe to her first lover. The closest observers may misjudge love, but I think that most of these affairs were unimportant and soon over. Yet I doubt that any of these nine women remembers her adventures as sin. Perhaps as folly. Most likely as extravagance.

Literature

WHILE I was still in the University, studying literature at arm's length, I could not avoid the errors which make most literary history too simple, and false. The academic historians of my time were always hunting for what they called influences. If they could find a writer dealing with a subject that an earlier writer had used, and in something like the same spirit and language, they were at once certain that the earlier had influenced the other. The hunt was easy, and what they found strengthened their belief that literature was a dignified tradition which nothing new ever interrupted. It went on like a university, with young writers endured like young instructors till they had settled down to being professors. The academic historians made much of what they called the background of writers. Reconstruct the age in which a writer lived and there was no further mystery. You had then become a contemporary of the writer and understood him—though you could not understand one of your actual contemporaries, and never tried to. The age was like the sand molding the body of a buried man. The academic historians forgot that if you touched such sand it collapsed and lost the impression of the body, and that in any case the man was dead.

The writers I knew, after I left the University, seldom reminded me of those I had read about, as I had read about them. These were often undignified, violent, and incalculable:

frivolous when I expected them to be serious, inarticulate when I expected them to be eloquent, drunk when I expected them to be sober. They did not talk about living for their art. They had lived for it till it was second nature. They talked about technicalities, markets, money—like any other professionals. Some of them seemed to me to have no clearer idea of what they were doing in their books than a river in its necessary course. Those who were aware seemed less like deliberate workmen than like men possessed, or like men in love. A passion urged them for reasons of its own. The best writers were never, as persons, as much better than the worst as their books promised. Excellence in a writer appeared to be a knack that had not too much to do with the man. The ancients must have meant that when they spoke of inspiration, using a more reverent image.

I was like an anthropologist who had learned all he could from reading and reasoning about some unfamiliar tribe but who now went to live with it. I remember the first shock I had. A man I knew wrote negligible little books to uplift their readers to the level of the platitudes. He referred to his work so lightly that I supposed he put no more value on it than it deserved. One day he insisted that I call on him. He lived, I found, in a library packed with dictionaries, encyclopedias, and the heaviest books of learning: philosophy, history, science. Tentatively, at first, he asked me what I thought of his own books, none of which I had ever read. He did not take that humorously. Instead, he got one after another and read me flat paragraphs. "Isn't that as smooth as Emerson?" he asked me about one. "Isn't that as true as Plato?" he asked about another. I was so embarrassed I did not know what to do with my face. By and by I found out what he was at. He knew I was editing the Cambridge History of American Literature. "And I don't suppose," he said, really asking, "that there will be anything in it about me." I told him that we did not deal with living writers. He thought that a pity, for he had laid the plans for a great work, in eight volumes, on education. It would take a long time and terrific labor, but he hoped to win the Nobel prize for literature with it, and trust to that and royalties the rest of his life.

I thought then that he was a special case. It turned out, as I learned more about his tribe, that many of its members were much like him. They wrote as well as they could and did not know why their work was not thought as good as anybody's. I had read of writers, tongue in cheek, who tossed off inferior but popular books for money. I never met one. Plenty of good writers would have liked to do it, and tried, but they were not successful. To succeed, a writer had to believe that he was at work on a masterpiece. Rupert Hughes published in the Bookman an angry open letter to me about my underestimate of his novels, when Fielding, who had written the same kind of novels, Hughes implied, was famous now that time had done him justice. Writers who were merely excellent complained because they were not more generally read. Everywhere I found confusion about the claims of popularity and excellence. I concluded that they had no indispensable connection. To be excellent a writer had to satisfy the best minds; to be popular, to please the most minds. A writer might do both, or either without the other —or of course neither at all. The process was the same, whatever the result. The difference was in the man who wrote.

For four or five years I studied that process more than anything else, and wrote about it as I found it in most of my American contemporaries. It was a kind of anthropology. I

could not often get help from what my subjects told me, because they did not know themselves, would not speak out,
or did not understand the bearings of my inquiry. The writer
who told me most about himself—herself—was Mary Austin.

I had written about her, for the Century, praising the
abundance of her spirit but saying that her art seemed to me
inferior to her prophecy. She sent me word that I had made
her out a seer without saying how good a cook she was.
Would I dine with her and let her tell me more about herself? But she was ill the summer of 1923, had to leave in
July for Santa Fe, and wrote to me from the train.

2

"It seems decreed that I shall say what I wish to say to you
by letter, under conditions in which you can't very well talk
back.

"I have been rereading your books as a prelude to my lectures, and find your approach so much like mine that I might
have written some of these things myself—except for one
important point.

"I think you do not make enough of the prophetic spirit
of literature. Always it seems to me that the difficulty for
American writers, more than for writers anywhere, is that
in our rapidly changing environment we cannot always
strike a successful compromise between the old literary forms
in which the public finds itself at home, and the *becoming*
state of the public mind, putting forth prophetically in the
mind of genius.

"You see, I feel that you haven't quite done me the jus-

tice that it is important to me to have just now. I haven't
made any special clamor for appreciation, but I need it now
chiefly because I am now entering the third and probably the
last phase of my work, and an estimate of it which I felt was
based on complete understanding would be of immense
value to me.

"First of all, I question the grounds of your criticism that
I haven't combined all my gifts in one characteristic piece
of work. I honestly wonder if genius of every description
isn't tending toward greater variability, in our immensely
complex life. We have almost left behind us, in America, at
least, the old notion that everybody must have a 'career,' a
definite program of life to which every expenditure of energy
must conform. Isn't it the approaching ideal that we should
become more plastic to the thought-stream of our time?

"I ask to know, as our friend Hashimura Togo says. I
don't really know.

"May I tell you some of the dominating influences in my
life which may perhaps lead you to a different conclusion
about me in one or two particulars? I don't believe I am an
example of 'stubborn wilfulness,' if anything I have been too
pliant, responding to the push of the hour with any kind of
book that seemed to be demanded by the Powers to which
I have devoted my life.

"To begin with, I grew up in a small Illinois town, not far
from Spoon River, where I never saw even a good reproduction of a good picture, never saw any kind of play except
Uncle Tom's Cabin, never heard any good music, and had
few books. Then at eighteen I went deep into the desert
where all these restrictions were intensified, with the addition that for ten years I scarcely met an educated person.

"I was thirty-eight years old before I ever met any literary people, and two years older before I met any one who could have influenced my work. By that time I had written half a dozen books, and had probably passed the point where I could have been influenced very much in any case.

"The result of this utter isolation was that I had no notion of a literary career, of how success was attained and a standing among other writers secured. I had, rather, developed a mystical, desert-dweller's attitude toward the Friend of the Soul of Man, which had probably a good deal of superstition in it. I wrote what I was inwardly prompted to write, and for years longer it did not occur to me that a literary career should be self-directed.

"I left California in 1906, had three years of European travel, had recognition in London, and in 1910 came to New York.

"During the next ten years I was largely distracted by the necessity of mastering the new environment, and by the secret sorrow which for twenty-three years made a pivot for my personal life, and kept pulling me back to California when my material interests all lay in New York.

"I think I had better tell you about this. I have never had any objection to having it known, but never wished to burden my friends with it. Possibly you know that my only daughter paid the penalty which has to be paid by the children and grandchildren of men who rejoice in the nickname of 'High Roller.' She was always an invalid, and at the age of eleven I was obliged to put her in a private institution, and for the sake of everybody's comfort to say when asked about her that I had 'lost' her. But to keep her and to watch over her was, until three years ago, my chief private care.

"In many practical ways it had much to do with the variable character of my work. Still, in justice to myself I must say that of my sixteen books all but two were undertaken from genuine creative impulses.

"In The Lovely Lady, having written a psychoanalytic story of the influence on a man's whole love life of the first woman who impressed it, long before psychoanalysis had been heard of in this country, I was induced by a publisher to work it over into what he considered publishable form. It spoiled the story without producing popularity, and did me this service, that it saved me from allowing a publisher to interfere with my work again.

"In The Young Woman Citizen I yielded to the persuasion of the Y. W. C. A. to write, because I needed the money they promised me, a promise which they never kept. I also thought that by revising the book every two years as was agreed, I could find an outlet for opinions that I wished to keep out of my creative work, which may prove an advantage yet.

"For the rest of my work I shall have to claim full responsibility. If it is bad art, then it is the fault of the artist, and you do well to say so, but I wish I felt surer that you had read it all as thoughtfully as you seem to have read Upton Sinclair, for instance, or Floyd Dell.

"Because several times I have had the experience of having my work treated as a total failure only to discover years later that it was simply ahead of its time. There was The Arrow-Maker, which is now conceded to have been the first of the new type of poetic drama, and The Flock, which at first was read by no one that I could discover except Theodore Roosevelt, and is now making its way through the European universities into our own.

"And I don't know if my novels are imperfect because they are failures to achieve the old type, or merely tentative attempts to create a new type. I don't know. I hoped you would know, but I suspect you of not being sure. Do artists ever know?

"I have a notion that those writers who say, Go to, I will now do a new thing, never do really produce the prophetic form. But if you could firmly say that you see a forward drift in my work it would help me greatly to realize it. I can be reconciled to knowing my work is inferior to the best of its type, but it would break my heart to discover that it does not point a true direction.

"I have wondered more than a little what you really meant by saying that I needed a surer science. Because I have some time since discovered that I often fail with our Intellectuals by my deliberate avoidance of the patter of professional scholarship.

"I am wholly committed to the literary statement of truth for reasons partly stated in something appearing in the August Bookman three years ago, when, after my daughter's death, I set myself to ordering the years that are left, I made my first move the capture of the intellectual audience, and I found that I could do it only by reducing my range about half and by turning their own vocabularies against them. I don't see how I can use any more science than I do until we have a more scientific reading audience. Even at the Convention of Scientists in Santa Fe I don't expect to be able to tell all I know about rhythm.

"If you have found out any way in which an American writer can be really learned and still get printed, I wish you would pass it on to me, for I can't find it. That's what Science Service has been organized for, to find the way, and we'd all be grateful to you if you would point the way.

"Well, these are the things I wanted to know of you.

Don't imagine you are going to get out of answering them when I come back.

"In the meantime get ready to write an essay on the problem of self-direction in the management of a literary gift, because I know an editor who is going to ask you for it. Shall a writer take his direction from within as I do, from without as Robert Chambers does, or shall he plan a career as a business man plans a business in view of the main chance?

"I hope this isn't too badly written. At the speed we are making it isn't easy always to land on the keys."

3

ONE of the most perceptive and reflective minds in America could not quite understand the literary process in the single instance about which it knew the most. Nobody could understand the whole process. Though it might be essentially the same, it worked always through individuals, who, whatever the literary historians might think, were never the same. No new book was exactly like an old one, any more than a new baby was. Types persisted, but each fresh example had to be alive with its own vitality. A writer could be influenced by his predecessors only when he found in them what was already in him waiting to be roused, and what he did with it was measured by his power not by theirs. So with the age in which he lived. Of course it gave him forms and idioms, and turned his attention to prevailing ideas, as it determined the language he used. But all these affected dozens of writers to no advantage, unless they were original enough to add something out of themselves.

These originalities were what interested me. I was not the most effective kind of critic. More and Babbitt, Sherman and Mencken, Lewisohn and Van Wyck Brooks, all demanded that literature take more certain courses toward more certain ends than I felt any need for. They took part in controversies. I never did. Though I had favorites among contemporary writers, they were those I understood best rather than those I sympathized with most. Edmund Wilson called me amiable. I was not. Instead, I was so arrogant that I did not particularly care how anybody besides me chose to write. As an anthropologist I took nature as I found it, pleased with variety and leaving to the moralists to say which varieties must be kept, which discarded.

But all men, being finite, are moralists, and want some kinds of excellence to prevail. Close in temper to the speculative part of the Younger Generation, I prized the same excellences as they. Only, I could not satisfy myself with critical argument. I had, as I put it, to do something about American literature.

As to the older writers, I wanted to revise the canon. I edited selections from Edwards and Franklin and Paine and Irving and Hawthorne, bringing down what seemed to me to be still alive in them from the high, dingy shelves of their collected works. I arranged Whitman's poems for the first time in chronological order, as nearly as I could, and published them. I made a redaction in one narrative of the books said to be by Davy Crockett. Herman Melville had been unbelievably neglected. Having done, for the Cambridge History, the first detailed study and the first bibliography of his work, I set Raymond Weaver at Columbia to writing the first life of Melville. (But between 1915 and 1917 I saw several copies of the first edition of Moby Dick offered in New

York bookstores for a dollar each, and, being short of money, bought only one, badly water-stained and cheaper still, and then cut that up to save myself the work of transcribing a long passage. A Melville letter which I bought for two dollars I later sold for a hundred.) I supervised a whole school of doctoral dissertations besides Weaver's, which outgrew the academic form and became a book. I had more graduate students in American literature than any other teacher had ever had, and I can seldom visit an academic community without meeting one of them—now himself a teacher and too often teaching what I taught then. With Mark I wrote American and British Literature Since 1890, which was only a textbook but which was the first general introduction to the new literature in English on both sides of the Atlantic.

As to the younger writers, I was the earliest critic who studied many of them systematically. In Contemporary American Novelists, written for the Nation, and in Many Minds, written for the Century, I was in at least half the chapters dealing with writers who had not before been studied as a whole, only reviewed book by book. Criticism was not enough. I left the Nation in 1922 to be literary editor of the Century, not only for more money and less work, but also for the chance this gave me to publish what I liked as well as to talk about it. The conservative monthlies had been slow in recognizing the new literature. Now for three years the Century was almost an anthology of it—at any rate, in poetry and fiction. A Lost Lady and the Venetian Glass Nephew appeared as serials. There were stories or sketches by Sherwood Anderson, Floyd Dell, Dreiser, Edna Millay, Katherine Anne Porter, Ruth Suckow, Elinor Wylie, and poems not only by Edwin Arlington Robinson, Robert Frost, Amy Lowell, and George Santayana, but also by Elinor Wylie,

Maxwell Bodenheim, Stephen Vincent Benét, and Mark Van Doren. The Nation and the Century helped establish a new canon for American literature in the minds of readers both of the new style and the old.

All men are moralists. I was so much a partisan of the new literature that when, in November 1924, I was elected to membership in the National Institute of Arts and Letters, I declined the election. The Institute did not seem to me to have any weight and in ordinary times I should not have cared whether I was a member or not. But now I knew I would rather be outside with Mencken and Cabell and Dreiser and Sinclair Lewis than inside with its traditions. Edwin Arlington Robinson had been left in the Institute, a kind of waiting-list for the American Academy, when at the annual meeting just held a patriotic professor had been elected to the Academy. I knew I had no business in any academy which ranked professors above poets.

No, field work with the tribe of writers was more to my liking. The unexpected came up every day.

At a luncheon at the Brevoort for Sherwood Anderson the classic antagonists Sherman and Mencken were for the first and last time in the same room. Friends of both proposed to introduce them and watch the fun. Sherman agreed. I should have expected Mencken to say: "Nonsense, bring him up, and let me confound the fellow and all his works." But Mencken refused to meet Sherman, who he said had called him pro-German during the war and had put him in real danger. He would have nothing to do with a dirty fighter. . . . Glenn Frank, my colleague on the Century, told me that he had once been an assistant to Billy Sunday. The summer before Frank went to college he had given himself up to saving souls in Illinois. Then he had gone to Northwestern, taken to reading Darwin, Spencer, and Huxley, and within six months had lost all interest in salvation. "How did the change come about?" I asked him. "As soon as I stopped talking about it I stopped believing it." . . . Elinor Wylie was in love with Shelley, not in the usual sense of the term in such cases but so near to literally in love with him that he stood between her and living men. "Are you sure," she said to me, "that if I had lived in his time and had known him, Shelley would have loved me?" She was flushed and excited and I had to yes with all my might—though she laughed a little. . . . Edgar Lee Masters came to dine with me and, without any satiric anger, told humorous and affectionate stories of Spoon River and its people. . . . Floyd Dell said that once when he was talking with Masters and Dreiser he had tried to argue that beauty was not necessary in literature, that the rough truth would do, and that both of them had cried out against his argument. If literature was not beautiful it was not literature. They aimed always at beauty. . . . Edwin Arlington Robinson read as many detective stories as he could lay his hands on during the winters when he was not writing poetry. Learning that he had never read Trent's Last Case, I gave him the book. He was touchingly delighted, but accepted it only on condition that he might give it to some one else. He collected no books or any other property. . . . When Heywood Broun heard that I had written about him for the Century, that seasoned and scarred controversialist, as I thought him, could not wait for the essay to be published but came to the office to read it in the proofs. . . . Zona Gale first planned, in making her stage version of Miss Lulu Bett, to have the heroine married twice as in the novel. But she, or her producer, realized that on the stage this was impossible. The playbill might say whatever it would about the lapse of months or years, but the audience would not be able to forget that it had just seen this woman married and would either be shocked or tickled. The play could not do what the novel had done. . . . Sherman told me that when the Pulitzer prize committee was considering William Ellery Leonard's Two Lives they felt they ought to give it the prize but were afraid of its plain speaking. They were not willing to admit this even among themselves and so rationalized their more timid choice. Two Lives, they reasoned, was a long poem. A long poem must have a great subject to be good. This one did not—that is, its subject was what they thought unpleasant—and consequently was not a good long poem. A long poem that was not good was less deserving than short poems which had attempted less. Moreover, Amy Lowell had never received the Pulitzer prize for poetry. They gave the prize that year to her for a volume of posthumous miscellanies. . . . At a time when Paris was next to New York as the American literary capital some friends and I took James Joyce to the Grand Prix at Longchamp. "I don't suppose," he said, looking down from the grandstand through strong binoculars at field and track and concourse, "that the good Lord ever gave a man such a desire to see and such blind eyes to see with." Then he asked us to point out some mannequins to him. We pointed out two or three pairs, bright and bold, and in a few minutes he could catch sight of as many of them as any of us, and as quickly. . . . After I had written about George Santayana in the Century and, thinking of a non-philosophical audience, had reduced the rich universe of his many books to something so close to axioms and formulas that it embarrassed me, he wrote that he wished I had been disposed to make my study simpler. . . . For the last volume

of the Cambridge History I had planned a chapter on Popular Bibles, and had asked Woodbridge Riley, a good scholar,
to write about the Book of Mormon and Science and Health,
the only modern gospels and both American. As soon as
the volume was published the Christian Scientists, who had
more vigilant watchmen than any other sect, came upon the
publishers with their soft, firm pressure. Riley was not orthodox and he was lively about the origins and doctrine of
Christian Science. The publishers were worried. As the editors had done their work for a fee, not for royalties, and had
no further legal interest in the history, there was little they
could do. The publishers explained in the newspapers that
their house had inadvertently hurt the Christian Scientists and
that the chapter would be suppressed, though not the section
on the Book of Mormon which would not be resented. Now
the Latter Day Saints had to resent it, whether any of them
had yet heard of the chapter or not. The first printing was
suppressed and the publishers had a more discreet person
write a smoother chapter. Writers, I learned, had to face more
kinds of censorship than I had realized. But I might have
expected this.

4

THERE are as few good writers among the many who want
to write as there are good lovers among the many who fall in
love. Writing is like love in this: a writer falls in love with
his subject. He may calculate in advance to his mind's content about the subject it would be wise or prudent to choose,
as a man may calculate about a woman. But for the writer,

as for the man, calculation alone is of little use. More than his mind is needed. Let him reason out a proper subject as he will, he will stand inert before it unless his nerves start and his blood stirs. Only love could carry him through the labor that goes into a book. Only love could make him, at least for the time, as obsessed as he has to be if life is to pass from him into the book, which otherwise is merely black words on white paper. Because he loves he may be often unreasonable. I have seen writers as angry at a stubborn subject as they could be at a bad-tempered mistress. And writers are almost never just when their books fail to please. The fault is not in the book but in the reader.

Actually there are no books which everybody is obliged to read, no book, except perhaps of technical information, which anybody cannot do without. The writer may have been compelled to write, but not to publish. Once he publishes his book another process begins. If it is striking enough in what it has to say, and clear enough in its way of saying it, it may get at once as wide a hearing as it will ever have, like a newspaper. If it is quiet and profound it will be heard more slowly, less as the day's news than as truth about which there is no hurry. If it is original in thought and language it will have to overcome the resistance both of those who do not understand it and those who, understanding it, dislike it as troubling or subversive. Most of the books published are of course not striking, not profound, and not original. But all books face the same fortune: they reach as large an audience as they can interest to the point of buying or renting or borrowing them, sooner or later. A writer is lucky if he is striking enough to be read at once, profound enough to be read a long while, original enough to overcome resistance and set new fashions. He is unlucky if he is none of these things. But he cannot compel readers to read since they do not compel writers to write. There is free trade between them.

These are the essentials of the process. As it involves human beings there are frequent accidents, happy or unhappy. Here is the story of one of those accidents in which I had a hand.

In the spring of 1927 Edwin Arlington Robinson had published over a dozen volumes of verse since his first one over thirty years before. Whoever knew poetry knew his name. But except for the flutter of curiosity that President Roosevelt had roused by his excited review in 1905, Robinson had always been only a name, if that, to the larger public, and his books, year after year, had sold no more than two or three thousand copies each. Merlin, his first Arthurian poem, had pleased so little that his publishers had forced, or allowed, him to find another for Lancelot. Now he had written Tristram. A literary historian, knowing of this third book's success, would probably say either that Robinson from the failure of the others had learned to tell a story more dramatically or that the public, though obtuse at first, had gradually become aware of the power and magic of his theme. The historian would certainly then examine the three poems and find that Tristram was more dramatic than the others, and he would find in the critical opinions of those years the evidence of a rising tide of recognition. The historian would be partly wrong. The episode of Tristram's success was a happy accident. Robinson had written his poem as he had written the others, and with no thought that it would have greater popularity than they. The year 1927 was little more ready for Tristram than 1917 had been for

Merlin or 1920 for Lancelot. But circumstances conspired and the accident turned into triumph.

Harold Guinzburg, that charming young Cæsar among publishers, had organized the Literary Guild and had asked me to be editor with associates whom I was to choose. The Guild was a book club to which the members subscribed as to a magazine, and got each month a book selected by the editors and furnished by the club at a cost which, though no book could be bought separately, made the twelve cost less from the Guild than through the bookstores. The bookstores objected to what they thought unfair competition, and the publishers from whose lists the books were to be selected were dubious about it. For the third book I decided that we must make a choice which would surprise the public and give the Guild a reputation for taste and courage. I read Tristram and felt sure that it was the book. Krutch, one of my associates, agreed with me as soon as he read it, and Elinor Wylie eagerly concurred even before she had.

Behind the scenes of the affair were various mixed motives. The editors, knowing that the Guild had been organized for profit like any business, were afraid that if its circulation became large they might be urged or tempted to aim at a more popular audience than they had in mind for the kind of books they wanted to select. The choice of Tristram put them in a strong position with their critics and their consciences. A book club which sent its members a narrative in blank verse by a distinguished poet was itself distinguished. My strongest motive was a desire to make Robinson known as I thought he ought to be. But I was also the responsible editor and I had to consider the interests of the Guild as well as of the writers selected. If the Guild failed it could do nothing for them. I had to consider Guinzburg, whose money was in the venture. Refusing to own stock in it myself, so that I could not be influenced in my judgment by any thought of dividends, I felt I must not gamble at another man's expense. What Guinzburg thought I do not know. He was such a publisher as most editors only imagine, and he never by word or look questioned, to me, any editorial decision. Yet he cannot have helped wondering whether the selection of a long poem by an austere poet, so early in the Guild's career, might not frighten more subscribers than it satisfied. He had another problem. The publisher of Tristram reduced the price of the book. Anybody would be able to buy it for one-twelfth of the cost of an annual subscription to the Guild. If the bookstores complained they would be told that the publisher had merely sold so many thousand copies to the Guild, as he would be glad to do to any other customer. Guinzburg, bound to offer the subscribers each month more than their money would buy in the bookstores, thought of sending the subscribers along with the Tristram another volume about Robinson and his work. This would not only add to the value of the May selection but would also make it a literary event impressive to the subscribers. We asked Mark to write it, in three weeks. Both Mark and I remembered Swift's lines:

> "Read all the prefaces of Dryden
> For these our critics much confide in,
> Though merely writ at first for filling,
> To raise the volume's price a shilling."

The Guild did still more to make the appearance of the two books an event. It arranged to hire a theater on the Sunday evening nearest the day of publication, invite Robinson's friends and admirers, and all influential journalists, and have the poem read, or as much of it as would take no longer than a short play. Friends of Robinson, not the Guild, thought of Mrs. August Belmont (Eleanor Robson), also his friend, for the reader. Fine actress and great lady, she would mean as much to many in the audience, and to the newspapers, as the poem. The evening came and the theater was crowded. Mrs. Belmont's voice had never been a purer silver. Though Robinson was too shy to be present at the reading, he nerved himself to come to the reception afterwards in the lounge of the theater. For the first time I noticed how tall he was, a Maine pine harried by the tumultuous occasion. The next day the newspapers all over the country told how America had at last discovered a great poet and honored him.

All this strategy would have done little if the poem had not met the expectations of the curious. It did. The Guild's special edition was sold out quickly. "How many copies did you say you wanted?" Robinson had asked me, incredulous. I told him twelve thousand and he shook his head in sympathetic anxiety. "I hope you don't have too many left." In a letter at the end of March he had written: "I hope that you and your brother made out somehow to understand my appreciation of all your interest and effort—in the matter of the book—which is all the more gratifying to me for the reason that the whole thing was a complete surprise to me. It will cause some profanity on the part of your subscribers, but we'll hope that most of them will take it calmly and kindly." In June he wrote: "I hope you are not getting too many bad wishes and brickbats for putting 210 lines [pages] of blank verse on your list. Perhaps you will let me know about that." I reassured him. "It is gratifying," he answered, "to know that Tristram has made friends with your subscribers, and that you have no regrets for turning him loose on them. I haven't yet succeeded in telling you how much I appreciate your action in this matter, and all it means to me, but you will be tired of hearing about it if I say any more, and so I won't—for the present." Out of the countless enthusiastic letters that had reached me about Tristram I selected about a hundred and had them copied for him, with one that had run to an essay. "Thank you for the letters," he wrote in July, "and for the rather surprising essay, all of which I have read with interest. The epistolary 'essay' was at times a little too 'metaphysical' (sic) for my comprehension, but probably my own intellectual limitations were responsible for that. I should like to believe that you are not too heavily burdened with left-over volumes of my poem and that those you have will eventually be disposed of. And I am glad that so many like it." Not only the Guild subscribers liked it. The trade edition within a few months sold over fifty thousand, his Collected Poems were reissued in one volume and in five, his next long poem was sought by avid collectors when it appeared, and for the rest of his life he had renown and tranquillity.

He had the envy of some other poets. One of them said to me: "Well, I see Robinson has sold himself down the river." By this the sneerer thought he was saying that Robinson had diluted and cheapened his work for the sake of a vulgar audience. This was obviously not true. He had never even thought of a larger audience while writing Tristram, and in his later poems he wrote as if nothing had happened. What the minor poet was saying, rather, was that he himself had liked thinking that he and Robinson were equally unread and that, now he could no longer think and say it, he must find the cause in Robinson not in himself. I do not know whether Robinson ever felt the envy directed at him. It was a quality he seemed to lack altogether. Four years after Tristram he did one of the most considerate things I have ever heard of one poet's doing to another. Mark had published his Jonathan Gentry. Robinson, who had read the reviews as well as the poem, took it on himself to write to Mark about the many reviewers who had said that he showed the influence of Robinson. He had himself, he said, noticed nothing of the kind. He thought he would use this opportunity to say so because when he was young he had often been distressed and bored by reviewers who said he wrote under the influence of this or that poet when he knew he did not.

5

THE plainest statement of a truth may convey as much error as the most intricate falsehood. Once in Kansas a man I had met on a train asked me where I lived in New York. I said in Greenwich Village. He licked his lips. "Did you ever go to one of those parties they have there?" Nothing could satisfy him, I saw, but a tale of more-than-Roman orgies as imagined in Hollywood. His mind was already made up. I could not have given him any true impression of a party where, while there might be more drinking than real thirst and more caressing than real desire, the people would have come together less for these than for talk about their trades, gossip about their neighbors, and general conversation which might be honest and serious as well as free and lively.

I can myself hardly realize, after living fourteen years in Greenwich Village, that for fourteen years before that I had lived in New York with less knowledge of the Greenwich section than of the Left Bank in Paris. It was fabulous and remote. I took visitors by bus to Washington Square and back to Morningside Heights. I occasionally went by the Subway to dine at an Italian restaurant in Tenth Street. But what first made me want to live in Greenwich Village was the houses I looked down on as I passed over them in the Elevated on the way between my flat near Columbia and my office at the Nation in Vesey Street: picturesque, small, weathered houses excitingly unlike the piled-up tiers of flats on Morningside. Mark and Krutch, still bachelors, shared the top floor of a house in Barrow Street. The Canbys had a house in Charlton Street, which architecturally belonged in the American wing of the Metropolitan Museum and which stood on ground which Aaron Burr had onced leased from Trinity. In 1922 I moved into the Charlton Street house which the Canbys had left and I had bought. Five years later, having sold it at a profit, I moved to a house in Eleventh Street which a single family had occupied for fifty years.

My Greenwich Village has nothing to do with the noisy night clubs of marauding tourists. It might be a small town. Many of my closest friends have been my neighbors. Ludwig Lewisohn and his first wife had a house in Jane Street. So did the Shermans before Stuart's death in Michigan in 1926. Elinor Wylie and William Rose Benét after their marriage in 1923 lived in Ninth Street. Mark, married in 1922 to Dorothy Graffe of New York, lives in Bleecker Street near Eleventh. Krutch, married in 1923 to Marcelle Leguia of Hendaye, lives in Twelfth Street. I have seldom dropped into the Brevoort or the Lafayette without seeing some one I knew. My children went, like most of their friends, to the City and Country School near by. They know the dogs, janitors, ice-men, boot-blacks, taxi-drivers, barbers, confectioners, and other shopkeepers of the neighborhood precisely as if this were a small town. Everybody goes to the neighborhood theaters for movies. Here are all the comforts of a small town without the bondage. Greenwich Village has city standards of privacy at home, and its people can, if they choose, have close friends elsewhere in New York. Their best friends need not know each other.

Far from idling in Greenwich Village, I worked harder my first five years there than ever in my life. In Cornwall we sold the old parsonage and moved to a farm on Cream Hill which had a larger house, an orchard, and a red cottage which I used as a study. The family moved from New York to the farm the first of every June and stayed till the end of September. Life at Threeways, the parsonage, had been austere and rustic. Life at Wickwire, the farm, was less rustic and gayer. Mark and Dorothy, the Krutches, the Gannetts, the Canbys came to spend their summers in Cornwall. Elinor Wylie and Benét, Ruth and Stuart Sherman, Grace and Sinclair Lewis came to visit. There Lewis outlined his plan for a new American Academy which was to have William Randolph Hearst as president and Otto H. Kahn as secretary. There he got a crowd together at the boat house and preached an Elmer Gantry sermon on Greenwich Village. One of the finest of Sherman's Letters to a Lady in the Country describes a week-end at Wickwire. We drove to Cornwall, too, for week-ends in the spring. Spring crept up Cream Hill from the village to the farmhouse about a hundred feet a day. One week-end the apple blossoms would be white in West Cornwall, the next at Wickwire only four miles away. We drove to Cornwall for week-ends in the fall, and saw what the season did to the country week by week, setting it on fire and then dulling it to winter colors.

Cornwall laid its hand on Greenwich Village, and with Cornwall, Hope again. "At each new turning season," I wrote in the heyday of the Younger Generation, "I ask myself what annual phrase in the great epic of the year most pricks the senses: the stir of sap in the maples, the earliest robin coldly foraging across a bare lawn, crocuses or cowslips or trailing arbutus in the muddy wood-lot, willow bark suddenly ripe for whistles, garden soil warm and dry enough to risk seed in it, apple blossoms and lilacs like music with their fragrance—the bright, young, green procession from March's equinox to June's accomplished solstice; or the higher pomps of summer, red and yellow—berries luxuriant on the hills, wheat in the head, corn haughty with the pride of its stature, meadow-larks that cry continually as cherubim, evenings spangled with fireflies and alive with shrill bats and angry night-hawks and repining frogs, the spare smell of mown hay, keen acrid dust flung through light air by the lean hands of drouth; or golden, purple, imperial autumn— the incredible blue of fringed gentians, apples for hungry hands, grapes dewy and fresh on tingling mornings, gardens giving up their wealth to ready cellars, birch fires crackling on a hearth which had nearly forgotten them, leaves so scattered that every foot sounds like a marching army, wild geese off for the south with eager bugles, a frost transmuting the world in a night; or white and black and dusky winter— sounds heard muffled over deadening snow, the privacy of long nights, the sweet, bitter coldness of cheeks when the blast strikes them, blood triumphantly warmed by exercise even in zero weather, the crisp flesh of fruit dug from pits hid deep underground, the ringing blades of skates, the malicious whine of sleigh runners, fat companionable snow-birds with an eye on the pantry window, barns warm with

the breath of ever-ruminant cows: which is best? Is there any
choosing? Shall we all vote for the nearest? Perhaps this is
what I do when in this season I make my choice for the sun-
downs of August, which, by some keenness in the winds that
then waken, clearly though not too brusquely prophesy, in
the midst of a consoling splendor, that the epic has an end:
August of the blazing noons, August of the cool nights."
Hope and Cornwall in one landscape of set prose. I strike
out a few soft words and let it stand.

In that same post-war time I came nearer than ever before
or since to putting my whole unguarded heart into published
words, in my portraits of my three daughters: Anne as the
Scholar, Margaret as the Gypsy, Barbara as the Barbarian, in
Other Provinces.

"Doubtless," I wrote of Anne—and of all of them, "I see
her sadly from without and mistake the drama of which, like
every human being, she feels herself to be the center. Yet
certain strings in me so vibrate to certain of her moods and
deeds that I have to trust the emotions and judgments which
they waken. Recognizing that kinship, however, I dare not
presume upon it. It helps me to understand her fierce will,
her hot rebellions, her tireless quest for knowledge, her res-
tive desire always to be acting through some form of art;
but it can go no further. There is still the mystery of her
golden beauty, the marvel of her flame-like youth setting out
upon the paths of the world which will eventually dim it.
Is she cool now? Fevers will run through her. Is she fiery
now? Winter will touch her sooner or later. In those days I
can be of no avail, great though my longing may be. Something new has been fashioned out of the stuff which makes
the race, yet it can at best only slightly vary an ancient
process. Powerless even now in all that essentially concerns

the Scholar, I watch the process working with her. This delicate clay, caught up by what hands for what purposes, advances in what must seem a tentative direction toward what must be an unguessed fate. As I hang dumbly over the spectacle, the Pities and the Ironies come from the wings of the theater and stand beside her where she, unaware of them, plays her ingenuous part. The Ironies, with hard eyes, smile at the long plans they see her laying and tell each other that such plans are brief and brittle. The Pities, with kind eyes, weep to see her plans so long, for they too know how soon they will be broken. And this, no doubt, is as much as may be expected of life for any man's daughter: that now and then the Pities and the Ironies, their glances meeting above her head, may agree concerning her."

6

ON AN afternoon of March 1925 Anne, then nine, was playing in the garden behind the house in Charlton Street with Margaret and Barbara and some visiting children. One of the boys had a bow and arrow and was aiming at a wall. Anne, coming toward him on roller-skates, ran into him or between him and his mark. The arrow struck her full in the left eye before the lid could close.

Irita came at once from her office, and Stuart Sherman with her. I was speaking that afternoon in New Jersey. When I got back they were just leaving for the hospital. I held Anne on my knee in the cab, asking her too often whether her eye hurt her. She had cried when the arrow struck her, but she did not cry again. No, it did not hurt, she said.

The doctor was to meet us at the hospital with the surgeon. Neither was there yet, and we went into the nearest waiting-room. The clerk at the desk did nothing. Nobody came. Time whirled around me. After how long I do not know—probably a few minutes—I went to the clerk and asked when the child's room would be ready. She looked me over and un-hurriedly called an interne.

The interne came, all leisure and insolence, "Are you sure," he said, "you can't pay anything?"

I did not at first take in what he was saying or why he said it, and I only later realized that we had gone into a waiting-room for patients with no money. If I had taken it in then I should, with the whole hospital on my back, have choked him till his eyes lost their sneer and his contemptuous tongue its speech. At the time I hardly noticed how his manner changed when I told him I did not care about the cost. Then the hospital sprang to life. Let the poor wait and the children lose their sight.

The doctor and the surgeon came. The arrow had entered the pupil and torn the iris. The surgeon must operate at once to save the wounded eye, if it could be saved, and the other eye, which also was in danger. They wheeled Anne, still quiet, away to the operating room. Now for eternity.

They wheeled Anne back, limp with ether, her gold hair tumbled, her blue eyes covered, but the pink still indomitable in her cheeks. The surgeon had had to cut away a part of the iris and that pupil would be a little larger than the other. He could not tell yet how much sight would be left, if the eye recovered. Nor could he tell whether it would recover. If it did not, he felt he must tell us, he might have to remove it altogether for the sake of the right eye. In a week he would know. After a longer eternity.

Hours like days, days like years. The boy who had shot the arrow prayed in his church, his mother told me. Prayers for a pagan, blind to the bright world.

In spite of the black bandage Anne's face glowed. "Will you do something for me? Of course I can't read, but I would like to have my book of the Three Musketeers here. I could keep it under my pillow."

I said I would bring the book, which she knew almost by heart. And I said: "I don't think D'Artagnan would be any braver than you are, if he had had his eye hurt."

"Oh no," she said. "If he had been only hurt as much as this he wouldn't even have gone to the hospital." In the worst times, remember heroes.

Friends of Robert Frost were giving him a dinner on his fiftieth birthday, and I had promised to be chairman. As I could do nothing for Anne, I might as well do what I could. By some momentum of the will, with some involuntary muscles of the mind, I got through the dinner, though I cannot remember a word that was said or even the names of the speakers I introduced. Nobody seemed to notice anything strange about me. The fever of horror may be cold, too deep to burn in the cheeks.

That evening, while others talked, I sat down with horror. Horror kept holding up before me a glowing face with a murdered socket where a soft eye ought to be. Horror would spare me nothing, and would not let me reflect that the art of the surgeon could conceal the wound. Horror went further and showed me both gay eyes lost. In the darkness Anne stumbled and must be led. In the darkness she had to live shut out from the light of the sun and the colors of the earth. I saw her desperate with rebellion, whether she were blind or only marred in her beauty, cheated of her hopes for work and love. Would she, who demanded so much of herself as of others, want to live with these imperfections? Should I want her to? Might she not ask why I, her father, had not somehow protected her? What could I answer? In my cold fever I told myself that a man who did not protect his daughter did not deserve to have her to love and be loved by. I must not want what she did not want. If she wanted not to live I must be willing for her to die, I must believe that was better. Sitting there, while others spoke of poetry, I tried to open my heart and let Anne go. I could only pretend with my mind that my heart opened. It held tight, and my mind could not coax or comfort it. But my mind began to prepare itself for resignation.

(Mad mind. Yet Paul told me that he went through the same frantic reasoning when his son Peter had infantile paralysis—had it and recovered without a trace.)

They took off the black bandage. The left eye had lost some of its vision but no more than the right, untouched and tireless, could make up for. The larger pupil made the hurt eye look merely bluer than the other. Most observers would never see the difference. Whatever went through Anne's young mind, she showed no sign of worry or despair but serenely played with dolls, during her recovery, while she had read to her volume after volume of the Three Musketeers and Twenty Years After and the Vicomte de Bragelonne.

7

BESIDES my grief I remember nothing else at the Frost dinner except the sympathy of Elinor Wylie, who knew about Anne and who half-raised, for a moment, my buried spirit. She

had the tact to speak to me apart from the others, understanding that I could not bear the weight of any general sympathy. Only a few words, but as hopeful and encouraging as
words could be. I had said, when I first met her two years
before, that she looked like iced chalk, and she had been
pleased with the comparison. But now she was the warmest
flesh and blood.

Later, when I could, I wrote to tell her what she had been
to me that night. She answered from New Canaan, 8 April
1925:

"If any word I was empowered to say proved of the slightest help to you, I am very proud. Thank you for telling me.

"You know that this tragedy touching—but I will not believe ultimately dimming—the brightness of Anne has come
to me like a personal sorrow—no, it is a personal sorrow,
because of my feeling for the darling child, & for you & Irita.
I wish I had the words in which to say the hundred thoughts
& indeed prayers which are in my heart."

Let me tell the story of Elinor Wylie, that pure yet troubled genius, as truly as I can. It is several stories. She was a
legend before she was a fact, and the legend came to New
York ahead of her. Sometimes she seemed to be living up to
it, with little mystifications about herself. At other times she
would feel transient compunctions and tell her closer friends
things they would not have thought of asking for. It was
hard, knowing her, to disentangle fact from legend, and either
from the rôles, romantic or realistic, which she alternately
played. I am not too sure that I have disentangled the four
stories, though she often confided in me and though I have
since her death tried, so far as research at this distance can
go, to make one clear story out of them.

Because the legend said she came from Philadelphia she

let most people believe she had been born there, or in suburban Rosemont. When the Hall-Mills murder case made Somerville, New Jersey, conspicuous, she told me that was where she had actually been born, as an amusing secret. She let it be thought, too, that she had been born in 1887. But one evening, at a party, she drew me into a corner and asked me what day in September was my birthday. I told her the 10th. She knew the year was 1885.

"Then I'm really three days older than you. I was born on the 7th. Nobody knows but Bill. You won't tell, will you? Do you think I'm an awful liar?"

I did not consider it a lie for any woman to misrepresent her age, but I said only that I did not think this was a lie. And of course I would not tell. I had a policy for her confidences. Whatever she told me as a secret I kept to myself till I had heard the same thing from three other persons to whom she had told it.

A single confidence did not bind her. She told me that she had been married at eighteen, when she should have said twenty to agree with what I already knew about her age. And because I had written a life of Peacock, Shelley's friend, and because she not only loved Shelley but identified herself with him, she identified me with Peacock, and at times dramatically assumed that I was seven years older than she, as Peacock was older than Shelley. She knew better, but it was a pleasant fiction. When I gave her my first edition of Nightmare Abbey, in which Peacock had laughed at Shelley, she took it almost as a gift from the satirist to his subject.

Shelley so obsessed her in her final years that she liked to think he had been her earliest and only hero, but in 1924 she told me that her first hero was Darcy in Pride and Prejudice. She admired him for his pride, for his refusal to be hoodwinked by his love for Elizabeth into overlooking the disadvantages of marrying into her family, and for the delicacy with which his love in the end showed how strong it was. Gerald Poynyard in Jennifer Lorn is partly Darcy. Though Elinor Wylie respected the passions, she respected minds and manners too.

She had grown up among minds and manners. The eldest of the five children of Henry Martyn Hoyt and Anne McMichael of Philadelphia, she was a great-granddaughter of Morton McMichael, who had been mayor of the city, and a granddaughter of another Henry Martyn Hoyt who had been governor of Pennsylvania, and a daughter of the Solicitor-General of the United States. Taken at two from Somerville to her Philadelphia suburb, she lived there till she was twelve, and then in Washington till she was twenty-five. She went to Miss Baldwin's School in Bryn Mawr and to Mrs. Flint's (now Holton Arms) in Washington, and studied drawing in a class at the Corcoran Museum of Art. Before her marriage she spent the summers with her family at North-East Harbor, Mount Desert, Maine. When she was eighteen (but she told me sixteen) she and her sister Constance went with their grandfather, Morton McMichael, for the season in Paris and London. He introduced them to his friends Sir Henry Irving and Ellen Terry, and to Bram Stoker, who dedicated the Jewel of Seven Stars to the two girls. Elinor Wylie never mentioned Ellen Terry or Irving or Stoker to me, but she said that her grandfather, that year and other years, had been a good part of her education. The rest of it, she said, came mostly from her father. She had as a girl been both taught and petted by older men.

She missed this after her marriage to Philip Hichborn, son of Admiral Philip Hichborn, in Washington in 1905. William Rose Benét, then at Yale with her younger brother Henry, says he saw her in Washington while she was a bride, and thought her happy. Later she believed she had not been. "I didn't know what love and marriage meant," she told me. "The other girls talked about such things, but I would never listen. My marriage was a prison. I felt stifled. There was no room for my mind at all. I had to get away. While my father was alive, I had him to turn to. But after he died I was desperate, and I ran away with Horace. He was twenty years older than I, and father as well as husband to me." (Horace Wylie was only fifteen years older.)

She told me this, sitting beside me while I drove her and Benét from Cornwall to Waterbury. "I left my baby when I ran away," she went on. "That was the one thing I have ever done that I think was bad. Other things, no. I would do all of them over again. But that was utterly bad. I was a bad woman. And now I would rather have a child that I could think of as really my own than anything else I shall ever have. I tried to have children after I married Horace, but not one of them lived. I have had a miscarriage since I married Bill. The doctors say that anything like that again would be the same as putting a gun to my head." I think all this seemed the truth to her, but I know now that before her last miscarriage she was sometimes hysterical with fear and resentment.

The Hoyts, the McMichaels, the Hichborns, and the Wylies were so well known in Philadelphia and Washington that the elopement of Elinor Hoyt Hichborn and Horace Wylie in December 1910 raised an enormous scandal. Newspapers did their worst. As Horace Wylie's wife would not divorce him, the lovers had to leave the country, to live quietly as Mr. and Mrs. Waring in England near the New Forest. Some paper invented stories of a wild residence in Corsica, which neither of them ever saw, though they went now and then to France. After two years Philip Hichborn killed himself. "Of course," Elinor Wylie said, "if Philip had killed himself over me he could not have waited two years to do it." But the scandal had another episode of melodrama to increase it. Scandal followed her all her life, ready to lift its head from old files of news at every step she took: when she and Horace Wylie came back to Boston in July 1915 and after his divorce were married the next year, and when they lived two summers in Mount Desert and a winter in Augusta, Georgia, and when in 1919 they returned to Washington where he obtained a minor post in a Government bureau.

No newspaper, so far as I know, ever noticed a literary coincidence of the year 1912, when Philip Hichborn's stories were collected and published as Hoof Beats in Boston, and Elinor Wylie's (really Hichborn's) Incidental Numbers were privately printed in London. Some one more inquisitive than I will have to ask those who know what the coincidence means, which of the books was issued first and which of them led to the other if either did, and what motives were involved in this sad rivalry the year Philip Hichborn died.

The poems of Incidental Numbers had little of Elinor Wylie's magic. She was not precocious, and in a sense she was still at school, with Horace Wylie and rural England for her teachers. The fashionable world is full of women who write bad poems with good intentions, and Elinor Wylie at twenty-seven had only begun to outgrow her world, though she had run away from it. Eight years later she had outgrown it. Even if Washington had forgiven her, I think she could not have gone back to it, as she sometimes thought she could have. In any case, she was not forgiven, and she had few friends outside her family. Then in 1919-20 she renewed her acqaintance with Benét, and met Sinclair Lewis, who was in Washington writing Main Street.

Through them she learned of a world which would not hold her past against her, and in 1921 she left Washington for New York. It meant a separation, and two years later a divorce, from Horace Wylie. A love which was almost a classic had passed like any other. The story of it was not three pages long, as here, but a dozen years. (Pinch a story too tight, and the life goes out of it.) Much as Elinor Wylie told me about herself, she never told me about the end of this chapter. Only about her respect and affection for Horace Wylie, whose name she kept for herself as poet. Servants and strangers might call her Mrs. Benét, but I never heard the words Elinor Benét, and now, writing them, I see them for the first time and for the first time realize that they were her name.

She made her way at once into the literary society of Manhattan. What in Washington had seemed shocking, in New York seemed dramatic. Almost nobody knew quite what her story was, but everybody knew she had a story and thought of her as some kind of heroine. Her poems began to be noticed and applauded. The first one I saw was the Eagle and the Mole in the New Republic, and I read it over and over, excited as I had been at Edna Millay's Renascence in the Lyric Year in 1912. I think now, as Benét thought then, that Elinor Wylie should have had the Nation's poetry prize for 1921, but her crisp notes were lost in the clamor. Benét told me about her poems, self-consciously, and I guessed she was more to him than a new poet. I knew nothing else about her, except the vaguest legend, till I first met her late in 1922.

Mary Colum and Jean Wright planned a meeting at the

MacDowell Club where many poets were to read their work to a large audience, and I was to be chairman and introduce the poets. Elinor Wylie was one of them. She looked like the white queen of a white country. White-faced in white satin, she had no color but in her lustrous eyes and her bronze hair. She seemed restless and remote. Introducing her, I said her poems were like bronze bells. This delighted her. She read with a shy fire, but her voice was actually higher in pitch than her verses. Clear and fresh, it was not sweet, and in heightened moments it might be shrill. Shelley's voice was sometimes shrill.

I did not happen to see her again for another year, at a dinner just after she and Benét came back to town from a short honeymoon. That evening she was neither queen nor poet, but a laughing woman. On the way home in a taxi she and Mary Colum made such fun, with such lively and inventive malice, of a dull Englishman who had been at the dinner that I felt insensitive for having noticed only that he was another dull Englishman.

The summer following Elinor Wylie and Benét came from the Canbys' house at Yelping Hill to Wickwire. That day the Puritan marrow of her bones was in her mind. It was raw and windy after a hot week, but she refused to wear a coat and walked about wth bare arms, deliberately cold. At heart she was New England, she declared, like the first Hoyts in Massachusetts. At the lake she insisted on swimming all the way to the float, though it was too far for her, and she reached it breathless. In swimming clothes she had an angularity which did not appear when she wore her usual dress and looked stately. She was immensely pleased when I told her that Anne—this was before Anne's accident—had asked me if that was the lady who had written My love came up from Barnegat.

The Century published as much of her work as she would let me have. Gideon's Revenge was her first short story, Miranda's Supper her longest poem. Its cheeky assonances upset one of the older editors.

"Thank you for the Century check," she wrote from Peterborough 12 September 1924, "which was fifty better than my pessimism had predicted.

"It's a great relief that you think the poem improved, & I hope it will do you no discredit.

"For the novel, it goes on fairly well, & I believe you'll like it. I shall have the first part completely finished for you to see when I come back, & the rest mapped out quite clearly.

"It's not another Jennifer—but perhaps that's as well."

The novel was the Venetian Glass Nephew, which was to be a Century serial and was to furnish her some money she needed for the house she had bought in New Canaan, Connecticut.

"Can the Venetian Glass Nephew help me at all, as yet?" she wrote from New Canaan 3 October. "I find I have unexpectedly to pay the *interest*, as well as the *paying off*, on the mortgage. There *is* a difference, though it takes an expert to understand.

"What a pity that these sordid things exist in a world where we are going into the 18th century next week-end! Both Bill & I are longing to see the lovely house [Wickwire] again—and it was so nice seeing you & Irita last Monday.

"P. S. Of course I hope you can manage this advance, but if you can't, don't picture me as suicidal in consequence. It is my reprehensible nature to welcome excitement & change, & the idea of being melodramatically foreclosed & forced to find another—& of course a better—place to live is in itself attractive to my mind. But one must do one's duty, hence this letter."

Without telling the treasurer of the Century all the facts in the case I managed the advance for the whole novel when only a third of it was written. At Wickwire that week-end she gave me the first part, and I left the others to read it in the library. She was in more suspense than I realized, for her sharp ears overheard me laughing aloud as I read, and she called out in such glee that I had to go back to tell her how brilliant I thought it was.

She wrote the rest of the book in New Canaan, working after the three Benét children had left for school and before they came home. Elinor Wylie was not one of those spawning writers who pour out loose first draughts and then trim and tighten them. She began a sentence on her typewriter only when it was finished in her mind and needed no corrections. In the entire manuscript there was hardly a change, even of a syllable, to the page. And—as I have told before— she made only one copy, which she sent to me, and which I sent to the Century's printers in New Hampshire. She liked the risk. There was the further risk that the serial began in the magazine before the book was done. It had to be done, and of course it was. I never trusted another writer so far as that.

From Peterborough on 12 July 1925 she wrote me about her next novel.

"I should rather say we *could* come for the August 1st week-end—it'll be wonderful, & Ruth & Walter [Bartlett] can take us. I believe the current idea is to start Friday late, & spend the night on the way, so expect us fairly—not too— early on Saturday. It will be grand to see you & Irita again,

& I shall certainly have breeches this time & shorter hair, & be—practically, if you can be *him* practically—Shelley.

"My new novel—the one before the witch one—is shapind [shaping?] in my mind as my most glorious work, & one of God's most glorious."

She had often talked about a novel dealing with the Salem witches, one of whom was an ancestor of hers. "But it isn't about the witches," she said, "so much as about the witch-hunters. They were the evil ones. They found what they were looking for because they created it out of themselves. You know who the real Man in Black was. Why, it was Cotton Mather." She had suffered from witch-hunters herself, I imagined she was thinking. But that must be put off for something still closer to her. She could hardly bear to put it into words, and she pledged me to total secrecy. There had never been such an idea for a novel. Suppose Shelley had not been drowned in the Gulf of Spezia, but had been picked up by an American boat, and had decided to go incognito to America, not back to his wife, whom Elinor Wylie hated. To write the book would be almost to have Shelley for a visitor and to show him America, which Elinor Wylie loved.

"We had a wonderful time," she wrote again from Peterborough on 6 August, "as you & Irita know. As soon as I hear from Bill, which will be in a few days, I'll let you know about the week-end to which I invited us. If at all, it will be the twenty-eighth.

"*Don't forget to send me that American book* when you've done with it. It would be invaluable to me in my (Shelley) business.

"I have written another short story as an anchor to windward, in case the other is unsaleable. It is a modern story six thousand words long, done in three days, & will I hope be bought by the Companion or the Pictorial.

"Kiss the children for me—although I never dare do it myself!—& give Irita my love & bread & butter & jam respects."

And two days later:

"I have just heard from Bill, & he can come on Friday the 28th. Shall I arrive at Hartford Thursday evening or Friday morning? *Can do* either, as the high mandarins say.

"You are mentioned in a footnote to Shelley and the Unromantics. You are becoming famous, what?

"This is nice that the person—male or female?—who wrote it says of Peacock. 'He liked the flavour of the imperfect world & the preposterousness of peccant humanity.' That's the principle upon which I write my own immortal works!

"If I sell both stories I shall have you to thank for scaring me—unconsciously—about the Tudor one.

"If I told you how much I love you—you admit you would never believe it!"

The Tudor one was a story she had written about Mary Tudor, sister of Henry VIII, and Charles Brandon. Elinor Wylie had told me that week-end and I had spoken of When Knighthood Was in Flower. She had never read the book. When she found it too was about those lovers, she got into a panic for fear she would be thought to have stolen her plot. She ran to her husband and cried on his shoulder and swore she could never publish the story. Later she was cooler and did publish it.

I sent her books, for the Orphan Angel, about the America of the early nineteenth century. There were no pains to which she would not go to be accurate. After all, she was setting the stage and preparing her house for Shelley.

"Thank you," she wrote from Peterborough on 12 August, "ten thousand times for the noble collection of Americana, which has saved my life & Shelley's.

"I have looked up the trains, & the morning one is impossible, leaving at 5 A. M., so I will take one which reaches Hartford at 7.15 P. M. & is the only other train. Tell me, therefore, whether it will be more convenient for you to meet me Thursday or Friday.

"I was really much impeded for lack of proper material, & these books are a happy release. I am working myself deaf dumb blind & lumbagoishly lame, but am otherwise well & contented."

Then on August 20:

"Thursday it is then, at Hartford, at 7.15, with me alighting dinnerless from the train, & a silver moon ordered in advance.

"This is funny, really, because Bill & I—or rather I, for Bill although eager is innocent of fault—invited us this time. However, you must bear with it, I suppose.

"I shall have something to show you—two friends of mine —Shiloh and David Butternut, also a poem, although not entirely a new one.

"That is noble, your freedom from the base cares which oppress us. I felicitate you, & literature. Did I tell you that the Brandon story was to take the veil forever, but that I had sold the other in three days, & I had written it in four? This sounds like Solomon Grundy.

"Your skepticism remains a charm."

My freedom from base cares meant only that I had left the Century and was spending the whole summer in Cornwall. As to literature, I do not know that she ever read anything I ever wrote, unless it was about her. My skepticism was a joke between us. She insisted that she loved me and I that I doubted it. It was a joke, too, that she had invited herself.

Her plans had to be changed and she wrote again the 24th:

"You will perhaps be relieved & perhaps be sorry to hear that you needn't meet me in Hartford after all, because I'm going down to New York on business & will come up on Friday with Bill. I shall miss you & the moon, however, & I'm sorry.

"But I have a nice funny little book for you."

After her return to Peterborough she was late in writing to me, and then apologetic.

"When we came back to Peterboro," she wrote "Some day in September" (the letter was postmarked the 14th), "we dived head-foremost into a variety of complications, & I've been working like a nigger even since, & hardly coming up even for air. Which is to say that Shiloh and David have been my only correspondents.

"Were you cross with me? I can't tell you how scared I am of making people cross—silly, because no one has been really cross to me for some fifteen years—nor how wonderfully well my selfishness worked out for us in that stop-over at Springfield. But I am still a little conscience-stricken & quite timid when I think of your part in it.

"My darling lovely novel can't be finished, after all, because Mrs. MacDowell is closing the colony on the 22nd, & the children are returning the 26th. I know, I know, how infinitely sweeter & more valuable real people are than the products of one's fancy, but in this case I am prejudiced. My hero is not entirely the product of my own fancy. Some god became imaginative indeed at his creation, & went aside from the beaten track of button-moulding in making him. Which is true, if metaphorically mixed.

"You will perceive perhaps that I am depressed. I believe that it is a mistake to work throughout one's vacation. I don't *see the necessity*. West Cornwall was a bright oasis, as I told Irita.

"Every day I am reminded of you by the invaluable books. I could have done nothing without them. When—do you happen to know, since you know so much—did they first have steamboats on the Ohio? In 1822 do you think?

"Do not be angry with the most abject of your admirers."

I cannot have been angry with her, for I have now not the slightest recollection of what she here refers to nor what my part of it was. My best guess at the mystery is that their stop-over in Springfield obliged me to drive them a long or unusual way to some train they would otherwise not have taken. Her conscience made her exaggerate—her conscience and her jittery dread of disapproval.

From New Canaan she wrote the two longest letters I ever had from her, and the last except one, a year later, so malicious about some friends of ours that I spare them.

"Your review," she wrote without a date but with a postmark 5 October, "appeared just after my weeping eyes were looking their last on Peterboro, & though it served to stanch my tears it was impossible to write to you in mid-air, as it were. Three days with Grace Conkling, another three with the dear old Commodore in New York, & a week in New Canaan without servants have not advanced my correspondence, & it is with a stiff & enervated hand that I now seize a very bad pen & indite you these few lines.

"I love you & I love your review. I suppose I ought to be afraid—from the point of view of royalties—to be called erudite, but I adore it in reality. And your quotations from the wretched glass creature were so charming that you almost made me want to read the book itself. Yet not so charming, after all, as your own setting for them, which is a pretty compliment and happens to be true.

"I am heartily disgusted with the—really you must forgive me, it is the only possible term—gutless Virginio now that I have him between dull commonplace blue cloth covers, & if I did not believe that Shiloh & David were more alive & kicking I should be sad indeed. Thus it is to write a book under bad conditions & when one is tired—the lack of vitality is all too apparent in the tale. But what is one to do—sell matches? I have three little stepchildren, kind lady, & a mortgage on my house, & extreme astigmatism, & I feel as if I had a shawl over my head & chilblains. I suppose in addressing you I should rather say 'kind sir' but I was thinking of some sort of district visitor.

"You see I am writing out of a purple thundercloud of gloom, which your review has lit with lovely flashes. The trouble is—a book half done & a steep impassable prospect of finishing it this winter. All my plans were changed for us at the eleventh hour by the rich & powerful people who mould our lives.

"I'm sorry that I'm beginning to imitate Shelley in this melancholy fashion. Poor darling Shelley, I have not his other virtues to make my dejection forgivable! Nevertheless, please forgive me. And accept my thanks for the lovely gift of the review."

She wrote again the 6th:

"I've just heard that you are in town after all. I'm so sorry that I didn't know it Saturday, for I sent you a fairly long letter to Cornwall, & we all know what the Connecticut mails are. Perhaps it may reach you in time for Christmas.

"It thanked you for your brilliant and benevolent review of my immortal works, & it contained certain stanzas written in dejection by an unfinished novel.

"I hear—from another of your devoted admirers—that you are looking tired. There is nothing so restful—or so distressingly dull—as a regular bread & butter job. Your present way of life, while far more remunerative than mine for example, probably resembles it in discovering that it is harder, while pleasanter & more exciting, to do your own work than the other man's. Yet that—my own work—is precisely what I am fervently pining for at present. To do no work at all—except the other woman's, the dear classic dishwashing, dinner-cooking woman—is incomparably the hardest.

"Did we not make a mistake in our youth—which was so very nearly contemporaneous—in becoming what Miss Sinclair & the Peterboro servants call *creators?* What a noble shoemaker—to choose a trade at random, or because shoemakers are always liberals—would not you have made, & I how excellent at contriving artificial flowers or the peepshow scenes inside Easter eggs! You will say that these also savour of creation, but our present trouble—if indeed your impeccable admirableness will accept the word—springs from our stubborn attempt to utilize our wretched minds, to make unpleasant greyish convolutions work for us instead of trained & agile fingertips & the beautiful rhythmic strength of habit. 'How lovely is benign stupidity!' as no one really ever wrote.

"Two years ago the New Republic would have had a poem from me on this subject; now you must put up with a dull letter. It is hard on you, dear Carl, & I hope it is hard on the New Republic."

The Benét children went to California to live with their aunt Kathleen Norris, and Elinor Wylie finished the Orphan Angel, sitting up all night to write the last words in a flat in Bank Street and the next day sailing for Europe. Her novel, selected by the Book-of-the-Month Club, brought her more money than she could have expected to earn by her precise and delicate art. She spent what she was afraid was a guilty share of it for Shelley letters. This was paper his hand had touched. This was ink that had come from his sacred pen. She loved Shelley. He would have loved her if he had known her. They loved each other. She fiercely defended him once when I said I sometimes found his self-pity tiresome. She wrote her sonnets A Red Carpet for Shelley. She wrote essays about him and a short story, A Birthday Cake for Lionel—Lionel who is in effect Shiloh ten years older. Returning to England in 1925, ten years after she had left it, she thought of herself as almost Shelley, perhaps a friend of Shelley, returning to England ten or so years after Shelley's death in Italy. From this came Mr. Hodge and Mr. Hazard, her fourth novel. It had its origin, she told me, in two words spoken by a stupid man from Oxford, who, hearing she was writing sonnets to Shelley, muttered "Poor Shelley." She heard him. Her revenge was to pillory him as Mr. Hodge, who in the novel hears that Mr. Hazard is writing a sonnet to Milton, and says "Poor Milton."

During her last three years Elinor Wylie lived—with summers in England—in a flat in Ninth Street, her drawing-room dominated by its memorable silver mirror and her study at the back as austere as her style. Nobody worked harder than she. Four novels and four books of verse in seven years are proof enough. But her evenings were free, and she had countless friends. There were of course many Elinor Wylies. I can claim to know only one of them.

My Elinor Wylie had as sure and strong an intelligence as I have ever known. It was impossible to bring up an idea that she had not had or did not instantly understand. It was impossible to bring out a fact that did not fit into something she already knew. No formal scholar, she had a scholar's instinct for exactness. She could not be comfortable imagining steamboats on the Ohio in 1822 unless she knew they had been there, or imagining a volume of Plato into Mr. Hazard's pocket in 1833 unless she could find out that such pocket volumes then existed. She asked me the minutest questions. Had I ever come across any account of a frontier blue-stocking who might be a model for one of the women who courted Shiloh on his travels? I had, in A New Home—Who'll Follow? She was sorry that the book was about Michigan and a time later than 1822, but she used it, transforming what she used.

"This young lady," Caroline Matilda Stansbury Kirkland had written of Eloise Fidler, "was not as handsome as she fain would have been, if I may judge by the cataracts of ash-coloured ringlets which shaded her cheeks, and the exceeding straitness of the stays which restrained her somewhat exuberant proportions. . . . Her dress was in the height of fashion, and all her accoutrements *point device*. A gold pencil-case of the most delicate proportions was suspended by a kindred chain around a neck which might be called whity-brown; and a note-book of corresponding lady-likeness was peeping from the pocket of her highly-useful apron of blue silk—ever ready to secure a passing thought or an elegant quotation. Her album—she was just the person to have an album—was resplendent in gold and satin, and the verses

which meandered over its emblazoned pages were of the
most unexceptionable quality, overlaid with flowers and gems
—love and despair. . . .

"Miss Fidler wrote her own poetry, so that she had ample
employment for her time while with us in the woods. It was
unfortunate that she could not walk out much on account
of her shoes. She was obliged to make out with diluted inspiration. The nearest approach she usually made to the study
of Nature, was to sit on the wood-pile, under a girdled tree,
and there, with her gold pencil in hand, and her 'eyne, gray as
glas,' rolled upwards, poefy by the hour.

"And, standing marvel of Montacute, no guest at morning
or night ever found the fair Eloise ungloved. Think of it! In
the very wilds to be always like a cat in nutshells, alone useless where all were so busy. . . . And then her shoes! 'Saint
Crispin Crispianus' never had so self-sacrificing a votary. No
shoemaker this side of New York could make a sole papery
enough; no tannery out of France could produce materials
for this piece of exquisite feminine foppery."

Now Elinor Wylie's version in the Orphan Angel:

"Miss Rosalie Lillie was seated upon the woodpile in an
attitude of negligent grace; her fine eyes were fixed above
the distant tamarack-trees in contemplation of some winged
chimæra of the mind. A gold pencil-case was suspended by
a delicate chain around the lady's creamy throat; a notebook
peeped out from the pocket of her blue satin apron, and a
gilded album lay within reach. Under a furred cloak her at-
tire was frail and silken; she wore thin-soled bronze slippers,
and her hands were encased in gloves of primrose kidskin.

"Miss Lillie was a singularly lovely girl; her features were
regular and her figure tall and classically formed. She had
a rich abundance of chestnut hair and her velvet eyes were

the color of purple-brown pansies. She looked very expensive and unsuitable against a background of enormous forest trees and ragged rail fences; the smoky November sun picked out the Italian cameo upon her bosom and increased the splendid damask of her cheek."

The document wanders, the work of art marches. One stroke, and the lady is mounted upon her woodpile. Another, and she is contemplating some winged chimæra of the mind, not merely rolling her eyes. Stroke by stroke, the portrait is laughingly perfected. Kind epithets increase the lady's beauty. Her useless shoes become thin-soled bronze slippers. Her nondescript gloves appear as primrose kidskin. Her merely gray eyes turn to the color of purple-brown pansies. She is no longer the object of homespun ridicule. If she looks very expensive and unsuitable against her background of trees and fences, that may not be, the overtones imply, entirely her fault, but partly the fault of nature for being so vast and of the works of man for being so small and mean.

What Elinor Wylie did with Eloise Fidler in making her over into Miss Rosalie Lille she did with all the subjects of her art, and, for that matter, with her life. She both wrote and spoke with a lovely, amused formality which baffled the downright. But life had two or three times got out of hand with her, and had been tragic. She could never forget that. It kept alive the perpetual contradictions of her nature. She was a woman who had beauty and genius. Beauty compelled her and genius compelled her, both of them without always giving her simple motives for her compulsions. Doubly driven, she was doubly sensitive. Two careers side by side in one woman. No wonder she often seemed ruthless, often hysterical, habitually bewildering. Within a few moments she could be suspicious and ingenuous, insolent and tender, capricious and steadfast, desperate and hilarious, stirringly profound and exquisitely superficial.

And there was her vanity, which might have been unendurable if she had not so freely admitted it and laughed about it. Before her sister Nancy Hoyt came from Washington Elinor Wylie made me promise—and everybody else, I suppose—that I would faithfully tell her if I thought Nancy more beautiful than she. Once when Jacqueline Embry of Kentucky was visiting in New York I took her to call. Elinor Wylie could hardly wait to ask her guest to show her bronze hair and let it be compared with Elinor Wylie's own. At a large dinner a strange and tactless Russian woman said: "Mrs. Benét, I have heard you were not really beautiful, but I think you are." Elinor Wylie, disregarding the present compliment, wept that anybody could ever have said that she was not beautiful. One evening at a large party at Dreiser's studio she felt herself neglected. She could not bear being less than first in any company. Nothing on earth would do but that a few of her close friends should join her in another room and hear her read some poems—say some poems, as she always put it. Her friends humored her in such tantrums of vanity, and went to all lengths in flattering her. She liked flattery as much as a lizard likes the sun. "How can she take it," Jacqueline Embry asked me, "in such spoonfuls? Even if it is the very best butter?" Perhaps the friends who humored and flattered her the most were sometimes bored by her vain tantrums. I know I was, though I admired and adored her.

In June 1928 when I arrived in London Elinor Wylie was already there, living in her tiny house in Chelsea. She had asked me to meet her the first evening at Osbert Sitwell's, where she was to be. Barely off the boat, I misjudged the occasion, which was for Sunday evening, and did not dress. The whole evening was spoiled for her by my improper tweeds—or so it seemed. "But you did bring evening clothes, didn't you? I am giving you a party this week, and I've already asked everybody to meet you, and I can't bear to have you come in this brown coat." I told her I should not think of wearing it, but she would not be reassured, as she did not listen. "Please don't wear the brown coat to my party." She made me think of an anxious young girl who had planned something that was to be very grown-up and correct and was afraid that one of her guests might treat it as if it were for children.

Her house in Chelsea when I got there was in total confusion over water streaming from a broken pipe. She had writers not plumbers for dinner. After I had telephoned the water company for an emergency repairman, she forgave me my mistake of Sunday evening. "Nobody but an American," she announced with fantastic extravagance, "would have known what to do. And no American but Carl would have known how to do it in London." I felt like a disconcerted elder brother in the face of his sister's bragging.

When the others left she asked me to stay behind to hear her say some new poems she had written. They were sonnets, she told me. So, sitting in her Chelsea drawing-room, I heard a dozen or so of the nineteen sonnets which she later called One Person, and which belong to the supreme love poetry in English or in any language. I heard them, and I read them, too much moved to notice that one of them lacked a line. In her passion she had lost count. It was as strange in her, most accurate poet, as if she had forgotten to tend her hair or hands.

At first reticent and watchful while I heard and read, she was quickly warmed by my excitement over the poems, threw off her secrecy, and—then and at a later dinner in Soho—told me the story behind them. I must know the whole story, she said. There was a man—she told me his name—whom at last she loved absolutely. To me she did not make him sound glorious, though she tried. All the glory was in her. She had never been in love before, she was sure. She had only been loved. "I have believed me obdurate and blind To those sharp ecstasies the pulses give: The clever body five times sensitive I never have discovered to be kind." This in one of her sonnets. In her speech, the same thing in troubled yet exultant prose. Now at last the pulses had wakened in her blood and her senses leapt. Little enough had actually come of it. Jealous circumstances had kept the lovers apart, and they had been alone only in a forest. Three trysts: "And afterwards," she said, "you won't believe it, but we realized that we had met under an oak, an ash, and a thorn." Little could ever come of it. She would not disrupt her life again. This must remain a radiant experience of the mind. But it did not belong solely to her mind. It was flesh too, and it tore at her. She cried out against the cruel separation. "I don't want much. I don't expect it. I could be satisfied if I could know that sometime, maybe when we are very old, we could spend the same night under one roof. It would not have to be together. Only under the same roof, peacefully. Is that too much to expect? Don't you think I could dare to hope for that?" I soothed her as well as I could, but she was overwhelmed by the most shaking emotion I ever saw in her. Even Shelley could not help her: "A woman by an archangel befriended.   Now must I end the knightly

servitude Which made him my preserver, and renounce
That heavenly aid forever and forever."

Love is what it means to the lover, not to the bystander,
and I could not question the reality of the tempest which
wracked her. All that she had written in the sonnets she said,
in rushing sentences. "And am I not your child who has
come home? And am I not your hound for faithfulness?"
At last, she said, she had learned to feel humble and obedient.
"O dear my lord, believe me that I know How far your
virtues have outnumbered mine." She herself was nothing
beside him, who had borne everything. "The little beauty
that I was allowed"—what was that to his "degree of noble
and of fair"? How could she deserve, how comfort him?
"How is it possible that this hand of clay Though white as
porcelain, can contrive a touch So delicate it shall not hurt
too much? What voice can my invention find to say So
soft, precise, and scrupulous a world You shall not take it
for another sword?" "To educate me fitly for your bride"
an eternity might be enough. In the meantime let him be
patient with her. Let him make what use of her he could,
though he only set her like a timber in his house to "bear a
little more than I can bear." Her words rushed and tumbled, and her eyes were wild. She was as pale as a priestess
at the mercy of her oracle, flaming through her.

I never saw her alive again, and I remember her best for
these perfect sonnets and her broken commentary. What she
and the sonnets together said was that this final love had
come to her like first love, and had dissolved her to her
youngest elements, but that she was no less a poet than before, and she could instinctively find ripe, skillful words for
emotions which ordinarily go no further than sighs and
tears, timid raptures and pitiful despairs. For once in the

world, youth knew and age could. The heart of sixteen spoke
with the tongue of forty.

I went to Paris and Cannes for a summer among the expatriates. I heard mysteriously about her that she had had
a fall and had hurt herself, but could get no more detailed
news. Back in New York, I still heard only uncertain rumors.
She had had a stroke, the rumors said, and one side of
her face was paralyzed. Her friends could not believe she
would ever survive disfigurement. When, in December, she
came home, I did not go at once to see her, but telephoned
her and asked when I might. This would allow her to choose
the time, or to put it off indefinitely. She said she was not
well and was very busy but that she must see me early in the
coming week. She died that Sunday night, as swiftly as
the curtain falls after a tragedy.

Tragedy and triumph. Now she would have to drag out
no long old age, beauty fading, strength fraying. Her end
was as neat as her art. Perhaps she had been beaten in that
early career from which she had turned, at thirty-five, to
poetry, but she had outlived her defeats. No poet of her
time would be longer remembered, and no woman. In her
last scene the poet and the woman in her had shared a
triumph beyond which neither could hope to go. Lift the
trumpets upon this peroration. Let the black curtain fall.

Her dead face was lovely and serene and proud. Those
who were to miss her most took their tone from her, as
they had when she was alive, and bore themselves grace-
fully as well as seriously at her funeral. Death became her,
and they could not wish for her a life which she might not
herself desire. The lives of the immortals are not measured
by their fevered years.

A young man was speaking softly. He was Philip Hichborn, he said, her son. He had been brought up to think she was evil, a mother who had recklessly left her child. Two years ago, in England, he had gone to see her. (She had told me about that. He had come to see her, and had been silent, and had hated her, she thought.) Now he was saying that when he had seen her he had believed her beautiful and magical, and had not known what to say or how to say it. He was sure she had thought he did not love her. But he did, at sight. He had since then read her books and had found out all he could about her, and he had determined that this Christmas he would visit her again. At last they would be mother and son. "And now it is like this." There is no death quite complete. However it ties its ultimate knot, some loose strand dangles in the wind of life.

III THIRD WORLD: NEW WORLD?

Boom
Depression
Resolution

Boom

HISTORY is written by the survivors. It is they who look back along the tangled line of the past and see all roads leading to their present. They may remember the lost and dead with tragic pity or with romantic grace. But Greeks not Trojans tell the story of Troy, and Normans not Britons the story of Arthur and his knights, and white men not red the story of the American aborigines. When there is no pity or grace, there is generally self-congratulation. We are alive, and this is how it came about. Memory justifies the survivors. Remembering what choices they made, they feel successful. Memory simplifies. Forgetting the blind confusion in which they chose, they do not see how they could have chosen differently. If the thing is so obvious now, it must have been more or less obvious then. The surviving historian of events in which he had a part wonders why he did not see the changes that were just ahead, and often believes he did. Not content to be a historian, he may claim that he was once a prophet.

I have lived in three worlds one after another, and in none of them did I foresee the next nor the catastrophe which marked the change.

Not till after the outbreak of the war, which surprised me and everybody I knew well, did we realize that there had been an unusual peace. When it was gone we valued it. The most seductive argument in favor of making war was that

this would be the end of wars and would secure peace forever. Though the peace which followed the war looked dangerous to grave observers, not many people were grave about
it. At first they danced in the streets, and then they went on
dancing, less madly but not much more thoughtfully. The
new peace was flushed and prosperous. Though both the
flush and the prosperity were false, they came to seem as
natural as the peace before the war. One President of the
United States called them a return to normalcy. Another
President saw in them the revival of the homespun habits
of industry and thrift. A third President was sure that they
had come to stay. Let the people eat chicken. Millions of
them ate it. Prices and wages were high, the standards of
living higher. Credit was the very air. Buy now—a house,
an automobile, a radio—and pay later. Do not put off en-
joying the things you ought to have. The salesman was the
serpent in this Eden. It was merit, he argued, to run into
debt: enterprise and courage. It cost only fifty dollars a year
to owe a thousand dollars and have a thousand dollars'
worth of goods and satisfactions. If men waited till they
could pay outright for what they wanted, they merely did
without it. Better to commit themselves at once and then
force themselves to save and pay. Sooner or later the matter
of payment would have taken care of itself. Sooner or later.
Almost nobody worried about the duration of this era of
easy credit. It would continue under its own power, indefinitely.

When you drive from Chicago west toward Denver you
may not realize, at sight of the first Rockies, how high above
sea level you already are. The continent is tilted under you
and you have been climbing an imperceptible slope to the
foothills. So Americans, riding the boom toward the crash,

were most of them unaware. And many of them, even when Wall Street suddenly became a slaughter-house, were far from seeing that this was more than a temporary episode. A day or two after it I arrived in Kansas City and Logan Clendening met me at the train. I suppose he had lost money, and I know I had. But we spoke of the affair as one of many amusing things we had to talk about: only one of many, and not the end of a world.

2

THE late twenties were a golden time for writers. It is true that no books were sold as the historical novels of the turn of the century had been. Old-fashioned publishers often asked me, hopefully, if I saw signs of a return of history to fiction. They thought history could turn the old trick if it were given a chance, and they seemed not to understand that the movies and the radio and cheap motors and good roads had changed the reading habits of the nation. But many books were sold, and more different books sold widely every year than ever before in America. The Book-of-the-Month Club and the Literary Guild alone called for two new books each month, as many, in the best years, as seventy thousand copies of some of them. This meant that two dozen writers every year had from the book clubs what amounted to prizes of several thousand dollars each in addition to their ordinary earnings, which might be further increased by larger sales through the bookstores. There were smaller clubs for Catholic, scientific, and religious books. There were various annual literary prizes, the most notable those of the Pulitzer committee, all of which made books conspicuous in the newspapers. Individual publishers held prize competitions. Magazines gave frequent prizes for poems, stories, articles. And no writer knew when his book might not be profitably sold to Hollywood.

All this of course was business as well as literature. New men were in the field that had been sedately cultivated by the older publishers. New publishers watched for new writers and sought them out with contracts in their hands. It was enough to say of a book that it was a first novel, and many a first novel was published by many a writer who never wrote a second. Established writers were the game of rival publishers, who no longer let each other's writers alone, as formerly, but now lured them away if they could. They promised greater sales, wider publicity, handsomer books, and richer advances. Publishers were willing to take risks. Volume after volume of minor poetry appeared, as much because there were more publishers than usual as because there were more poets. Articles that should have been left in the newspapers and magazines that first printed them were collected into books. Eccentric and special works of erudition reached a curious public that in different times would have never heard of them. There was a lively traffic in first and limited editions for collectors who were willing to lay their books away unopened—in mint state, dust wrapper and all—to rise in value. Contemporary manuscripts and autographs brought good prices. Even the fashionable world heard of writers, and Park Avenue asked them to dinner.

For writers this was a dangerous prosperity. They got in the way of living, while they wrote, on money which their publishers had advanced in the hope that their books would earn it. Having written a book, a writer, having spent his advance, had at once to get more money and begin another book. If a book did not sell as well as the publisher had expected, he was likely to blame the writer not himself. If the book sold better, the writer seldom looked upon it as a windfall, but changed his scale of living as if every year could now be counted on to bring him in as much. In either case the writer was making himself trouble for the future. I reflected that writers were like the farmers I had known, living on what they were to have and thinking themselves better off than they were.

Writers were only a part of literary society in New York. Besides publishers there were also editors and agents, and a swarm of hangers-on and camp-followers. Literature was a local industry as in no other American city. Literature was news. Literature was gossip. The columnists wrote as often about new books as about any other single topic. Newspapers and magazines, with an eye to book advertisements, gave space to book reviews. The leading reviewers had influence, or were thought to have it, and were courted by publishers. Most of the reviewers were honest enough, though they might not know much about literature and might fall into loose enthusiasms over books which were better than the daily run. Reviewers had a professional standing and the best of them were touchily independent of advertisers. Sometimes they were so independent of writers that their reviews had less to do with the books in hand than with their own ideas.

I have often wondered why it is that the only reviews which ever give instant delight are the ferocious or feline ones, like—to take recent instances—Michael Gold's of Thornton Wilder or Dorothy Parker's of Christopher Morley. Readers who have enjoyed the books reviewed or who have not read them and know nothing about the issue are equally pleased by the critical assault. It is not quite like watching a fight. Rather, it is like watching a public execution, and it seems to fascinate. But the sympathy of the reader is almost never with the writer. Is it simple sadism? Or is it a kind of latent envy which the inarticulate feel toward the articulate? All men want to speak and be listened to. Most men cannot. Writers have an unfair advantage. When a writer is put at a disadvantage it is poetic justice.

The boom times in literature saw the rise of the literary tea. Suppose a publisher was about to issue a new book which he thought important or promising. He would give a party, at his offices or at a hotel, late some afternoon. Such parties were called teas because liquor was then illegal, but tea, if served at all, was always neglected for the cocktails and highballs which New York never thought of giving up during prohibition. The guests invited were friends of the writer and the publisher, and the reviewers, with the inevitable hangers-on. Except for the writer and publisher all literary teas were alike. The same guests came at about the same hour, had the same drinks and canapés, talked with the same persons on more or less the same subjects, swirled around the room at the same drifting velocity, got more and more talkative under the same stimulus, and left for the same trains or the same engagements elsewhere. In the busiest seasons there would be two or three teas a week, possibly one every day. I do not believe that any one of them ever did any real good to a book, but they did no harm and they held the literary profession together in a compact society.

Teas had less to do with the profession than with the business of literature, and nothing with the art. The artists seldom went there except when they had new books to be

celebrated. They kept to themselves, working hard, and preferring a few friends to many acquaintances. Writers who do
not happen to be friends meet no oftener than other men
of a given calling. I have had as wide a knowledge of American writers as any man of my day, and yet I have never
even seen George Santayana, Edith Wharton, Allen Tate,
Ernest Hemingway, Clarence Day, Ezra Pound, T. S. Eliot,
Robinson Jeffers, Gertrude Stein, Scott Fitzgerald, Hart
Crane, Booth Tarkington, or George Ade. I have seen none
of these writers more than once or twice: Edna St. Vincent
Millay, Eugene O'Neill, Ring Lardner, Vachel Lindsay,
Erskine Caldwell, William Faulkner, Clifford Odets, Thorn-
ton Wilder, Michael Gold, S. N. Behrman, Laurence Stal-
lings, Elizabeth Madox Roberts, James T. Farrell, Upton
Sinclair. Nor any of these more than a dozen times: James
Branch Cabell, H. L. Mencken, Theodore Dreiser, Willa
Cather, Joseph Hergesheimer, Robert Frost, Edgar Lee Mas-
ters, Amy Lowell, Carl Sandburg, Sherwood Anderson, John
Dos Passos, E. E. Cummings, Thomas Wolfe, Van Wyck
Brooks, Thomas Beer, Logan Clendening, Maxwell Ander-
son, Robert E. Sherwood, William Beebe, Glenway Wescott,
Waldo Frank, Pearl S. Buck, Carl Becker, Sidney Howard,
Ellen Glasgow, George S. Kaufman, William Allen White,
Zona Gale. With many of these I have long been good friends.
Writers do not need to be forever talking face to face to know
each other. Their writings are conversations, and when they
meet they go on talking from where they left off reading.

Not all writers were prosperous during the boom. Literature perpetually has its Grub Street for those who have not
yet succeeded, for those who never will, for those whose
vogue has passed. But in the last years of the twenties there
were many writers in New York, not merely the more pop-

ular novelists and playwrights, who could afford flats in town, plain farmhouses in Connecticut, and summers every year or so in France where francs were cheap. If you sat in July before any cafe in Montparnasse you might see anybody you knew in Greenwich Village and not be surprised. Or on the Croisette at Cannes. Or in the gambling rooms of Monte Carlo. There was gambling at home. Suddenly in the winter of 1928-29 writers were chattering about Wall Street. Money without work. They put their capital in stocks and watched it grow. One writer I knew inherited ten thousand dollars, gave up writing, played at buying and selling, and had enough—on paper—to think he was losing fifteen times that amount when finally he lost it all. I heard somebody tell Edwin Arlington Robinson how to make a hundred percent on his money. He said he would rather keep what he had. "You buy this stock," a broker said to me at a party, "and hold on to it. It is selling at fifty now, and it will go to a thousand." I bought some at fifty, sold a part of it, to the broker's disgust, at a little over a hundred, and for the rest was glad to get anything I could. The world was upside down, and rich men were imagining more greedily and wildly than beggars.

3

NOTHING is so hard to remember as a fever. Not only have its fantasies and distortions gone but they seem to have taken a part of the memory away with them. We remember some of the things we thought—if it was thinking—but not how or why they came and went through our minds. Then they made a kind of mad sense. Now they have lost it, and when we try to recall them we cannot be sure that any form they take may not be supplied by our later and other selves.

In 1925 I had for twenty years seldom worked less than twelve hours a day, and often more. I did not regard such industry as a virtue because I knew it was a passion. It was a passion in three parts. One part of me had been student and teacher and editor, to make my living. Another had been a scholar, to gratify my curiosity. A third had been a writer, to fulfill a restless instinct. This last I always had a guilty sense of neglecting. Classes must be met, issues of magazines must be got out, works of scholarship must be ready when promised. But writing, it seemed, could wait.

I would not let it wait, I resolved in 1925 when I was forty, but would give up the Century, be an editor no longer, and write. That year I published, besides the textbook written with Mark and a small book on James Branch Cabell, the volume of stories and sketches Other Provinces at which I had hinted in the final words of Many Minds the year before: "His fourth volume of more or less formal criticism being now completed, he plans, so far as it may be permitted him, to withdraw to other provinces."

"Just now," I wrote, "I am tired of authors. The documents they offer me are at once too voluminous and too explicit. By their volume they tell me a great deal more than I need to be told. By their explicitness they tell me a great deal that I do not care to reveal. If I had been disposed to make a wanton use of secrets, I could have started a dozen scandals. Being in no way thus disposed, I have been discreet. Discretion of this kind, however, suggests to me the hunting done by princes: the game is rarely savage and the sport is invariably public. To engage in it you do not have to get up at unpleasant hours or go to outrageous places or run the risk of disappointment or danger. The whole enterprise has rules as definite as those of a court function. Well, an author is public quarry, and a critic, though not precisely a prince, is bound to observe the regulations. And as a prince must now and then want to get away from the royal beaters and try his luck in the open field, so a critic now and then wants to leave all books behind and fix his scrutiny upon men and women whom he can study without seeing them through a medium already prepared. I am such a critic and I have temporarily forgotten the rules."

Everybody praised these sketches, nobody bought the book. The same thing was true of The Ninth Wave, my one novel, published the next year. I was amused and irritated by the efforts of friends and reviewers to find autobiography in it: amused when they were wrong, irritated when they were right. The story was not autobiographical except that in it I had tried to imagine what my life would have been if I had not stayed in New York but had gone back to the University of Illinois and remained there as professor. Two or three of the characters were more or less from life, but not their actions. Where I drew most upon my own experience was in the account of those moments in which Kent Morrow finds certain of his ideas turning suddenly into convictions. These had all been my moments, my ideas, my convictions, before I ascribed them to him.

I should have liked the accident and triumph of success for The Ninth Wave, but though I was disappointed I was still a critic. Whatever art I had, or had shown in the book, was too low-voiced to be heard far. I thought of my closest successful friends. Ludwig Lewisohn could utter the pain and rebellion in his heart, raising it to something universal. I could not put pain into words, but, at least in public, had to hide it with an Indian silence. Sinclair Lewis was more swiftly sensitive than I. A novelist, he told me once, had to feel strong attraction or antipathy at sight for people or he could not represent them with the necessary force. I had too often a Dutch indifference to persons or situations unless they crowded or actually threatened me. Elinor Wylie had a nimble mind which assembled a beautiful multitude of images to enrich her prose. I had a gaunt ardor for lucidity and wanted my style to be always like air or water. And after all, men take air and water for granted unless they need them worse than they would ever need a novel of mine. Art must not be too low-voiced. If it is, it amounts to no more than reverie in the artist and might as well not have been offered to the world.

But I was disappointed that my ventures into other provinces had interested so few, and I was not one of those happy writers who console themselves with thinking that their work is too good for many readers. Writing, I saw, would not be enough for me to live by. And it did not fill my days. When I had written all morning I had energy left over that called for action. Harold Guinzburg came, late in the summer of 1926, to Cornwall with his plans for the Literary Guild, and before he left I had agreed to be its editor. Back to the workbench, I grumbled, more relieved than discontented.

What followed was a year of such activity that for the first time in my life I seldom thought of writing. I wrote two chapters of a large history of American literature for which I had signed a contract and taken an advance—to pay a debt for my father—and then wrote no more. Plenty of scholars before me had thought business a nuisance and then found it a fine excitement, but I had of course to find it out for

myself. This was movement. As a writer I sat solitary at a
desk, originating whatever came to me. But as a man of business I sat more often judging things that had arisen outside
of me and came for my decision. They never left me alone.
A scholar could step aside and meditate. His pace was his
own. But in business a man had his pace set for him by outward events and must keep up with them or be overrun.

The pace of this business was the helter-skelter of the
boom. As it increased it changed my whole tempo. I no
longer spent deliberate mornings in my study but hurried
to my office to see what was happening. There were long
lunches and argumentative afternoons. In the evening I was
keyed too high to settle down. The boom had brought the
speakeasy to its noisy, smoky, alcoholic eminence. It will not
be believed, but it is true, that I had never been in one before
the first day of 1927. After that I slipped more and more into
the current formula for a New York day. After work, somewhere for cocktails. When the party broke up there would
be several persons who had no further plans, and thought,
thanks to cocktails, that they could not bear to separate.
They would rush off somewhere else to dinner, in an oblig-
ing speakeasy, eat if they could, drink more than they should,
and talk forever and forever. I had a head for liquor, when
I took it, but I was always bored by drinking. Drinkers rarely
say amusing things. What they say seems amusing only to
other drinkers. The fun of alcohol is less on the tongue than
in the ear. But the speakeasies were the essences and centers
of those hectic times, and there I wasted long nights without
realizing how long they were.

What I see now never occurred to me then: that I had
worked too hard for too many years and needed a holiday.
I took the holiday without realizing what it was. The times

prescribed, not quiet days in the country, but stirring nights in town. Let the driven brain relax. Let it open itself to the sensations that poured round and over it. Work could wait. When I was forty I had gone to a doctor for a physical examination. He put his stethoscope to my heart, listened, and then said: "Bring this back again in a hundred years and I may be able to do something for you." I assumed an eternity ahead of me to work in. I could always work when I had to be alone. In this lively company I would loaf and be at ease. Spend time, not hoard it.

Reasonable as I now make it sound, I was then not reasoning. My holiday was a headstrong flight from the forms by which I had lived. I went less frequently to Urbana than I had been used to. Though I sank money in my father's troubled affairs I did not bother to understand them thoroughly, nor Frank's, which were involved, and I did not guess that the depression among the farmers would be repeated in New York. I seldom saw Guy, busy in Detroit. Paul, married in 1925 to Jessie Hess of Wilmette, was a broker in Chicago and came several times a year on business to New York. Otherwise I might not have seen him. I saw Mark at odd times, and my own children fitfully. I drifted from some of my old friends and made new ones. I went Friday afternoons to lecture at Columbia, but the University was almost as remote as Hope. I spent a whole idle summer in Var and the Alpes Maritimes. From Cannes in a light car I explored the coast from Toulon to Ventimiglia and inland to the hill towns growing out of their rocks. From my terrace in the sun I could see the citadel on Ste. Marguerite where the Man in the Iron Mask had lived with his secret. A little further lay St. Honorat and the monastery once famous throughout Christendom for its learning.

Neither interested me so much as Grasse for its perfumes, and Monte Carlo. Then in February to Nassau with Alice and Harold Guinzburg. Days on the coral beach of Hog Island, nights at roulette. Caring nothing for games of skill, I delighted in the sly ins and outs of chance. Anything might happen. Time began all over with each spin of the wheel, each clattering of the ball. No past with its burden. No future with its threat. Now, now, now the wheel spun and the ball clattered and the lucky number leapt out of its unfathomable, unpredictable mystery. As soon as the number came you wondered why you had not known it a second before, and yet about the next number, an instant off, you were as ignorant as if it were a thousand years away. Life on a hair-line. Life by the split-second. But I was a wary gambler. I bet on the numbers of my daughters' ages—eight, eleven, thirteen—for I knew that one number was as good as another, and I stubbornly quit a winner, even of small sums, as often as I lost. It was chance that excited me, not money. After too much order and system, after too much planning and foresight, I welcomed pure and arbitrary chance.

What I remember best from the last years of the boom is mathematics and music: the mathematics of roulette, the music of popular songs. I had never gone much to the theater. Now I went constantly. Most of the plots have sunk out of sight in my memory, but any number of songs still run along my nerves. It was at a party that I first heard Water Boy. I was sitting in a crowded room talking to Paul Robeson. Somebody asked him if he would sing. He got up, stood so close to me that my head was only a foot or so from his diaphragm, and sang. This was not merely a throat singing. It was a great body living a song. Was it only my

fancy that I heard a race remembering? Millions of black
voices moaning and laughing? They had come down through
time gathering power until they flooded America. The best
American music had sprung from them. I was not Negro,
but I was American, and these ancient black voices were in
some dim way a part of me too. They were a part of Jerome
Kern, composing Ol' Man River. I heard Show Boat a few
days after it opened. Ol' Man River was already a classic,
neither new nor old. No, it must be old. Listening, I could
not believe I had not always known it. Some day I would
remember. Now the words and music did more than run
along my nerves. They swept through me, blood and bone.
Men planted, men sweat and strained, men got weary and
sick, tired of life and afraid of death, but the river rolled
on, silent, surviving them. Here was a cool halt for peace in
the midst of a feverish, dissolving time.

Depression

IN THE midst of the general depression each man had a depression of his own.

I did not foresee the crash of October 1929, but by April of that year I had come to feel, not understand, a deep trouble and division in my mind. If this were fiction I could account for all that happened to me. I might say that the death of Elinor Wylie—the first person I had seen dead since I left Hope—touched me with a cold thought of mortality. I might tell how private passions and treasons wounded me. I might, even, claim to have been a prophet who saw catastrophe at hand. But, since this is history, I can point to none of these things alone. All of them together are not enough. I turned aside because the times were dissolving, and I, premonitorily, with them.

I felt the change begin as irritation. There were too many parties in the winter of 1928-29, too many meetings of the same people in the same places, saying the same things. Gradually, then suddenly, I was tired of them. Irritation became disgust at the counterfeit high spirits, the headless activity. I had a revulsion from alcohol. What was the matter with people's minds that they had to do so much to rouse them? What was the matter with people's minds in general? On every side a noisy sterility. The good writers were men and women still, but the little writers and the hangers-on were a race of mules. They had, like mules, the impulse to

create but no power to do it. Frustrate, they were wilful
and envious. Often intelligent, they used their wits only to
deny. They did nothing, but they sneered at those who did.
They suspected any generosity or heroism or devotion. Above
all, they distrusted and feared the common life. Life was
terrible, they said over and over, refusing to specify or to
distinguish. It sounded to me as foolish as if they had said,
without specifying or distinguishing, that all was right with
the world.

My disgust was not for particular persons. It was worse
than that. It was a general soreness, as if my skin had worn
away and left my nerves bare. Because I had heavy work
to do, I could not irresponsibly escape. I had no philosophical antipathy to mankind, and I thought of such antipathies
as sickness. I did not want to yield and run. By main strength
I held out till my soreness had become a sickness too. Then,
almost without planning it, on a day's decision, I found a
penthouse and turned hermit.

If this were fiction I might say that I went into a retreat
to think things out. It still is history. I have never in my
life thought things out, nor have I known anybody who
ever did. I have always had to live them out, thinking as
I went along. In my penthouse I was less a philosopher than
a bear licking his wounds while nature healed them.

Penthouses are a legend. Mine was hardly more than a comfortable tent on a roof opposite my office. It was one large
room, and half its walls were windows. Though comfortable, it was a tent. In winter, when the steam was cut off
at night, the cold came through the thin walls and I had to
work in an overcoat or go to bed. In summer the sun made
the room an oven and I worked in next to nothing. But I
lived in the sun, which men in cities rarely think of, and I

could look at the stars—I seldom did—and observe the changes in the moon. I had perfect privacy, for I saw, on my own terms, only those I wanted to see.

Every afternoon I crossed the street to spend two or three hours at my office. Two or three hours, I had learned, are enough for any office. The rest of the time is wasted in argument for its own sake, without use. As editor I knew my mind, in the midst of whatever distractions, and I worked fast. Whoever had to see me could come while I was there. Whatever needed to be decided could wait till afternoon. If it could not, the telephone. I answered it during office hours, but at other times not unless I chose. Except for the work by which I lived my days were free.

Free for a solitude which had no map or calendar. Now was the time to empty out my mind, like cluttered pockets, and take stock of what I had. Now the time to review my learning. Now the time to understand myself and my life. Masterly processes, and all beyond me. I felt nothing clearly but a strong instinct to rid myself of tangible bondages. I resigned from clubs to which I no longer could bear to go. I gave up my class at Columbia after fourteen unbroken years. I sold off many of my books, in a rush of distaste: dust gathering more dust. Even the farm at Cornwall faded from my desires. I had built walls and fences, made and kept a garden every year, pruned trees or cut them down, dug ditches, set out hedges, trained vines, and in house and study been by turns mason, carpenter, painter, plasterer, plumber, glazier. I had felt rooted and mortised in the farm. All this sense left me, as in a paralysis. When, during the years of my hermitage, I went to Cornwall, the farm was strange and dim to me. I noticed the signs of my neglect, but I felt only pin-pricks of conscience.

Most of the time I stayed in New York, winter and summer. The hours of the day had ceased to matter. I got up when I naturally woke, worked, looked after my office, often spent my evenings alone, sometimes busy, sometimes in the ache of solitude, and went to sleep with the grateful thought that now for some hours I would not think or feel. I went to the movies with my daughters. I dined with my family or with a few friends. My friends were perhaps mystified but they were kind. Not one of them ever asked me why I lived alone, and only one ever asked me how I liked it. I had visitors, who dropped in at odd hours of the night. There must seem to be something priestly about a hermit, for I found them telling me the most secret things about themselves, men nearly as much as women. One night it was a man and woman, married but not to each other, who were running off to Reno and came to ask a blessing. If I had no visitors, and could not endure myself alone, I would go out and wander through the streets, determined not to come back till I had seen something incredible. One night I saw an elephant walking up Ninth Avenue with a red lantern at its tail to warn off traffic. If I were hungry I stopped and ate. I had fixed hours for food no more than for sleep.

But I could not be idle. I would write the life of Swift, that great solitary. Twenty years before, a student at Columbia, I had wanted to write about him but had given it up, baffled. Ever since I had thought of it as a thing I would some day undertake, and had made many notes. Now Swift rose in my imagination, substantial and alive, and compelled me. For four months I stopped working only long enough to keep an eye on my office and at intervals to eat and sleep. I would wake possessed, work till three, cross the street for two resented hours, come back and take a nap to get the office out of my mind, and work again, it might be till day-light. I finished the book on the day I had set for the end.

Though it was a life of Swift, it was also a tragedy which might have called its hero by some other name. Twenty years of reading about Swift had taught me less than a year's experience of solitude and silence. A biographer looks in his heart as a poet does. I had no thoroughgoing mis-anthropy in my nerves and had to guess at Swift's. I had to guess at the fury of his hate, which was out of my reach, and his will to rule, which was alien to me. But I understood his pride, his reserve, his directness, and his solitude. His story, as I saw it, was the story of a man of genius who failed when he tried most and succeeded when he tried least. No wonder he had been misjudged. He misjudged himself. But I wondered that so few of his biographers and critics had been willing to take him as he was. On all but two or three points he had been frank and explicit about himself. That was the difficulty. He had told the truth about his extraor-dinary self and had not been believed. It is easier to reject the extraordinary and fill in the ordinary. The truth is too strong and wild. Muffle it, sweeten it, round it out. I did my best not to do that. I told the story as it came and it shaped itself into a tragedy because it was one. Some other day I would write a biography which was a comedy. Frank-lin would be its hero: a man of genius who rightly judged himself and never failed, because he had a talent for success.

The collapse of Wall Street did not at once affect me, and my income in 1930 was larger than in 1929, and in 1931 larger still. My own depression was far more than simple economics. It was surfeit and lethargy, soreness and inert-ness together. In any company I grew restless and slipped away to be alone. But when I was alone, time settled down upon me and I was endlessly conscious of it. I could not forget it and hurry it. It ticked off its slow seconds with obtuse monotony. Except for the Swift I did no work under the compulsion of a theme. I had to drive myself, minute by minute, never sure when I would slump again into dejected brooding. I did not begin the Franklin as I had planned, but excused myself by writing, in one year, thirty introductions to books by other men. Like a savage, I would be fiercely active for a day or so, then sluggish for more days. I had lost the steady rhythm of civilized work.

I had no systematic thoughts but I had recurrent dreams. One dream, rather, in several forms. It was a dream of fear. I had never suffered from baseless fears, apprehensions, nightmares, and had never come nearer to them than in an occasional flicker of doubt that my good luck could last. Now fear visited my sleeping mind. Suddenly I would notice, dreaming, that there was a disorder in the sky. Any second there might be a collision fatal to the earth. I stood among innumerable men and women looking up in a hideous uncertainty. I knew no astronomical mathematics while I slept. All was mad chance. Special horrors emerged in different dreams. The moon lurched toward us and we waited for the unspeakable crash. Or a planet shot by, missing us but for a dreadful time shutting out the light of the sun and compressing the atmosphere till we could not breathe it. Or an obscene island—was I remembering Swift's Laputa? —hovered over us, with men fighting on it and falling bloodily over the edge. Sometimes the island had come out of space. Sometimes it was only a part of the earth which had detached itself and whirled away defying gravitation. Sometimes it was the act of men, a mammoth flight on impossible wings. But always there were strife and confusion on the island, in a malign parody of life on the earth. And always it was the sign of anarchy in the heavens, which had lost their order and obedience.

2

EVERY man watches his own weather. I saw the signs of the new time in its literature.

If governments, which use so many experts, were wiser, they would use experts to study and interpret the national literature which shows the national imagination working upon the national predicament. Writers need not be prophetic but they may be seismographic, recording tremors of opinion while they are still sensations to most people, finding the earliest clear words for roiled emotions. What writers begin to say, what they give up saying, what they emphasize, what they disregard, what they announce, what they assume: these are mental and moral news. They are guide-posts to history if not straw votes for the next election.

The older writers of the twenties seemed to be checked by the collapse of 1929. Sinclair Lewis, the most seismographic of them all, that year published Dodsworth, but it had been written before. Not for four years did he write another book, and not for six did he write as if he felt the groundswell of the age. Dreiser for two or three years concerned himself as much with his autobiography as with the world around him. Cabell, fifty in 1929, formally closed his long chronicle of Poictesme. Eugene O'Neill turned back to the ancient though modern story of Electra. Edwin Arlington Robinson, awarded the gold medal of the National Institute in 1929, went his old way. Mencken had collected so many American absurdities that the American Mercury began to resemble a museum: young men said they were post-Mencken. In 1929 A Farewell to Arms was in a sense a farewell to the expatriate decade: Ernest Hemingway and the other expatriates would soon come home. I met Thomas Wolfe just after Look Homeward, Angel, and he roared against the Americans who had wasted their years in Europe and had never noticed that America was magnificent.

After the dinner to Sinclair Lewis before he left for Sweden to receive the Nobel prize late in 1930 a few of his friends took him away to a smaller party. It was like old times, we said. He and I recalled another dinner in the days of Babbitt when three or four writers had been invited along with Leopold Stokowski and a tableful of musicians. Then Lewis, after dinner, organized an impromptu meeting of a Rotary Club. As chairman he introduced Mencken as General Pershing with a message from the Army, George Jean Nathan as a representative of the Ku Klux Klan, me as the bishop who had come to dignify the revels. Now he organized an hour on the radio, with a standing lamp for a microphone. I was the announcer and he was most of the entertainers. Like old times. The whole company had the odd sense that there were classics present. Writing books had been the day's work. Had some of the books got into history?

Lewis was conscious of this, as he always is of whatever may be in the minds of anybody near him. He told the Swedish Academy: "There are young Americans today who are doing such passionate and authentic work that it makes me sick to see that I am a little too old to be one of them." He mentioned names: Ernest Hemingway, Thomas Wolfe,

Thornton Wilder, John Dos Passos, Stephen Vincent Benét, Michael Gold, William Faulkner. "I salute them, with a joy in being not yet too far removed from their determination to give to the America that has mountains and endless prairies, enormous cities and lost far cabins, billions of money and tons of faith, to an America that is as strange as Russia and as complex as China, a literature worthy of her vastness."

The twenties had their classics and the Younger Generation had children of their own. The pendulum of the generations swings fast in literature, and a decade may bring revolutionary changes. The young after the war wanted to live freely. The young after the crash wanted to live at all. The villain in the drama of the twenties had been dullness. The villain of the thirties was poverty.

"Everywhere around me," Thomas Wolfe remembers in his Story of a Novel, "during those years, I saw the evidence of an incalculable ruin and suffering. My own people, the members of my own family, had been ruined, had lost all the material wealth and accumulation of a lifetime in what was called the 'depression.' And that universal calamity had somehow struck the life of almost every one I knew. Moreover, in this endless quest and prowling of the night through the great web and jungle of the city, I saw, lived, felt, and experienced the full weight of that horrible calamity.

"I saw a man whose life had subsided into a mass of shapeless and filthy rags, devoured by vermin; wretches huddled together for a little warmth in freezing cold squatting in doorless closets upon the foul seat of a public latrine within the very shadow, the cold shelter of palatial and stupendous monuments of wealth. I saw acts of sickening violence and cruelty, the menace of brute privilege, a cruel and corrupt authority trampling ruthlessly below its feet the lives of the poor, the weak, the wretched, and defenceless of the earth.

"And the staggering impact of this black picture of man's inhumanity to his fellow man, the unending repercussions of these scenes of suffering, violence, oppression, hunger, cold, and filth and poverty going on unheeded in a world in which the rich were still rotten with their wealth left a scar upon my life, a conviction in my soul which I shall never lose.

"And from it all, there has come as the final deposit, a burning memory, a certain evidence of the fortitude of man, his ability to suffer and somehow to survive. And it is for this reason that I shall always remember this black period with a kind of joy that I could not at that time have believed possible, for it was during this time that I lived my life through to a first completion, and through the suffering and labor of my own life came to share those qualities in the lives of people all around me."

Writers did not need to experience poverty to imagine it. It filled the imagination because it filled the air. Americans at large had been badly trained to face it. There had been hard times before, want and unemployment, but during a long era of prosperity they had come to be thought of—if thought of—as peculiar to certain seasons and occupations. This depression was almost universal. It was mass poverty. Following so sharply after the boom, it affected men as if the land had failed them and had started to sink below the sea. The bubble of easy credit had gone like any bubble. A man who had sometimes uneasily reflected that he owed more than he ought, but had dismissed it from his mind, now desperately saw that he owed more than he could ever pay or would ever own. Pay debts? He was not even sure he could buy food. Americans increasingly imagined the ex-

tremes of hunger and nakedness. William Faulkner might
have written novels if there had been no depression, but the
depression brought him many readers who once could not
have endured his brutal stories. Here was a whole society
that had lived too long at a depression level. The study of
it was a kind of dark anthropology. If all life should come
to this in a horrible collapse! Or if all life should establish
itself at the margin of existence and go on there forever, as
in the Chinese novels of Pearl Buck!

The prospect was intolerable. By 1932 many of the younger
writers in New York were communists or inclined to communism. Russia, at times confused with Utopia, had given
them an example and Karl Marx a set of precepts. Some
of them knew little about either Russia or Marx, but they
had found what seemed a way out of the American disorder. Marx charted a course of inevitable development. The
bourgeoisie had in its day risen above the feudal aristocracy.
Now the proletariat would rise above the bourgeoisie. Let
revolution come, bringing with it the climax of class struggle
and then the end. After that, a final peace. Russia had made
a beginning. In a disorder far worse than America's it had
powerfully planned a new society in which every man was
to be employed and no man could be made rich by the labor
of another. Compare that with planless America, bankrupt in
the midst of all its plenty.

The younger writers compared them. There was a whole
literature about Russia. But America must have a new literature too—as Americans had declared when the republic
was young and generous. Now, as then, there were countless
programs saying what the new literature would be like.
There were more programs than performances. Criticism
can start faster than creation. This criticism talked about

the doctrines the coming literature was to further and sometimes forgot that good books are written only when there
are good writers, and that good writers appear, by an arbitrary rule of nature, only when they happen to.

Nobody could have foreseen that Tobacco Road would be
to the thirties more or less what Main Street had been to
the twenties. Nobody did foresee it. The novel made no great
stir in 1932. The play in December 1933 seemed a strange
experiment for Broadway. Jean Wright, who saw it at the
first matinee, told me to hurry or it would be taken off and
I would miss it. I went to the second matinee. The audience
that afternoon was shocked but fascinated, on the edge of
laughter but not sure whether it could be decent to laugh at
comedy so broad, misery so deep. I did not feel in the audience any general horror. New as such characters and situations were to the American stage, they did not seem entirely
new to the imagination of the spectators. The depression
was four years old.

I had talked with Erskine Caldwell a few weeks before
and had found that he did not then think of himself as
furthering any doctrines. "I am glad," he had said, "if the
communists like my books, but they are not propaganda."
Later he was more conscious of the implications which
critics saw in his work. One of the least articulate writers,
when it came to talking, that I have ever known, he seemed
to have no theories whatever. His only argument was that
his stories told the truth about lives he had observed, in
Maine as well as in Georgia. Some of his short stories had
reminded me of salty folk-tales. He seemed to me to have a
strain of folk-telling in him.

I had a special interest in his argument. When the New
York Society for the Suppression of Vice had brought a re-

port against God's Little Acre, and the publishers asked me for an opinion, I had said in a letter to them: "I do not know Erskine Caldwell, but he is unmistakably a serious artist who has chosen to write what he believes to be the truth about a phase of American life. The truth, I believe, should always be accepted as justification for literature." Magistrate Greenspan, dismissing the complaint and clearing the book, had said: "In this book, I believe the author has chosen to write what he believes to be the truth about a certain group in American life. To my way of thinking, *Truth* should always be accepted as a justification of literature." The magistrate had confirmed the critic almost word for word.

Many people saw the play, during its long run, with many motives. For some it was a document and an arraignment. For some it was rank sex. For some it was a monkey house, burlesquing the human race. Works of art do not have each of them a single meaning. They mean what they mean to various minds, who may disagree enormously about them. But the triumph of Tobacco Road made it plain that Americans, educated by the depression, could now imagine, and savor, forms of life which American literature had habitually left out of its record. Poverty was not obsolete or foreign. Poverty was here and now.

Caldwell's tough realism about Southern farms, James T. Farrell's about Northern cities in the Chicago trilogy Studs Lonigan: the depression was not sectional. Farrell, articulate and deliberate, avoided the formulas which too often, in the novels of the time, made the class struggle too much like old-fashioned melodrama. The trilogy is the whole history of a young American who barely lives into the depression and dies a muddled bystander. To read it was to know it must be true. I gave it to Frank, who had no experience of cities, and he said it was the truest story of a young man he had ever read. True and troubling. Here was a wilderness in America, still to be civilized—if it ever could be. The depression would make it worse.

Some of the communists were sure that only a revolution would make it better. There were such disagreements as to the aims and ways of the revolution that it looked far off. The victims of the depression had been unbelievably patient. They could still remember the good days which they had had or thought they had. Hold out till such days came back. The older America was stubbornly rooted as an example in the national memory. The revolution would have to take place there.

The literature of the twenties had been chiefly concerned with freedom for individuals. Its heroes, oppressed by a life which they thought rigid and unimaginative, had rebelled, demanding the right to live, love, work as instinct told them to. They assumed they could do this if society would let them alone. Society was strong enough to do without them. It ran, somehow, like its machines, which the rebels condemned. For the thirties, when so many of those machines had stopped, and society seemed to have fallen into impotent disorder, the problem was how individuals could be joined in a common effort to survive. Trade unions were one obvious answer. The theatrical season of 1934-35 in New York filled the stage with strikers as heroes, and Clifford Odets was a hero among playwrights. But the collective mood in the new literature was general. Mere freedom would not serve. Starving men could not eat it, freezing men could not wear it, homeless men could not lie down to sleep in it.

Let the twenties have their freedom. These were sterner times.

Yet it was a writer of the twenties who wrote the thirties' most timely book. Sinclair Lewis, who is an epitome of thoughtful America, had tried for three years to write a labor novel and had found he could not. Nor could he assimilate the age and make out any issue clear and dramatic enough to rouse his total energies. The menace of fascism supplied an issue. It can't happen here, people said. But it might. America had gangsters and might have a gangster government. America had a tradition of vigilantes and might revive it to put down, in the name of law and order, new demands for justice to the underprivileged. Lewis imagined the coming of an American fascism and called it, ironically, It Can't Happen Here. At a moment when hostile parties were drawing together in a united front against war and fascism he precipitated the argument in a story which was a warning and might be an inoculation against the disease. The younger writers, excited by his powerful support, should not have been surprised. After all, Main Street had dealt with fascism in the village, Babbitt with fascism in business, Elmer Gantry with fascism in the church. The twenties had not realized what fascism might become, but they had resisted it in all the forms they knew.

3

AFTER the war there had been a conspicuous Younger Generation, or a generalization called that. After the crash the youngest generation took no special name. It had, like the

Younger Generation, its rebels against old ideas. They favored communism or at least opposed war and fascism. The new rebels against old manners were less conspicuous than those of the twenties. These could take for granted various freedoms which the past decade had won. They could not always use them. They had been the freedoms of a leisure class. Its heroes had gone their ways with easy pockets, at the expense, ordinarily, of the elders who complained about this restlessness. The elders of the youngest generation had less money. The youngsters barely understood that there had ever been a lavish age.

A young man whose father I had known in high school brought his wife to see me during the summer of 1934. The two had written a novel which I guessed was in part autobiography. Would I read it and talk to them about it? Talking about the novel, which had its whole scene laid in the depression, I spoke of the differences between that and the boom. I saw a look in the young man's eyes as if he did not quite follow me. It checked me for a moment. Then he said: "Of course we don't remember the boom at all."

Of course they could not. They had been in school then, and heedless. They, or at any rate the boy and girl of the novel, had lived at college on a dwindling surplus and had taken their first independent steps in a depression world. Before the war a similar hero, married at the end of college, would have found a job and gone to work to support his wife and the expected children. After the war, he would have had a fling in New York or Paris, looking for a freedom which his Main Street denied him. For the depression hero there was neither a job at hand nor money to frolic on. He and his bride, with what they could scrape together, bought an untrustworthy automobile and set out for a nomadic honeymoon. It would be cheaper to travel than to pay rent. America was full of nomads of the depression. The bride and groom had adventures, but they were hunting for a job.

All the youngest generation was hunting for a job. Nothing about the depression came so close to most Americans as unemployment. A job was buried treasure, the pot of gold at the end of the rainbow, the beauty hidden in the wood, the prize on the top of the mountain. To many it was the needle in the haystack, and they became sluggish and helpless, or dissolute and criminal. They will color American life for years, whatever revolution or recovery may come. But most of those I knew kept up the hunt for jobs. The hero in a symptomatic play said to the girl he was engaged to: "Do you know what I think about all day? A job. And do you know what I think about at night? I don't wish I had you in my arms. I wish I had a job." The audience applauded as at no other point in the entire play. I noticed in the movies that whenever there was a strike on the screen the audience was on the side of the strikers, no matter how the story was presented. These men were fighting for the right to work and be paid for it.

I watched the course of an episode which was exciting my daughters and their friends. One of the boys, just out of Yale, had set his mind on a particular job which he wanted more than any other. To his friends, I gathered, this was romancing: at a time when any job was a success, to aim at a first choice among jobs. He got his job, and there was a happy tempest in the group. My daughters looked upon college as amateur and dilettante compared with actual work. "Why should I go to college to study literature," Anne asked, "and maybe use textbooks you and Uncle Mark

wrote? I already know you." After high school she went to
work with a publishing house. Margaret, who at fourteen
had illustrated a book for children, by eighteen had a thoroughly professional temper and a job. Barbara, wanting a
better horse than she had, decided to write a book and earn
the money herself. She wrote it in a month the summer before she was fifteen. But she used a pseudonym when it was
published, so that too many of her acquaintances might
not hear about it.

The majority of the boys I knew—sons of men with more
learning or talent than wealth—tried all sorts of jobs before
they found any that would suit and keep them. They were
chauffeurs and mechanics and lifeguards. They worked on
farms. They went to sea as sailors or stewards. They acted
as cooks and caretakers on pleasure boats. They found part-
time work in offices. The ingenious among them thought up
jobs and proposed them to possible employers. They were
full of ideas. It struck me that they were less like their
fathers than their grandfathers or great-grandfathers, setting out to make their fortunes. Back to shirt-sleeves.

One day when I was lunching with the staff of the New
York Times and some of the editors grumbled about the
youngest generation, I spoke of the active and inventive
boys I knew. The editors asked me to write them an article
on this hopeful return to an old American way of life.
When I tried to do it I found I could not. This was an old
American way, old and wasteful. Surely young men eager
to work deserved a chance to do it without hunting and
begging, without delays and disappointments, without re-
buffs and insults. Surely their society was to blame if it was
not organized to put young energy to its proper uses with
the least confusion. The old American way had been to turn

young men loose to scramble among the country's resources and learn that there was enough for everybody. But those sprawling times were gone, and a more scientific way was called for. I wondered why young men hunting for jobs did not hate their elders more than I saw them doing. Perhaps they did.

Whether it was a simple matter of money or whether it was a swing of the pendulum of manners, the youngest generation as I saw it was soberer than the Younger Generation I remembered. More than once, at parties, I observed that it was the survivors of the twenties, now well on in or toward their forties, who were boisterous. They seemed never to have outgrown the habit of being self-conscious in their freedoms, of wanting or hoping to shock somebody. The new arrivals of the thirties, still in their late teens or early twenties, were free without caring whether they were or not, and with little interest in shocking. More than once I caught them looking at these elders with surprise and, now and then, disgust. That old-fashioned Younger Generation.

There were ten years between me and the Scott Fitzgerald generation, thirty between me and my daughters and their friends. "Parents," Anne told me, "never know anything about their children." But the youngsters seemed to me to have an unaffected realism in their judgments which, so far as I knew, was new to youth.

They were realistic about money and marriage, those tests of realism. When I was a boy, boys would hardly ever admit, before girls, that they had no money, but would make up complicated excuses why they did not do what they could not afford. Now boys said they had no money, or had only so much, and let it go at that. Girls took such situations as they came—as girls no doubt would have done in my youth if boys had had less foolish pride. These girls might offer to share expenses, and the boys not be distressed. Possibly an increasing number of girls married older men, who could support them. But the girls who married men nearer them in age cheerfully assumed that wives would have to do some kind of work as well as husbands.

"How much were you earning when you were married?" a girl asked me. I told her. "Why," she said, pleased, "Tony and I will have that much." I saw that she meant the two of them together.

But the strident feminism of the twenties had disappeared. The two sexes were now pooling all their natural endowments. I heard two girls discussing a famous feminist. "She is one of those old battle-axes that hate men," one girl said, and they both laughed. Most of the feminists had given up talking about the war between men and women which James Thurber's drawings made into a joke. Yet beneath the surface there may have been a silent conflict. One young man said to me: "If all these women hadn't gone into business there wouldn't be any unemployment. There are just about as many men out of jobs as women in them." I wondered if women, now appearing to be feminine, might not be appearing so in an instinctive self-defense. Make war with the weapons you know best.

Margaret, eight or nine years old, said to me: "I'll tell you a dirty story if you won't get mad." I said I would not. "Do you know what this word means?" she asked, and spoke one of the words least often printed in English. I said I did. Then she told me her dirty story. It was out of the lowest and falsest folk-lore. For a moment I was horrified that she had heard it. Then I remembered that I had heard it from one of the hired men at Hope, when I was about her present age. It was not a very funny story, and I said I thought it was not. She agreed with me. "You must be careful about using that word," I said. "Some people think it is bad and would be shocked. Grandmother, for instance." "Oh," Margaret insisted, "I'd never say it before her. I wouldn't say it to anybody but you and Betty." Betty was the cook, colored, lively, and sensible. I could think of nothing else to do or say. When Margaret was seventeen I told her how horrified I had been. "You know," she said, "I had heard the story and didn't really understand it. I told it to you to see if you would say something that would help me to. But you didn't."

It seemed to me—but now the thirty years between me and the youngest generation makes me especially uncertain —that the youngest knew as much as the Younger about sex without feeling the need to talk so much about it. They had as children, most of them, been told whatever they asked when they asked it, and had little of the curiosity which before the war had been dammed up and after the war had spilled over. Sex was not now a thing to be ignorant about. Where there were divorces, unions without marriage, and homosexuality, the older boys and girls knew it as well as anybody. If love had lost some of its mystery, so had it lost some of its fear. Young love remained magical. The youngest generation discovered it as every generation does.

Barbara, born in 1920, when she was six or seven asked me: "What was the Great War about, and who won it?" If it was hard to answer these questions it was harder to think of all the others which her generation would have to ask and try to answer. My youth had been passed in the time of a long peace, in the confidence that life would go on peacefully, changing only to be better. She and her contemporaries lived, and would live, in a time of turmoil and doubt. Wars and revolutions. Brutal dictatorships. Imperialistic raids on backward countries. Conflicts between social classes. World-wide poverty. Unrest everywhere. Even if there should be, in America, a recovery within the forms of democratic government, it would mean a new attitude for Americans. Their republic could not seem to them a last achievement. Russia would have a newer model, and America would be among the conservative nations. Americans, who had always looked forward, would often look back to the golden age of prosperity which had built such cathedrals and universities and museums and railway stations and office buildings, such roads and bridges, such institutes and endowments, as could perhaps no more be undertaken. It would affect the whole national character. What marks men and nations is the balance between the past and future which they hold. When the past is heavier upon them, their pace is dogged at best. They run onward only when the future pulls, promising them that whatever has happened can happen again, and more.

Resolution

THIS history becomes difficult. A narrative is a line drawn between two points. They are not, as is often said, what has been and what is to be. Those are not two points, for nobody knows what is to be. The two points at the ends of a narrative are what had been and what was to be. The story cannot be told till after the events have taken place and the causes have shown themselves in the effects. The present is meaningless in itself. The narrator cannot represent it. Whatever he chooses to tell may turn out to have been of no importance. Unaware of the end, he may pass over present matters in which the future is perfectly implicit and yet prefectly invisible.

So, trying to tell about the depression while it lasts, I am not sure what values to put on what I have seen. If the outcome is to be revolution, then all those who have worked for recovery will have been reactionaries. The impatient future will think of them as blind, however the sentimental future may feel that they were romantic. If the outcome is to be full recovery, then those who worked for revolution will have been the blind ones, to be remembered with blame or sympathy by different survivors. And if the outcome is to be mere patched-up recovery, swinging unstably back and forth between recurrent booms and depressions, perpetuating grievances, then both those who worked for recovery and those who worked for revolution will have been too weak, and 1929 not a watershed in the course of time.

And I who tell this story, with no conscious desire but to be truthful, must be suspect. I had not suffered under the old régime. Though I had lived by my labor, I had been free to give years to my education and had become an expert. I had never been hungry or cold or homeless. I had never had to look for work, only to choose between kinds of work offered to me. I had done work which I enjoyed so much that it was better than play. My work had been recognized and rewarded. If, then, I did not welcome the prospect of revolution, it might be that personal comfort had dulled me to general distress. I thought that my instincts were opposed to violence—such as wars and revolutions—but what I thought instinct, I had to admit if I were honest, might be habit. Try as I might, I could not trust my mind in these affairs as I could in my own.

Yet I must use the mind I had. My mind told me that revolutions come only when incurable stupidity has caused intolerable suffering. I knew I should never stand on the side of the stupid as against the sufferers. But I could not feel the present necessity of revolution in America as some people did. It was enough for them, it seemed to me, to call it inevitable. Or they saw it as melodrama—the melodrama of the class struggle. Nobody could stay out, everybody must take a hand.

I had heard the same thing about the war, and I accepted this no more than I had accepted that. As to inevitability I was unconvinced. Nothing human was inevitable but death. Any changes that came to America would have to come through men, and men were minds as well as machines. They could affect the changes if they chose.

I did not want to avoid a decision by the lazy, timid trick of thinking there was something to be said on both sides. But I did not know, and I could not learn, enough to give me confidence. If I had been starving and bullied and desperate, I should have had passions to lead me. As it was, I could have no confidence except from knowledge. I lacked that, and I found nobody else who seemed to me to have it. I listened to dozens of schemes for revolution, and for recovery, and I was never able to think a single one of them through, let alone feel it through. I was not a creature of blind faiths, charging as happily in relative ignorance as in relative certainty. Sometimes I envied such men. No, I really did not envy them. I have never envied anybody anything. But I perceived that their work was not my work. I should try to understand them as they went along, but I could work only within the limits of my knowledge. I had, both by nature and from experience, the temper of the expert. And I was an expert in literature, not in government.

The last months of the Hoover administration were full of despair and the sense of imminent collapse. Dreams of fear came more often to my nights, and my days were troubled by them. I became less solitary. But wherever I went I ran into confusion. Perhaps it was New York. Toward the end of 1932 I left the ominous island for seven weeks of lecturing across the continent.

I had lived in New York half my life and I preferred it to all other cities I knew, but I had never become one of those New Yorkers who cannot breathe outside of Manhattan, except in Europe. I was an American from the Middle West who lived in New York to be near his market as a mining engineer might live near his mine. New York gave me the chance to do many kinds of literary work and did not hinder as much as it stimulated me. The noise and dirt seldom got on my nerves, nor the pressure of crowds. But I was an American first, a New Yorker afterwards, and I liked travel-

ing in America. By the end of 1932 I had seen a good deal
of every state east of the Mississippi and the first tier west
of it.

Almost all my traveling had been as a lecturer. During the
prosperous years the public had an appetite for lectures, particularly by writers and explorers. I had given the more or
less formal Clyde Fitch lectures at Amherst College and the
William Vaughn Moody lecture at the University of Chicago
and a Commencement address at the University of Kentucky
and a speech to the Phi Beta Kappa society at Leigh University. I had lectured at colleges and universities from Bowdoin in Maine to Tulane in Louisiana, from the University
of Minnesota to the University of Georgia. I had spoken before schools and clubs and forums. As a rule I went out
once or twice a year for a week or two of busy engagements,
covering thousands of miles, speaking to thousands of people.
An editor needed to know what was being read outside of
New York and what the readers thought of it.

This was my excuse, but I liked the excitement. I was as
much at home on a train as a sailor on a boat. There was no
kind of chance acquaintance with whom I could not enjoy
myself. The traders returning to Tennessee from the mule
fair at Atlanta. The strutting young fellow on his way to
join the St. Louis baseball team and wanting everyone to
know it. The Dutch-American who asked me for advice between Dallas and Amarillo because he thought I had a
Dutch face. The three young girls, members of some minor
dancing troupe, whom I invited to dinner on the long ride
to New Orleans, and who first primly asked permission of
their manager, a man who sewed all day on the troupe's
costumes. The child three years old, being taken from an
orphan asylum to foster-parents, which said to itself over

and over: "Going to find mamma, going to find mamma, going to find mamma." The Pullman porter who was reading the works of Thomas Paine which I had edited.

I liked the unexpected things that happened at the lectures. In a Chicago suburb, after I had lectured on modern biography, an old lady on the first row asked me what I thought of immortality. I was later told that she asked that same single question of all lecturers. In Richmond, with James Branch Cabell in the audience, I spoke enthusiastically of Jurgen. A woman not far from Cabell whispered to a friend beside her: "The nasty thing! Of course I haven't read it." In Fairmont, West Virginia, there had been a battle in the streets between union and non-union men a half-hour before I arrived, and I had to speak to an audience which could hardly listen to me for wondering whether the guns might not begin again just outside the hall. It was as hard to rouse them as it would have been to lift them. One of the women in the audience told me she was Stuart Sherman's sister.

I liked the entertainments planned for me in the towns where I spoke. In Lexington I was taken to call on Man o' War, not at the hour of the day when he regularly saw visitors but a whole hour earlier. He cantered around his paddock and came back and posed as if for a photograph. They gave me one of his cast shoes mounted as a doorknocker. From Nashville we drove out to see the Hermitage, home of Andrew Jackson. That hero of the rough frontier had one of the stateliest of all American houses. And there was the Old Capitol of Iowa, now used by officials of the University: why do so few Americans know about this masterpiece? In Titusville, Pennsylvania, where the first artesian oil well in America was drilled, I was shown the making of stainless steel. In Brunswick, Georgia, I watched Negro stevedores handling barrels of turpentine all night, singing an endless song of which their leader improvised a first line for each new stanza. At La Guaira—though this was not in the United States and it came later—I went on shore from a cruise on which I had gone as lecturer, and motored up to Caracas for lunch. A deputation of Venezuelan poets, hearing I was on the boat, came to greet me in French as bad as mine. They presented me, as a souvenir, with a jagged pebble shining with native gold. (During this voyage the news reached me that Edwin Arlington Robinson had died. I spent half of one of my lectures on a memorial account of him, in the remote Caribbean.)

In 1932 I gave my opening lecture in New Orleans, which once before I had explored with Sherwood Anderson and Carl Sandburg and Edward Tinker. Now, at the reception after the lecture, two young women insisted that I slip away with them and their young men to a night club. From New Orleans I went on to Fort Worth, then to San Antonio. I had wanted to see San Antonio ever since I was a child, when my father had come back from a visit to Texas and had told us, on our cold farm, of roses in December, of palm trees, and the Alamo. I had wanted to go there, at sixteen, from the Indian Territory, and had been prevented by a fever which I picked up among the Kiamichi mountains. San Antonio had become for me a kind of Carcassonne.

The San Antonio I saw was a merry kaleidoscope. Former students of mine turned up: one who had been in the first college class I ever taught, one in the last. They took me up to see the city from the sky in a small dirigible. For a weekend we never stopped. The Plaza of the Alamo is firm in my memory, with the Franciscan chapel which was a fort to Davy Crockett, the governor's palace, the cathedral, the

bridges over the winding river. The rest of San Antonio is
a flicker of remembered images. The doors painted blue in
the Mexican streets to indicate that marriageable girls live
behind them. The deer wandering loose in the quadrangle
at Fort Sam Houston, kept there by the sentries at the gates.
The little shrine, unrecognized by the Church, where simple
Mexicans believe that miracles of healing are performed.
The tower where Geronimo was a prisoner. The beautiful
Spanish buildings used as garages at the flying school. The
Mexican children in a schoolroom, singing unnaturally in
alien English and then suddenly finding their true voices
in a Mexican folk-song. The four missions south of San
Antonio, particularly San José de Aguayo, with its beautiful
carved window and the bell tower where I climbed the un-
forgettable stairway. The cockfight just outside the city limits,
with nobody but the county sheriff to mind, where a red
cock killed in one stroke and I talked with a woman who
must have known as much about the sport as any man.
The Mexican plaza Saturday night where scores of braziers
are set up to cook the burning food of the people, to the
sound of guitars. The great Municipal Auditorium, with the
hand of Mexico visible within the American glove of its
architecture. The terrace where I sat under a live oak till
late at night, talking to my friends, always aware of the river
whispering in the dark. The bats which, housed by the city,
fly out at dusk to devour mosquitoes.

From San Antonio to Dallas, with its regional arts. All
Thanksgiving Day I rode across Texas on the way to Denver,
and the next morning I hunted for Pike's Peak among the
mountains that rose out of the night. A poet in Denver told
me that the mountains were too big for literature. Writer
after writer had come among them, tried to write about

them, and lost himself in swelling words. In Cheyenne, between trains, I saw a Western movie: to this audience, this was realism. Having two or three days idle in Salt Lake City, I called on nobody who might have shown it to me, but studied it alone. Seen so close, it lost most of the strangeness it had in the Mormon legend. Again and again I was reminded of Hope and Old Settlers' Day. This was another Canaan which another wandering tribe had come through the wilderness to conquer. Latter Day Saints. But though they made a cult of the patriarchs, they seemed to me not to have lost their hold on live affairs. I thought this the best managed community I had ever seen in America.

Another day and night on a train to California. Mountains and deserts spread out in a landscape which changed so fast as the train moved that I was afraid to turn aside for fear I should miss some change, some splendor. Las Vegas in the dark. In the first light, the sun on groves of oranges and walnuts.

I lectured as far north as Fresno, I drove as far south as Agua Caliente, but I lived in Hollywood. All extremes meet in Los Angeles. At tea the first afternoon I met half a dozen writers I had known in New York. After my lecture that evening, there were at least a dozen persons I had known in Hope. Hope and Hollywood. My first teacher came to hear me speak, and one of my high school teachers. Southern California swarmed with cousins. I swam in the Pacific, picnicked on those mountains which look as if Hollywood had designed them, and spent a night in San Andreas Cañon beyond Palm Springs. A burning sun on drifts of snow, on palm trees as old as fossils, on the incomparable colors of the desert.

The landscape was unfamiliar, not the people, I dined

with Upton Sinclair, and he talked about technocracy, which had just broken into the news. One of my Oklahoma aunts was a cousin of Will Rogers. I went to see him, at the studio, working on State Fair. Phil Stong had been a student of mine at Columbia and the Literary Guild had chosen his book. Helping him revise the manuscript, I had suggested that since every other Jack at the fair had a Jill, Blue Boy ought to have one too, and Stong had invented Esmeralda. Somebody at the studio pointed her out as my granddaughter. I talked with Viña Delmar about the original of the sanitarium where the heroine of Bad Girl had her child. Anne had been born there. The writers of Hollywood were hospitable. Most of them were homesick for New York and asked about it. Rupert Hughes, who had once been angry at me, was now a friendly host. He introduced me to Earl Derr Biggers, whose Charlie Chan I knew as well as Sherlock Holmes. With Edwin Justus Mayer I discussed his Children of Darkness, which I was to include in An American Omnibus. He gave me the freedom of the lot where he was working, invited me to lunch with other writers, to hear Claudette Colbert retaking a scene in a sound studio. Many of the actors were homesick too, though Mae West seemed at home. I watched her making She Done Him Wrong. Dudley Digges told me about his make-up as a tong leader. He had been made to look so quintessentially Chinese that the real Chinese actors in the picture did not, in comparison, look Chinese at all. We recalled the days when Ludwig Lewisohn was dramatic critic of the Nation. Jean Wright, who had taught me most of what I knew about Broadway, was my chief guide in Hollywood.

Perhaps if I had been under some iron contract, and not merely a care-free visitor, I should have enjoyed myself less than I did. For me, Hollywood was a holiday. A producer said that a writer did not need to be crazy, but it helped. Later a writer said the same thing about camera men, and a technician about actors. Everybody said it about everybody else, and I thought it was true of all of them. Making a picture, many wills were in conflict: producers demanding profits, writers insisting that their stories be followed without change, actors wanting to appear in the most favorable light and to be constantly in it, directors fighting to keep the reins in their own hands. No one will was the general will, dominating the whole. Nobody knew enough about the process for that. The technicians, who knew the most, were too busy for speculation. Whatever plans might be laid in advance, unexpected developments might alter them. The process remained fluid, apparently chaotic, till the last. Then, suddenly, something emerged. Often it emerged as the hodgepodge that, to a logical mind, it seemed bound to be. But sometimes the product of these warring antagonisms might have unity and form, point or grace, even meaning. Hollywood was a good deal like nature. Hollywood was a good deal like human society.

When I was a very young man, too little conscious of my body to realize that I was nearsighted and needed glasses, I used to suffer from savage headaches, during which, ashamed of them, I drove myself more savagely to work. No headache could last forever, and I would keep waiting for the pain to ease. I never once noticed it begin to grow less, but would forget it and then be surprised to find that it had gone. So, at forty-seven, I found that the long ache of my own depression had left me. I had not thought my way out of it, nor been converted to healing doctrine, nor at last arrived at absolute self-knowledge. I had lived through it, without knowing how. And I had not noticed that it was clearing away before the winds of travel, activity, diversion. It had been there. It had gone. The sense of survival came up in me again.

Hollywood was as odd an antitoxin against spiritual malaise as I could imagine. There must be other elements in the cure. I remembered something James Stephen had once said to me. Americans, he thought, undervalued their Far West. Living on a small island, seldom going more than a few miles from home, he had often been freed and elevated by reading Western novels in which the scene might be a thousand miles wide. The size of life had something to do with it. Well, I had left a smaller island than Ireland and had moved thousands of miles through America. I was not mystical about mountains and deserts, and I knew that distances were illusions. But I knew, too, that I had changed and was happier, without being able to put my finger on a sufficient intellectual or moral reason. Was life better? Life was bigger.

On my way back to Chicago the train killed a wild horse somewhere in New Mexico. I got to Urbana on Christmas day and walked in on Christmas dinner. In New York I was another Trader Horn to my daughters, who asked about Hollywood as if I had been to Heaven. Mark was spending the winter with his family in Cornwall. I went for an early week-end there and filled their warm farmhouse with rangy stories. Nobody held it against me that I had been so long a hermit.

I did not give up all my solitary habits, but I felt the impulse to write again. In What Is American Literature? I tried to distill in one small treatise twenty years of study and reflection. The larger history, untouched for six years, had become an incubus. The world had changed too much for me to feel sure of any point of view from which to write, but the book had troubled my conscience and kept me from beginning anything else. Now I threw the idea overboard. I would review my contemporaries and edit them in Modern American Prose. I would digest the reading of my whole life and edit an Anthology of World Prose. Then I would write a book unlike any I had ever written.

2

LATE in October 1933 the telephone woke me. Mark said a telegram had come from Frank with the news that our father was dead.

He had been ailing since spring, denying that it was serious. In a letter to me at the end of June he had said: "Hoora! Hoora! Dad is on top again. Am all right but weak. Last Sunday Dr. Mason and Dr. Gray met here to decide whether it would be best to go to a hospital for a major operation of draining the gall bladder. I had decided before they got here that it would not be. It would be like trying to drive a wild mustang alone in a corral on a big prairie, so they decided to give it more time. The liver is almost natural size again, and the gall bladder is almost natural, and I can eat and sleep again. So all I have to do is to get strong. Get word to Mark and Paul. Frank went to Chicago last Friday and had a nice time. Am getting tired, so I will quit. Love to you all." And in the last letter he ever wrote, the middle of October, his penciled words straggling across the page: "I am in the dining-room writing on the table. Am getting better all the time now. An old rupture I had years ago came soon after you left and I have had trouble getting a truss, one to hold it up. They think registration [at the University of Illinois] will be greater than last year. Guess I will stop as about exhausted." Here his writing crumpled up. He must have rested, for his "Love to all" was more firmly written, and his signature much as it had been for all the years I had known it.

To the last my father never admitted the worse if there was a better to hold on to. But we were sure he had cancer, and I suppose he had, though he did not mention cancer to us nor we to him. Mark and I had gone to visit him, to drive back with Paul, who was already there. My father was not in much pain, though he was feeble, and he liked to lie quietly on a couch in the living-room and listen to people talking. Everything interested him, and he kept up his amused chuckle, particularly when we argued. Though he had been a Republican all his life he had voted for Roosevelt. These hard times could not last much longer. Things were looking up.

Toward the end, for the first time in seventy-six years, he was often tired. On the afternoon of his last day his heart almost failed. His doctor, who had been one of his young assistants at Hope, did what he could, but my father was a doctor too. He told my cousin Dorothy Knight—though not my mother—that the game was up. That night he slept, stopped breathing, and was dead.

Mark, Paul, and I arrived by train from New York, and Guy, ahead of us from Detroit, and Frank, from Villa Grove, met us at the station. Then the five of us went to see our father.

There was nothing to show that he was dead except that he did not notice us when we came in—that and the gray coffin and the bright flowers. "He was very tired," my mother said. "Now he can rest." She had said the same thing when we were children, and he had come in from a hard ride and lain down for a nap. We were used to seeing him asleep. We must be careful not to wake him.

It was different that evening, after the day's stream of visitors, when the family was alone again. We sat scattered around the long room, with my father at one end, talking as he had liked to hear us in the summer. Nobody was more clearly present than he was. Again and again I half-turned to him when something was said, to see how he took it. I had to look to realize that he was not breathing. I missed the chuckles that did not come when the others laughed. There was laughter and gaiety. His own immortal cheerfulness set the tone for us, mourning him.

My mother and my brothers and their wives went to bed on the upper floors of the house. I stayed with my father. We knew he would have pooh-poohed the ceremony of sitting up with him, and we did not observe it. But I was the eldest son, the eldest brother, and I felt an old responsibility. Of course my father no longer needed me, nor my brothers depended upon me. I stayed with my father out of instinct.

Looking at him, I could partly realize that he was dead. Alive, his hands had never been so still, his humorous lips so grave. But when I turned out the lights, and lay down on a couch in the dining-room, it was as if he were only asleep and I was within call. I would tell myself that this was more than sleep, and little terrors of death would run over me. But there was no great terror, and no disorder of grief. My mind understood. It had faced this for months and was prepared. My imagination was slower. It could not make itself an image of him as anything but alive. There in the dark I kept thinking I heard him breathe or stir. And other obscure senses in my nerves felt his calm and smiling presence. It quieted me and I went to sleep.

The next day the stream of visitors began again and lasted till the hour of the funeral. Urbana came, but there were more old friends from Hope, or originally from there, like us. That microcosm was still close-knit enough to come together in loving farewell to a good man. I noticed that of the six pallbearers four had once lived at Hope or near it. By some unconscious tact my mother had asked men who were a kind of index to my father's friendships. One was a professor at the University, one an athletic coach, one a county official, one a school principal, one a retired farmer, one a mechanic. More than half of them my father had helped in their careers.

The funeral moved to the church under trees which make the streets of Urbana green tunnels in the summer, tunnels now vaulted with the proud colors of October. The service for the dead. No, for the living. The funeral moved through longer streets to the cemetery, to the grave dug under an oak. Only the words of the minister were somber. The sun shone sweet and warm on the green grass and the harlequin leaves, the flowers of the funeral were gay, and on the faces of the mourners I saw friendly smiles more often than tears. My father was lowered into his grave.

But the strong roots of his life were already deeper in Illinois than this. Shallow death, which spreads a little earth over the body a man can no longer use. Deep life, rooted in subsoil and bedrock.

3

EVERY man who spoke to me about my father's death said, in one set of words or another, the same thing. He said that his own father's death had been for him like the burning of bridges, the cutting off of retreats. He discovered then, commonly for the first time, that he had always thought of his father as the point of life from which he was traveling and to which, believably, he might go back. This was as true of men quite independent of their fathers, or even hostile to them, as of the others. But after his father's death, each man of them said, he realized that he himself was a beginning, naked in time. He had been an individual. He had become a type.

In The Ninth Wave, seven years before my father's death, I had put into Kent Morrow's mind a conviction of my own. "People talked of children as springing from the bodies of their parents and leaving the rent carcasses behind. Surely the image was nearly as accurate when reversed. The seed of the father is in the son, Kent mused. It nourishes itself upon the stuff of youth, gradually grows stronger, and in the end breaks the shell and casts it aside. No one can say whether the individual who remains is more thoroughly son or father. By such subtle links the generations are bound one to another. It seemed to Kent that he had surprised Nature at one of the tricks by which she holds mankind to its narrow path. She had been working, as it were, behind his back, as she had worked behind the back of every maturing man since Adam."

If the individual became the type and the son turned into his father, what was I to do in this new world to which my father had been unable to adjust himself? His faith had duped and ruined him. He had learned his gait and direction from the national momentum of the last century, and in the troubled times he had not known how to move otherwise. Faith was the right counsel, and blind faith as good as any. I wondered if the strong instinctive faith in me was mine or only my father's, persisting. I felt in the whole country the stir of the New Deal. Men did not know whether what was being done would work, but they assured themselves that at last they were doing something. I could not agree with my mind that mere activity would do. I could not understand these activities. And yet my own depression had lifted and the general hope surged up in me in spite of my skeptical mind. America was alive.

When I tried to reason I found one assurance. Life, I had found again and again, was more inventive than any man. Lay your plans as carefully as you liked, and unforeseeable events might change them. Settle as profoundly as you liked into despair of the future, and it might surprise you with good fortune. So with nations, I could reasonably assume, since nations were many men. Despair and logic thought there would have to be a revolution to make America endurable. Life might turn out to be neither so desperate nor so logical. And if recovery came, it would be different from what the prophets said. They disagreed already. Powerful forces were in opposition, none of them willing to compromise. But history would compromise for them.

After the war I had tried to describe a man at home and at peace on the earth:

"In any winter of our discontent let us think of gardens.

The sun looks north again, March is stirring somewhere, and in a few stubborn weeks there will be another spring with loud, cheerful robins, insistent grass, and buds ready to turn pink or white at the warm touch of the advancing season. We have lived long enough on the stores we laid up from the harvest of last year. Like bears, we have grown thin in our hollow trees and must resume our occupations. Too much winter can destroy the genial sap that spring annually renews in the veins of men as surely as in trees. Cities, which have built strong barriers against the seasons, forget them, but they bring morals no less than the weather. The seasons are teachers that never cease teaching, and examples that never fail to move us. Our tempers follow the sun.

"Though it is true that the senses relax and ripen in a garden, a garden is more than a sensual delight. Roses grow there, and radishes; so does patience. That man who puts seed into a furrow at the same moment tucks his hand into the crooked elbow of Time and falls into step. He knows he must abide the days, must endure hot and cold, wet and dry, the ups and downs of immeasurable nature. Infected almost at once with peace, he feels his will surrendering its fretful individuality to the ampler cause with which he has involved his fortunes. He sees that he cannot profitably scold the rain; he cannot wear a chip on his shoulder and dare the wind to knock it off. The stature of his will shrinks when he learns how little he means to the rain or the wind, and the stature of his wisdom increases. Vigilant of course he must remain. He must take quick advantage of sunshine, as sailors do of the tides. He must foreknow the storm by its signs. In the long run, his prosperity will depend upon his eyes and hands, but he will be aware that he thrives by virtue of the patience with which he tends a process which is ageless and immortal.

"Nor will he be patient merely for hours or months. As the seasons depart and recur year after year, he will begin to realize what centuries mean, epochs and æons. It is the weather which varies, not the seasons. The gardener in his little plot looks out less feverishly at elections and revolutions than other men. He has seen clouds before and has lived through them confident of the sun. From an experience stronger than dogma he knows that just after night there is dawn, and that every winter is succeeded by a spring. What in another might be a shallow optimism is in him a faith rooted in subsoil and bedrock, bred and nourished in the vast, slow, undeviating habits of soil and sky. He is conservative because he has seen the seasons perennially pass one into another without convulsions. He is radical because each spring he has had to set the spade into his sleepy ground, has had to tear it open and establish the new harvest on fresh seed. Others may stutter about the strife of old and new, but the gardener sees old and new eternally linked together with human toil. He perceives that history continues, for he has observed the grass. He understands, not dimly but certainly, that the tread of armies or the din of melting dynasties and shattered governments may indeed touch him in his garden, may even drive him forth into desolation, but that the work of the garden and the duty of the gardener will go on. To the end of the world there must be seed and toil and harvests."

It would not do to take this bland post-war doctrine too literally now. There were not enough gardens to go round in America, and whole farms, whole countries, had blown away in the wind. Working out my metaphor in 1920, I had drawn it from Hope and my father. Hope had been dissolved, and my father defeated. The old order had come to a crawl, or so it seemed, and America was slow in getting under way again. In Europe all the ancient dark hatreds had risen out of disorder, with dictators to use them and call them government. The contagions of Europe might reach America. They had reached America in minorities who despised democracy as bungling and helpless, and who preferred this or that kind of dictatorship. Give us dictators and we could march again.

As to this my mind was straight and clear. I did not want to see any dictatorships imported to America, or copied here. The fascist kind had nothing to commend it. It was brutal to begin with and it did not look beyond brutality. The communist kind had the best aims, but it would have more to resist it in America than it had had in Russia, would probably last longer, and might lose the end in the means. The partial dictatorship of money which we already had in America had too much power, but it actually held no title to the government, and it could be curbed by the people if they seriously set about taking their own laws in their own hands. To ask for a dictatorship would be like asking for a war. It would cost more than any probable gain would be worth, and after it was over men would wonder why they had tolerated it.

I think there was nothing that was mystical and little that was traditional in my belief in democracy. It came down to this: that in the long run many heads are better than one. Ardent minorities are always sure they are right and benevolent. Sometimes they are. But when they have their way they either stiffen into a dry routine or else survive by assimilating ideas they once condemned. Even Russia, I could see, was no longer pure revolution. It had found that life is more varied than any one plan. Russia was learning from America how to carry out its programs in competent detail. America might learn from Russia how to design larger and wiser programs, so that all men might have work and no man have to work to fill another's pocket. For either country to shut its eyes to the other would be to overlook a natural human resource. There was health in them both.

They might shut their eyes, like the angry forces that were struggling for power all over the earth. There might be wars that no decent men wanted, dictatorships that were confessions of sick failure. If these should come to America, my mind would be straight and clear about them too. Then, more than ever, I should feel the need to look forward to what came after the madness or the emergency, when men found out again that they could not live without liberty and truth. Nothing would ever make me believe that these are thin abstractions. They are permanent realities. There was no well-being I would ever sacrifice them for. That would be like preferring the comforts of a cage to the dangers and pleasures of a native state.

I did not think that what was good enough for my father was good enough for me. I did not think it had been good enough for him. But there was a common experience of the older American order which now for the first time was mine too. After years of prosperity I had felt myself a failure, stopped, disintegrated, insecure. In Asia I might have called it destiny and sunk into resignation. This was America, where thousands of men had come out of similar defeats as a matter of course. I did not know how to doubt that I would emerge and survive. Perhaps it was not mere traditional optimism. Perhaps it was national stamina. I was a part of

America. If the whole was the sum of its parts, my obstinate courage might be a sign of what was happening to more than me. I must take the signs as I found them.

You who may be reading this book tomorrow or day after tomorrow will wonder why I could not foresee the events which lie between us and which you will think ought to have been plain to me. I strain my eyes into the dark and make out nothing: wars, dictatorships, revolutions, recoveries, compromises. I think that my own depression has left me. But this may be a moment of false ease, to be followed by years of misery and tedium. I think that the general spirit of America is putting behind it a dull confusion and beginning to free its great energies. But this may be wishes which I mistake for facts. I may have looked into the wrong American heart for a sign of what was happening to America. You know, and I do not. I have told you only what I know about these times.

Index

Abbotsford, 100
Abby, 126
Abolitionists, 27, 137
Academic life, 81, 83, 94-98, 106-08, 118
Addison, 100
Ade, George, 251
Agua Caliente, 289
Alamo, the, 287
Albert I, 103
All the Sad Young Men, 169
Alpes Maritimes, 257
Altgeld, Governor, 18
Amarillo, 285
Ambleside, 100
American Academy of Arts and Letters, the, 197
American and British Literature Since 1890, 196, 253
American Mercury, The, 267
American Novel, The, 151
American Omnibus, An, 290
Amherst College, 285
Amsterdam, 102, 103
Amy, 16
Anarchists, the Chicago, 18
Anderson, Maxwell, 251
Anderson, Sherwood, 154, 196, 197, 251, 287
Ankersmit, Hendrik, 102-03
Anna Karenina, 79
Annapolis, 95
Anne, 126
Anthology of World Prose, An, 293
Anthropology, literary, 187-89, 195, 197-200
Apeldoorn, 102-03
Archbishop of York, the, 126

Aria da Capo, 175
Ariosto, 141
Aristophanes, 141
Armistice, the, 119, 166
Armstrong, 24, 33
Arnold, Matthew, 100
Arrow-Maker, The, 192
Arrowsmith, 38
Arthur, King, 164, 245
Atlanta, 146, 285
Augusta, Georgia, 220
Austin, Mary, 133, 189-94
Authors Club, the, 159
Autobiography, difficulties of, 105-06
Automobiles, 48, 70, 121, 175, 247, 276
Avon, 161
Avon's Harvest, 160

Babbitt, 150
Babbitt, 147, 267, 274
Babbitt, Irving, 135, 195
Babylon, 147
Bad Girl, 290
Ballachulish, 99
Baltimore, 151
Balzac, 158
Bank of England, the, 101
Barbarian, The, 211
Barbour, John, 99
Bartlett, Ruth, 224
Bartlett, Walter, 224
Beard, Charles, 151
Bea Sorenson, 158, 159
Beatrice, 177
Beautiful and Damned, The, 169
Becker, Carl, 251
Beebe, William, 251

Beecher, Henry Ward, 177
Beer, Thomas, 251
Beerbohm, Max, 100
Behrman, S. N., 251
Belmont, Mrs. August (Eleanor Robson), 205
Ben-Hur, 49
Benét, Stephen Vincent, 197, 268
Benét, William Rose, 208, 209, 217, 219, 221, 222, 223, 225, 226, 227, 228
Bennett, Arnold, 154, 155
Ben Nevis, 99
Beowulf, 105
Beresford, J. D., 146
Best Short Stories of 1918, The, 156
Betty, 280
Biggers, Earl Derr, 290
Billy, 39
Birthday Cake for Lionel, A, 232
Blake, William, 77
Blue Boy, 290
Board of Trade, the, 55
Bodenheim, Maxwell, 197
Bodleian Library, the, 104
Boer War, the, 108
Bookman, The, 188, 193
Book of Mormon, The, 200
Book-of-the-Month Club, the, 123, 232, 247
Book reviews, 67, 127, 135, 136-37, 139-44, 145-51, 249-50
Books (New York *Herald Tribune*), 123
Boone, Daniel, 177
Bordeaux, 119
Boston, 150, 162, 220
Boston *Transcript,* 155
Boswell, James, 99, 100
Bourne, Randolph, 98, 151, 167-68, 172
Bowdoin College, 285
Bowery, the, 95
Brandon, Charles, 226, 227
Brearley School, the, 124-27
Brest, 119
Brevoort Hotel, 197, 208
British Columbia, 25
British Museum, 97, 101, 104
Broadway, 87, 95, 271, 290

Brooklyn, 128, 134, 160, 162, 165
Brooks, Van Wyck, 98, 136, 168, 195, 251
Broun, Heywood, 136, 198
Browning, Robert, 49, 141, 143
Brunswick, Georgia, 286
Bryan, William Jennings, 73
Bryn Mawr, 218
Buck, Pearl S., 251, 270
Burns, Robert, 100
Burr, Aaron, 208
Butler, Nicholas Murray, 95, 110, 167
Butz, DeWitt Clinton, 25, 48
Butz, Great-grandfather, 22, 23, 30
Butz, Jeremiah King (grandfather), 5-7, 18, 22, 24-28, 29, 30, 36, 44, 50, 52, 109, 110, 123
Butz, Mark, 25, 28-29, 48
Butz, Rebecca (Tillotson) (grandmother), 5-7, 9, 24-28, 109, 120
Butz, Wallace, 25, 48
Butz, Warren, 25, 48

Cabell, James Branch, 98, 151, 181, 197, 251, 253, 266, 286
Caldwell, Erskine, 251, 271-72
Caledonian Canal, the, 99
California, 70, 191, 232, 289
Cambridge History of American Literature, The, 108, 151, 187-88, 195, 200
Camelot, 150
Campbell, Colin, 99
Camp Dodge, 119
Camp Pike, 119
Canaan, 28, 289
Canada, 70
Canby, H. S., 123, 208, 209, 222
Cannes, 240, 252, 257
Cannon, Speaker, 18
Canon of American literature, the, 195-97
Canteen, the, 68-69
Canterbury, 104
Captain Craig, 163
Caracas, 287
Carcassonne, 287
Carlyle, Thomas, 100
Carol Kennicott, 146, 158
Cather, Willa, 98, 151, 251

Catherine the Great, 177
Catullus, 141
Central examinations, 15
Century Club, the, 150
Century Magazine, The, 148, 156, 162, 189, 196, 197, 198, 199, 223, 224, 227, 253
Chambers, Robert W., 194
Champaign, 87
Champ Perry, 158
Charing Cross Road, 101
Charlie Chan, 290
Charlton Street, 208, 212
Chaucer, 96
Chelsea, 236, 237
Cherokees, 25, 48
Chesterton, G. K., 97
Cheyenne, 289
Chicago, 18, 19, 27, 35, 46, 49, 55, 88, 246, 257, 272, 285, 286, 292, 293
Chickasaws, 48
Children of Darkness, 290
China, 15, 77, 268
Choctaws, 48, 68, 69
Christian Scientists, 200
Church at Hope, the, 2-8, 59-60
Church in Urbana, the, 58-60
Churchill, Winston, 105
Cincinnati, 7, 50, 88, 89
City and Country School, the, 208
Civil liberties, 138, 139, 302
Civil War, the, 5, 20, 22, 107, 179
Class struggle, 270, 272, 283
Clavering, 163
Clendening, Logan, 247, 251
Cleveland, Grover, 18, 19
Clothes at Hope, 35-37
Cockermouth, 100
Colbert, Claudette, 290
Coleridge, 154
Collected Poems (Edwin Arlington Robinson), 161, 206
College Widow, The, 87
Collier's Weekly, 161
Collison, 15, 33, 85
Cologne, 104
Colum, Mary, 221, 222
Columbia University, 75, 83, 88, 90, 91, 94, 95-98, 106-08, 109, 110, 114,

118, 123, 124, 125, 148, 162, 167, 175, 195, 208, 257, 262, 263, 290
Columbus, 151
Columnists, the, 88, 249
Commodore Hotel, 229
Communists, 168, 270, 272, 275, 301
Compleat Angler, The, 50
Conkling, Grace Hazard, 229
Connecticut, 123, 223, 231, 252
Constitution of the United States, the, 123
Contemporary American Novelists: 1900-1920, 151, 196
Coolidge, Calvin, 166
Cooper, James Fenimore, 49
Corcoran Museum of Art, the, 218
Corn-ploughing, 42-44
Cornwall, Connecticut, 123-24, 169, 209, 210, 211, 219, 227, 231, 255, 262, 292
Cornwall Center, 123
Cornwall Hollow, 123
Corsica, 220
Corydon, 175
Country doctor, the, 37-38
Crane, Hart, 251
Crane, Stephen, 97
Crash of 1929, the, 246-47, 252, 260, 264, 269, 274
Cream Hill, 123, 209
Cream Hill Lake, 124
Creeks, 48
Crinan Canal, the, 99
Criticism, academic, 135-36, 144, 149, 186
Criticism, journalistic, 135-36, 145-53
Crockett, Davy, 195, 287
Cuba, 20, 21
Culloden Moor, 99
Cummings, E. E., 168, 251

Dallas, 285, 288
Dancing, 63-64
Dandy, 36
D'Angelo, Pascal, 128-34, 160
Dante, 96, 141, 177
Danville, 18, 25, 35, 51, 53, 120
Darcy, 217, 218
D'Artagnan, 76, 214
Darwin, 198

David Butternut, 227, 228, 230
David Copperfield, 49
Dawson, Mrs., 158
Day, Clarence, 251
Decatur, 22
Deer-hunting, 26
Defoe, 96
Dell, Floyd, 155, 192, 196, 198
Delmar, Viña, 290
Democracy, 21, 80-81, 301
Democrats, the, 18, 48, 73, 137
Dentistry, pioneer, 23
Denver, 246, 288
Depression of 1893, the, 19-20
Des Moines, 119
Detroit, 121, 146, 257, 294
Devil's lane, the, 52
Dewey, John, 167
Diary, 125
Dick, 12-14
Dickens, 41, 49, 141
Dickinson, Emily, 177
Dictatorships, 301-02
Digges, Dudley, 290
Dodsworth, 266
Dos Passos, John, 168, 251, 268
Dostoevsky, 141, 156
Dreams, 264-65, 284
Dreiser, Theodore, 98, 135, 149, 178, 181, 196, 198, 251, 266
Druid Circle, the, 100
Drummond, William, 100
Dryden, 24, 103, 118, 204
Dullness as villain, 152, 268
Dumfries, 100
Dürer, Albrecht, 104

Eagle and the Mole, The, 221
Ecclefechan, 100
Edgett, E. F., 153
Edinburgh, 28, 99-100, 102
Education of Henry Adams, The, 145
Edwards, Jonathan, 195
Electra, 266
Eleventh Street, 208
Eliot, T. S., 150, 251
Elizabeth Bennet, 218
Ellis, Havelock, 77
Elmer Gantry, 209, 274
Eloise Fidler, 233-34, 235

Elsie, 126
Embry, Jacqueline, 236
Emperor Jones, The, 150
Enchanted Hour, The, 156
Enormous Room, The, 151
Erskine, John, 108, 116, 134, 167
Esmeralda, 290
Ettrick Hills, the, 100
Ettrick Shepherd, the, 100
Europe, first visit to, 98-105
Evangeline, 49
Everybody's Magazine, 156
Expatriates, the, 151, 240, 267
Expression in America, 148

Faerie Queene, The, 141
Fairmont, West Virginia, 286
Farewell to Arms, A, 267
Farm at Cornwall, the, 209-11, 262
Farm at Hope, the, 29-30, 31-50, 287
Farm at Villa Grove, the, 70, 84, 121
Farrell, James T., 251, 272
Far West, the, 292
Fascism, 274, 275, 301
Faulkner, William, 251, 268, 270
Faust, 140
Feminism, 181-83, 279
Feuds, 51-52
Fielding, Henry, 158, 188
Fifth Avenue, 91-94
Final examinations, 15-16
Fingal, Cave of, 99
First day in New York, 87-94
Fitch, Clyde, 285
Fithian, 33, 46
Fitzgerald, F. Scott, 150, 168-69, 251, 278
Five Tribes, the, 24
Flatiron building, the, 92
Fleet Street, 101
Flock, The, 192
Florida, 69
Folies Bergères, 104
Follies, the, 147
Food at Hope, 33-35
Football, 63, 64, 70
Foreign languages, 78-79
Fort Sam Houston, 288
Fort Worth, 287
Four Hundred, the, 87

Fourth Dimension in Criticism, A, 139-44
Fourth of July, 30, 44, 45, 47
France, Anatole, 159
Frank, Glenn, 197
Frank, Waldo, 251
Franklin, 195, 264, 265
Free Air, 155, 159
Fresno, 289
Frost, Robert, 98, 150, 162, 163, 196, 214, 215, 251

Gale, Zona, 154, 162, 198, 251
Galsworthy, John, 97
Gannett, Lewis, 123, 209
Gardens, 298-300
Gargantua, 140
Garland, Hamlin, 98
Garrison, Wendell Phillips, 136
Garrison, William Lloyd, 137
Genesis, The Book of, 141
Genius, The, 181
George V, 102
George Eliot, 100
Georgia, 271, 286
Georgia, the University of, 285
Gerald Poynyard, 218
Geronimo, 288
Gibbon, 49, 100
Gideon's Revenge, 223
Glasgow, 98, 101
Glasgow, Ellen, 251
Glaspell, Susan, 147
Glencoe, 99
God's Little Acre, 272
Goethe, 141
Gold, Michael, 249, 251, 268
Gopher Prairie, 146, 152
Gourock, 99
Graduate students, 95-96
Grand Prix, 199
Grasmere, 100
Grasse, 258
Gray, Dr., 293
Great Lakes, the, 69
Green, J. R., 49
Greene, Evarts, 79-80
Greenock, 98
Greenspan, Magistrate, 272
Greenwich Village, 177, 207-10, 252

Grub Street, 251
Guinevere, 164
Guinzburg, Alice, 258
Guinzburg, Harold, 203, 204, 255, 258
Gulliver's Travels, 49
Guy Pollock, 158
Gypsy, The, 211

Hackett, Francis, 155
Hague, The, 103
Haiti, 119
Hall-Mills murder, 217
Halloran's, 159
Happy childhood, a, 41-42
Harding, Warren Gamaliel, 166, 177
Hardy, Thomas, 160
Harper's Magazine, 156
Harrison, Benjamin, 18
Hartford, 123, 226, 227, 228
Hartshorne, 68
Harvard, 75, 81, 83, 98, 163
Hashimura Togo, 190
Hawthornden, 100
Hawthorne, 49, 195
Hay-making, 45
Hearst, W. R., 209
Hearst's Magazine, 156
Hebbel, Friedrich, 78
Hebrides, the, 99
Heine, 104
He Loved His Country, 156, 157
Helvellyn, 100
Hemingway, Ernest, 168, 251, 267
Hendaye, 208
Henry V, 140
Henry VIII, 226
Hergesheimer, Joseph, 251
Hermitage, The, 286
Hester Prynne, 177
Het Loo, 103
Hiawatha, 49
Hichborn, Admiral Philip, 218
Hichborn, Philip II, 218-20
Hichborn, Philip III, 240-41
Hippodrome, the, 109
Hired men, the, 33, 55, 60, 280
History, 245
History of a Literary Radical, 167
Hog Island, 258
Holborn Street, 101

Hollywood, 207, 248, 289-92
Holmes, Oliver Wendell, 49
Holton Arms, 218
Holyrood, 100
Homer, 141, 145
Hoof Beats, 220
Hoover, Herbert, 284
Hope, Illinois, 1-57, 58, 59, 60, 62,
    85, 103, 107, 123, 126, 152, 177,
    210, 211, 257, 260, 280, 289, 294,
    296, 301
Hope, New Jersey, 22, 109
Houndsditch, 105
House at Hope, the, 32, 37, 39-40
Houses of Parliament, 101
Howard, Sidney, 251
Howells, William Dean, 98, 136, 178
Hoyt, Anne (McMichael), 218
Hoyt, Constance, 218
Hoyt, Henry (brother of Elinor
    Wylie), 219
Hoyt, Henry Martyn (grandfather of
    Elinor Wylie), 218
Hoyt, Henry Martyn (father of Elinor
    Wylie), 218, 219
Hoyt, Nancy, 236
Huckleberry Finn, 140
Huckleberry Finn, 49, 50
Hudson River, 89, 94, 137
Hughes, Rupert, 188, 290
Hugo, Victor, 141
Huneker, James Gibbons, 97
Huxley, Thomas Henry, 198
Hyde Park, 101, 102

Ibsen, 141, 173
Idaho, 25
Illinois, 1, 17, 22, 28, 44, 50, 80, 85,
    121, 166, 190, 197, 296
Illinois, the University of, 61, 67, 70,
    71, 75-83, 86, 118, 119, 121, 254,
    294, 296
Incidental Numbers, 220
India, 77
Indiana, 2, 24, 49, 109
Indian blood, 24, 25, 109, 120, 255
Indian Territory (Oklahoma), 25, 48,
    68, 120, 287
Individual and type, 297-98
Influences, literary, 186, 191, 194

Intellectuals, 193
Inverness, 99
Iowa, 99, 286
Iowa, the University of, 286
Ireland, 98, 292
Irving, Sir Henry, 218
Irving, Washington, 49, 195
Isolde, 177
It Can't Happen Here, 274
Ivanhoe, 14

Jackson, Andrew, 22, 23, 24, 286
James, Henry, 98, 136, 178
James Branch Cabell, 253
Jeffers, Robinson, 251
Jefferson, 137, 177
Jeffries-Johnson fight, the, 100
Jennifer Lorn, 218, 223
Jewel of Seven Stars, The, 218
Job, The, 155, 156
Job, The Book of, 141
John Evereldown, 163
Johnson, Samuel, 82, 99, 100
Jonathan Gentry, 207
Jonson, Ben, 100
Joyce, James, 199
Judith (Hebbel), 78
Jurgen, 145, 147, 150, 181, 286

Kahn, Otto H., 209
Kankakee County, 28
Kansas, 19, 25, 207
Kansas City, 247
Kaufman, George S., 251
Keats, 154
Kenilworth, 100
Kent Morrow, 254, 297
Kentucky, 236
Kentucky, the University of, 285
Kern, Jerome, 259
Keswick, 100
Kiamichi Mouutains, the, 287
Kilmer, Joyce, 159
Kipling, 162
Kipps, 155
Kirkland, Caroline Matilda Stansbury,
    233
Knight, Dorothy, 293
Krutch, Joseph Wood, 118, 123, 148,
    151, 162, 203, 208, 209

Krutch, Marcelle (Leguia), 208, 209
Ku Klux Klan, 267

Lady Godiva, 100
Lady of the Lake, The, 67
La Guaira, 287
Lafayette Hotel, 208
Lake Louise, 146
Lake Poets, 100
Lancelot, 164
Lancelot, 160, 202, 203
Lardner, Ring, 251
Last Days of Pompeii, The, 49
Las Vegas, 289
Latter Day Saints, 200, 289
Leather-Stocking, 170
Lecturing, 285-89
Leffingwell, 163
Left Bank, the, 208
Lehigh University, 285
Leonard, W. E., 199
Leopardi, 141
Lessing, 143
Letters to a Lady in the Country, 209
Levin, 79
Lewis, Grace, 209
Lewis, Sinclair, 38, 98, 146-47, 150, 152-59, 168, 197, 209, 221, 255, 266, 267, 274
Lewisohn, Ludwig, 98, 136, 146-48, 151, 195, 208, 254, 290
Lexington, Kentucky, 286
Lilliputian Bazaar, the, 35
Lincoln, 42
Lindsay, Vachel, 98, 251
Lionel, 232
Litchfield, 123
Literary Guild, the, 123, 203-06, 247, 255, 290
Literary teas, 250
Little Rock, 119
Little Women, 49
Lloyd George, David, 155
Lodore, Falls of, 100
London, 97, 101-02, 104, 105, 191, 218, 236
Longchamp, 199
Long Island, 93
Look Homeward, Angel, 267
Los Angeles, 289

Lost Lady, A, 196
Louis XIV, 177
Louisiana, 285
Love in American history, 177-78
Love in Hope, 53-55
Love in the Younger Generation, 176-85
Love in the youngest generation, 278-80
Love in Urbana, 72
Lovely Lady, The, 192
Lowell, Amy, 98, 196, 199, 251
Lucian, 141
Ludgate Circus, 101
Lusitania, the, 114
Lyric Year, The, 221

Macbeth, 99
Macdougal Street, 150
MacDowell, Mrs. Edward, 228
MacDowell colony, the, 162, 164, 222, 228
Madame Bovary, 141, 154
Madison Square, 89, 90
Main Street, 145, 146, 150, 152, 153, 154, 155, 157, 158, 159, 174, 175, 221, 271, 274
Maine, 163, 271, 285
Maine, the, 20
Man Against the Sky, The, 145
Man from Home, The, 95
Manhattan, 89, 150, 221, 284
Manila, 21
Man in the Iron Mask, the, 257
Mannheim, 104
Manon Lescaut, 177
Man o' War, 286
Many Minds, 196, 253
Marine Corps, 119
Mark Twain, 49, 98, 150, 168, 178
Marlowe, Christopher, 76
Marx, Karl, 270
Mary of Scotland, 100
Mason, Dr., 293, 294
Massachusetts, 24, 222
Masses, The, 155
Masters, Edgar Lee, 98, 153, 154, 157, 198, 251
Mather, Cotton, 225
Matthews, Brander, 98, 136

Mayer, Edwin Justus, 290
McMichael, Morton (great-grand-
    father of Elinor Wylie), 218
McMichael, Morton (grandfather of
    Elinor Wylie), 218
Melrose, 100
Melville, Herman, 178, 195, 196
Mencken, H. L., 97, 135, 136, 149,
    150, 151, 162, 173-74, 195, 197,
    251, 267
Meredith, George, 96
Merlin, 164
Merlin, 202, 203
Merrimac River, 137
Methodists, 7, 16
Metropolitan Magazine, The, 156
Metropolitan Museum of Art, the, 208
Mexico, 70, 288
Michigan, 233
Middle Fork, 23
Milking, 42
Millay, Edna St. Vincent, 98, 150,
    168, 175-76, 182-83, 196, 221, 251
Milton, 143, 232
Miniver Cheevy, 163
Minneapolis, 146
Minnesota, 38
Minnesota, the University of, 285
Miranda's Supper, 223
Miss Baldwin's School, 218
Miss Flint's School (Holton Arms),
    218
Mississippi River, 285
Miss Lulu Bett, 198
Missouri Compromise, the, 16
Moby Dick, 195
Modern American Prose, 293
Molière, 141
Moody, William Vaughn, 285
Monte Carlo, 252, 258
Montparnasse, 252
Moon-Calf, 156
Moore, George, 135
More, P. E., 97, 135, 136, 195
Morley, Christopher, 249
Mormons, 289
Morningside Heights, 208
Mother, 156
Mount Desert, Maine, 218, 220
Mount Vernon, 109

Movies, the, 48, 88, 247, 289-91
Mr. Flood's Party, 161
Mr. Hazard, 233
Mr. Hodge and Mr. Hazard, 232
Muckrakers, 80
Mullin, Glen, 77
Munich, 103, 104
Murder at Hope, 51
Muskogee, 120
My Ántonia, 145
"My love came up from Barnegat,"
    223

Nashville, 286
Nassau, 258
Nathan, George Jean, 136, 267
Nation, The, 123, 127, 128, 129, 133,
    134-39, 145, 146, 147, 148, 149,
    150, 151, 157, 158, 160, 161, 162,
    171, 196, 197, 208, 221, 290
National Institute of Arts and Letters,
    the, 197, 266
Negroes, 137, 259, 286-87
Nelly, 36
Nelson, Lord, 177
Nero, 87
New Canaan, 216, 223, 224, 229
New Deal, the, 298
New England, 24, 49, 123, 222
New Forest, the, 219
Newgate, 101
New Hampshire, 224
New Home—Who'll Follow?, A, 223
New Jersey, 22, 26, 28, 109, 212, 217
New Lights, the, 7
New Mexico, 292
New Orleans, 285, 287
New Poetry, the, 145
New Republic, The, 155, 167, 221, 231
New York (State), 24, 28
New York (City), 35, 83, 87-93, 105,
    106, 109, 119, 124, 150, 156, 162,
    166, 169, 177, 191, 207, 209, 216,
    221, 228, 234, 236, 240, 249, 250,
    251, 254, 256, 257, 262, 273, 284,
    285, 289, 290, 292, 294
New York Evening Post, 136, 146, 158
New York Globe, 158
New York Herald Tribune, 123

New York Society for the Suppression of Vice, the, 271-72
New York *Times*, 277
Nietzsche, 141, 173
Nightmare Abbey, 217
Ninth Wave, The, 254, 297
Nobel prize, 188, 267
Nomads in America, 70, 276
Norris, Frank, 97, 178
Norris, Kathleen, 232
North of Boston, 145
Northwestern University, 197
Novel-writing, 66-67, 108, 254-55
Nuneaton, 100
Nuremberg, 103, 104

Oban, 99
Oberammergau, 104
O'Brien, E. J., 156
Obscenity, 54-55, 279-80
Odets, Clifford, 251, 273
Odysseus, 140
Ogden, 33
Ohio, 22, 229, 233
Ohio University, 147
Oklahoma, 120, 290
Old Capitol (Iowa), 286
Old Country, the, 20
Older America, the, 73-74, 80-81, 273, 277-78, 280-81, 301-02
Ol' Man River, 259
O'Neill, Eugene, 147, 168, 251, 266
One Person, 237-40
Oregon, the, 21
Orphan Angel, The, 226, 232, 234
Osages, 48
Other Provinces, 211, 253-54
Our Mr. Wrenn, 155
Outline of History, The, 151
Oxford, 75, 100, 101, 104, 105, 232
Oxford Street, 101

Paine, Thomas, 195, 286
Palm Springs, 289
Parents and children, 63-65, 85-87, 170-72, 176-77, 211-12, 215, 297-98
Paris, 75, 104, 199, 208, 218, 240, 275
Park Avenue, 125, 126, 248
Parker, Dorothy, 249
Parnell, 177

Parris Island, 119
Pascal D'Angelo: Son of Italy, 134
Passion Play (Oberammergau), 104
Pater, Walter, 100
Peacock, Thomas Love, 96-97, 104, 118, 217, 226
Penfield, 28
Pennsylvania, 218, 286
Pennsylvania Germans, 22
Penthouse, 261-66
Pershing, General, 267
Peterborough, 160, 161, 162, 223, 224, 225, 227, 228, 229, 231
Phelps, W. L., 136
Phi Beta Kappa, 286
Philadelphia, 216, 218, 219
Philippines, the, 21
Pictorial Review, The, 226
Pierrot, 175
Pike's Peak, 288
Pilgrim's Progress, 49
Pilot Grove, 15, 22
Pilot Township, 23, 24, 27
Pittsburgh, 147
Plato, 141, 143, 233
Plutarch, 49
Poe, 49, 143, 151, 177
Poet, ambitions to be a, 76-77, 83, 101
Poetry, discovery of, 76-77
Poetry, the persistence of, 134
Poets' Corner, the, 102
Poictesme, 266
Pope, 143, 167
Popular Bibles, 200
Popularity and excellence in literature, 188, 201-02
Popular songs, 258-59
Porter, Katherine Anne, 196
Potomac, 18, 25, 27, 33, 36, 44, 45, 47
Pound, Ezra, 251
Poverty as villain, 268-70, 273-74
Prairie people, 23, 24
Pride and Prejudice, 217
Prince, 39
Prohibition, 27, 180, 250
Pseudo-Boswell, 99
Publishers and writers, 248-49
Pulitzer committee, 199, 248

Queen Mary, 102
Queen Wilhelmina, 103
Quincy, 121
Quo Vadis?, 49

Rabelais, 77, 143
Radio, 48, 88, 247, 267
Reading, 49-50, 67, 76, 78-80, 144
Rebels against old ideas, 170-73
Rebels against old manners, 170-76
Recovery, 282, 284, 298, 302-03
Red Carpet for Shelley, A, 232
Reed, John, 98, 151, 168
Renascence, 221
Reno, 263
Repplier, Agnes, 136
Republicans, 5, 18, 19, 27, 73, 137, 294
Research, 107-08
Retired farmers, 1, 61-62, 84-85, 121-22
Revolt from the Village, the, 151, 152, 153, 168
Revolution, the American, 20, 80
Revolution, the French, 80
Revolution in America, 138, 270, 273, 282, 283, 284, 298, 302
Rhine, 104
Richard Cory, 163
Richmond, 286
Riley, James Whitcomb, 49
Riley, Woodbridge, 200
Rip Van Winkle, 178
Riverside Drive, 94, 110
Roberts, Elizabeth Madox, 251
Robeson, Paul, 258
Robin Hood, 14
Robinson, Edwin Arlington, 76, 98, 150, 159-66, 196, 197, 198, 202-07, 252, 266, 287
Robinson Crusoe, 49
Rochester, 146
Rockport, 121
Rocky Mountains, 246
Rogers, Will, 290
Roosevelt, Franklin D., 294
Roosevelt, Theodore, 76, 99, 114, 192, 202
Rosalie Lillie, 234-35
Rosemont, 217

Rotary Club, 267
Rotterdam, 102, 104
Roulette, 258
Roving Critic, The, 133, 139
Roy, 15
Royal, 85
Russia, 138, 164, 268, 270, 281, 301, 302
Rydal Water, 100
Ryksmuseum, 112

Sabotage, 167
Sachs, Hans, 104
Sainte-Beuve, 143
Saintsbury, George, 100
Sale, Chic, 68
Salem witches, 225
Salt Lake City, 289
Sam Clark, 158
San Andreas Cañon, 289
San Antonio, 287-88
Sandburg, Carl, 98, 251, 287
Sandusky, 22
San José de Aguayo, 288
Santa Fe, 189, 193
Santayana, George, 76, 196, 199, 251
Saturday Evening Post, The, 146, 156
Saturday Review of Literature, The, 123
Sappho, 182
Scandals at Hope, 53-55
Scarlet Sign, The, 156, 157
Schiller, 104
Scholar, The, 211-12
Scholar in business, a, 255-56
School at Hope, the, 8-17
Scotland, 98-100
Scott, Evelyn, 159
Scott, Sir Walter, 49, 100, 141
Science and Health, 200
Science Service, 193
Seattle, 146
Selkirk, 100
Shakespeare, 49, 100, 141, 143, 159
Shaw, G. B., 97, 141, 173
She Done Him Wrong, 290
Sheep-shearing, 48
Shelley, Mary, 225

Shelley, Percy Bysshe, 96, 100, 154, 198, 217, 222, 225, 226, 227, 228, 230, 232, 238
Shelley and the Unromantics, 226
Sherlock Holmes, 290
Sherman, Ruth, 209
Sherman Stuart, 81-83, 98-102, 108, 118, 135, 149, 169, 195, 199, 208, 209, 212, 286
Sherwood, Robert E., 251
Shiloh, 227, 228, 230
Show Boat, 259
Shropshire Lad, A, 76
Sinclair, Miss, 231
Sinclair, Upton, 178, 192, 251, 290
Sister Carrie, 145
Sitwell, Osbert, 236
Skiddaw, 100
Small town life, 70-73
Snyder, Uncle Tom, 7
Socialists, 73, 138
Socrates, 141-42
Solitude, 65-66, 77, 261-66, 284, 292
Somerville, 217, 218
South Carolina, 119
South Field, 91
Spain, 20
Spanish-American War, the, 20-21, 108
Spartacus to the Gladiators, 69
Speakeasies, 256
Spelling bees, 12-14
Spencer, Herbert, 198
Spezia, Gulf of, 225
Spoon River, 51, 150, 152, 190, 198
Spoon River Anthology, 145, 153
Sports, 70
Springfield, Massachusetts, 228, 229
St. Columba, 99
St. Honorat, 257
St. Louis, 285
St. Machar's Cathedral, 99
St. Patrick's Cathedral, 92
St. Paul's Cathedral, 101
Ste. Marguerite, 257
Staffa, 99
Stallings, Laurence, 168, 251
State Fair, 290
Stein, Gertrude, 251
Stephens, James, 74, 292

Stewart, James, 99
Stoker, Bram, 218
Stokowski, Leopold, 267
Stong, Phil, 290
Story of a Novel, The, 268-69
Strand, the, 101
Stratford, 100
Studs Lonigan, 272
Stuttgart, 104
Success in literature, an episode of, 202-06
Suckow, Ruth, 196
Suffragettes in London, 104
Sunday, Billy, 197
Sunday school at Hope, 4-8
Suppression of books, the attempted, 181, 271-72
Swedish Academy, the, 267
Swift, 141, 204, 263-64, 265
Swinnerton, Frank, 146
Sylvia, 126

Tagore, Rabindranath, 77
Talking and writing, 162-63
Tallahassee, 122
Tammany, 87
Tarkington, Booth, 158, 251
Tasker Norcross, 163
Tate, Allen, 251
Teacher, first, 9, 289
Teacher, the pioneer, 8-9
Tempest, The, 14
Tennessee, 118, 285
Tennyson, 49
Terry, Ellen, 218
Texas, 287, 288
Thackeray, 41, 49
Things, 156, 157
This Side of Paradise, 174, 175
This Simian World, 151
Thoreau, 118
Thorndike, A. H., 114
Three Musketeers, The, 214, 215
Three Soldiers, 151
Threeways, 124, 209
Threshing, 45-47
Thurber, James, 279
Thyrsis, 175
Tillotson, Great-grandfather, 22, 24-25

Tillotson, John, Archbishop of Canterbury, 24
Tillotsons, the, 24, 25, 44
Timber people, 23-24
Tinker, Edward, 287
Titusville, Pennsylvania, 286
Tobacco Road, 271-72
Tolstoi, 141, 158
Toulon, 257
Trade unions, 273
Trader Horn, 292
Trafalgar Monument, 101
Trail of the Hawk, The, 155
Translation, 78
Treaty of Versailles, 137-38
Trent, William Peterfield, 98, 108, 115-17, 118, 125
Trent's Last Case, 198
Trinity Parish, 208
Tristan, 177
Tristram, 202-06
Trollope, Anthony, 75
Troy, 245
Tudor, Mary, 226
Tulane University, 285
Twenty Years After, 215
Two Lives, 199

Ulysses, 150
Uncle Ananias, 163
Uncle Tom's Cabin, 143, 190
Unemployment, 276-78
Up Stream, 151
Urbana, 23, 58-74, 86, 87, 96, 107, 120, 121, 125, 126, 135, 152, 169, 177, 257, 292, 296

Van Doren, Abraham (great-grandfather), 28
Van Doren, Anne, 124, 172, 211-15, 216, 222, 276, 290
Van Doren, Barbara, 124, 211, 212, 277, 280
Van Doren, Charles Lucius (father), 1, 8, 10, 16, 17, 28-31, 32, 33, 37-38, 39, 41, 42, 49, 50, 51, 52, 59, 60, 62, 63, 64, 70, 84-87, 120-22, 257, 293-96, 297, 301, 302
Van Doren, Dora Anne (Butz) (mother), 1, 8, 16, 26, 28-31, 35, 36, 41, 42, 52, 60, 63, 64, 66, 86, 87, 119-20, 295, 296
Van Doren, Dorothy (Graffe), 208, 209
Van Doren, Frank, 17, 41, 62, 64, 86, 87, 118, 121, 257, 273, 293, 294
Van Doren, Grace (Gay), 121
Van Doren, Guy, 9, 12, 13, 14, 18, 20, 36, 37, 39, 40, 42, 60, 62, 63, 71, 86, 119, 120, 121, 257, 294
Van Doren, Irita (Bradford), 122, 124, 169, 212, 223, 225, 226, 229
Van Doren, Jessie (Hess), 257
Van Doren, Margaret, 124, 212, 277, 278-80
Van Doren, Mark, 17, 41, 51, 62, 86, 87, 118, 119, 120, 121, 123, 148, 151, 179, 196, 197, 204, 205, 207, 208, 209, 211, 253, 276, 292, 293, 294
Van Doren, Mary, 120
Van Doren, Paul, 22, 41, 64, 65, 86, 87, 119, 120, 121, 179, 215, 257, 293, 294
Van Doren, Peter, 215
Van Doren, Silas, 28
Van Doren, Verla (McCray), 120
Van Doren, William Henry (grandfather), 28
van Loon, Hendrik, 151
Var, 257
Vega, Lope, 141
Venetian Glass Nephew, The, 196, 223, 224, 230, 231
Venezuela, 287
Ventimiglia, 257
Vermilion County, 17, 18, 22, 27, 68
Vermont, 150
Vicomte de Bragelonne, The, 215
Victoria Embankment, 101
Villa Grove, 70, 84, 121, 294
Villard, Henry, 136
Villard, Oswald Garrison, 127, 136-37, 148
Virgil, 141
Virginia, 230
Vivian, 164
Voltaire, 141

Wall Street, 87, 252, 264
Walton, Izaak, 50
Waring, Mr. and Mrs., 219
Warwick, 100
Washington, George, 177
Washington, Martha, 109, 177
Washington, D. C., 51, 88, 137, 146, 150, 218, 219, 220, 221, 236
Washington Arch, 92
Washington Square, 91, 162, 208
Waste Land, The, 150
Water Boy, 258
Waterbury, 219
Waterloo Bridge, 101
Weaver, Raymond, 195, 196
Wells, H. G., 97, 151, 154, 155
Wescott, Glenway, 251
West, Mae, 290
West Cornwall, 209, 229
Western novels, 292
West Indies, 20, 21
Westminster Abbey, 102
Westminster Bridge, 101
West Point, 95
West Virginia, 286
What Is American Literature?, 292
What Price Glory?, 151
Wharton, Edith, 98, 155, 159, 251
Wheels of Chance, The, 155
When Knighthood Was in Flower, 226
Whigs, 5, 24
Whisperer, The, 156
White, W. A., 251
White House, the, 115
Whitman, 49, 82, 141, 143, 177, 195
Whittier, 49
Wickwire, 209, 222, 223, 224
Wilder, Thornton, 249, 251, 268
Will Kennicott, 158

Willow Walk, The, 156, 157
Wilmette, 257
Wilson, Edmund, 168, 195
Windermere, 100
Winesburg, 152
Wolfe, Thomas, 251, 267, 268-69
Woman by Candlelight, A, 156
Woman's Home Companion, The, 226
Woolworth Building, the, 109
Wordsworth, 143
World's Columbian Exposition, 18, 48
World War, the, 103-04, 107, 108, 113-24, 138, 173-74, 175, 197, 245-46, 280
Wright, Jean, 121, 271, 290
Writers as seismographs, 266-74
Writers in love with their subjects, 200-01
Wylie, Elinor, 98, 150, 196, 198, 203, 208, 209, 215-41, 255, 260
Wylie, Horace, 219-21

Xenophon, 141

Yale, 123, 219, 276
Yarrow River, 100
Yeats, W. B., 76, 100
Yelping Hill, 123, 222
Younger Generation, the, 149, 150, 166-76, 195, 210, 274, 275, 278
Youngest generation, the, 274-81
Young Man Axelbrod, 156
Young Woman Citizen, The, 192
Young Women's Christian Association, 192
Youth, the cult of, 149-50, 171-73

Zeppelin, 103

¶ Set in Linotype Granjon. Format by A. W. Rushmore. Manufactured by the Haddon Craftsmen, Inc., for the publishers, HARPER & BROTHERS, New York and London.